THE LANGUAGE
OF CRITICISM

THE LANGUAGE OF CRITICISM

*Linguistic Models
and Literary Theory*

Jacqueline M. Henkel

CORNELL UNIVERSITY PRESS

Ithaca and London

First published 1996 by Cornell University Press.

Library of Congress Cataloging-in-Publication Data

Henkel, Jacqueline Margaret.
   The language of criticism : linguistic models and literary theory
/ Jacqueline M. Henkel.
     p. cm.
   Includes bibliographical references and index.
   ISBN 0-8014-2656-1 (cloth : alk. paper)
   1. Linguistics. 2. Speech acts (Linguistics) 3. Linguistic
models. 4. Criticism. I. Title.
P123.H33 1996
410—dc20   96-25037

Printed in the United States of America

For
Sadie Berg
and
Camilla Henkel

Contents

Acknowledgments

I wish to thank the kind friends and colleagues who helped me with this project. My thanks go to Alan Altimont, Tom Cable, and Geneviève Escure for encouraging me to develop interdisciplinary interests; to Wick Wadlington and Bill Worthen for enthusiastic responses to early drafts; to John Wenstrom for many stimulating discussions about ordinary language philosophy; to Wallace Martin for insightful and generously detailed remarks on many chapters; to Judith Bailey for especially helpful editorial comments; and to Cliff Frohlich for imploring me to stop revising this book.

Portions of this book appeared, in earlier versions, as "Linguistic Models and Recent Criticism: Transformational-Generative Grammar as Literary Metaphor," *PMLA* 105 (1990): 448–63, reprinted by permission of the copyright owner, The Modern Language Association of America; "Promises according to Searle: Some Problems with Constitutive Rules," *1983 Mid-America Linguistics Conference Papers* (1984), pp. 181–94, reprinted by permission of the University of Colorado, Boulder; and "Speech-Act Theory Revisited: Rule Notions and Reader-Oriented Criticism," *Poetics* 17 (1988): 505–30, copyright 1988, reprinted with kind permission from Elsevier Science-NL, Sara Burgerhartstraat 25, 1055 KV Amsterdam, The Netherlands. I also thank the National Endowment for the Humanities for a summer stipend and the University of Texas Research Institute for two summer research awards which funded time for me to finish this book.

J. M. H.

THE LANGUAGE
OF CRITICISM

Chapter 1

Linguistics, Speech-Act Theory, and Literary Criticism

Metaphor is never innocent. It orients research and fixes results.
—JACQUES DERRIDA, "Force and Signification"

This book examines some connections—the initial attraction and ensuing disaffection—between linguistics and speech-act theory, on the one hand, and literary criticism, on the other. It focuses principally on a selection of specific, still-unsettled critical issues arising from the interaction between these fields, but it also considers the more general processes and aims of interdisciplinary borrowing.

Perhaps no one needs to be reminded that in the 1970s and early 1980s literary critics became enchanted with models drawn from both linguistics and ordinary language philosophy.[1] The precise cause of this interest is less clear, but certainly the sheer scientific and extradisciplinary cachet of these theories made them an attractive and authoritative means of escape from the methodological strictures of New Criticism. In an earlier stage, generally hostile to interdisciplinary methods, linguistics had merely supplied for specialized critics a detailed apparatus with which to carry out a more technical but essentially New Critical stylistic analysis (Thomas Sebeok's [1960] and Donald Free-

[1] American critics were importing structuralist methods by the mid-1960s, and mainstream theorists were expanding this interest to transformational-generative grammar by the mid-1970s, although linguistics had been a tool in a narrower variety of stylistic analysis since the early 1960s. Speech-act accounts of literary problems first appeared in the early 1970s. Although many books on the topic were still being published, the general appeal of linguistic criticism had begun to decline by the early 1980s, precipitated largely by interest in deconstruction.

man's [1970] well-known collections of linguistic criticism contain representative essays).[2] But the example of European literary structuralism began to suggest that the main business of criticism—and perhaps especially of a linguistics-based criticism—was not to explicate individual works. Critics who increasingly doubted that texts could be analyzed as stable artifacts without reference to authors or readers soon drew suggestively from a recently developed generative grammar, in the form of Noam Chomsky's *Aspects of the Theory of Syntax* (1965), later from speech-act theory, as outlined by J. L. Austin, then elaborated by John Searle in *Speech Acts* (1969).[3] Thus the generative grammar Samuel Levin initially applied to an analysis of syntactic and semantic "couplings" or equivalences in poetic language (1962) gave way to Jonathan Culler's more comprehensive critical framework, an analogous "literary grammar" of interpretive operations (*Structuralist Poetics*, 1975). The ordinary language philosophy with which Richard Ohmann established literary texts as autonomous entities (1971) later generated for Mary Louise Pratt a reader-oriented speech-act criticism that problematized the status of "literature" as a discrete category (*Toward a Speech Act Theory of Literary Discourse*, 1977).[4]

[2] For comments on the general hostility to linguistic criticism in the 1960s, see Nigel Fabb and Alan Durant, "Ten Years" 52. The references are to Sebeok, *Style and Language*; and Freeman, *Linguistics and Literary Style*. Other collections of the same period include Seymour Chatman and Samuel Levin, *Essays on the Language of Literature* (1967); Roger Fowler, *Essays on Style and Language* (1966); and Glen A. Love and Michael Payne, *Contemporary Essays on Style* (1969). A provocative, more theoretical early collection is Seymour Chatman, *Approaches to Poetics* (1973). Interesting later collections on literary stylistics are Ronald Carter, *Language and Literature* (1982); and Freeman, *Essays in Modern Stylistics* (1981).

[3] I refer, of course, to W. K. Wimsatt and Monroe Beardsley's well-known discussions of the intentional and affective fallacies; they argued both that the "intention of the author is neither available nor desirable as a standard for judging the success of a work of literary art" ("Intentional" 3), and that critical attention to the "psychological effects" of the work "ends in biography and relativism" ("Affective" 21). Thus, the work was something to be understood and appreciated on its internal merits.

[4] The first reference is to Levin, *Linguistic Structures in Poetry*, especially the essay "Coupling in a Shakespearean Sonnet" (also in Freeman, *Linguistics* 197–205), which draws from early transformational-generative grammar but relies principally on American structuralist methods. Although he essentially quarries the text in New Critical fashion, Levin does analyze the language of the poem without the immediate goal of a new interpretation (52) and refers here to the contribution of shared linguistic knowledge to the reading of the poem (54). He also treats his grammar of the poem as predictive (see Freeman, "Linguistic Approaches" 13) and in that sense anticipates later competence theories.

This is, of course, a rough history. In the Freeman collection Ohmann (in a 1964 essay, "Generative Grammars and the Concept of Literary Style" [reprinted in Love and Payne]) applied Chomsky's earlier *Syntactic Structures* to a stylistic analysis of prose. But in the same volume (in a translation of a 1965 essay, "Poetics and Linguistics"), Manfred Bierwisch was already developing a notion of "literary competence" from Chomsky's *Aspects*

Soon thereafter, the developing interest in poststructuralism and deconstruction encouraged further attention to the linguistic foundations of such critical methods. In short, this period saw an enthusiastic proliferation of material on a variety of linguistics-related topics: first (principally in the 1960s) collections of stylistic analyses demonstrating a range of linguistic methods, later (mid-1960s to mid-1970s) structuralist anthologies and summary-analyses of formalist and structuralist texts (Fredric Jameson's *Prison-House of Language* [1972] or Robert Scholes's *Structuralism in Literature* [1974]), a series of influential books of critical theory (the 1970s and 1980s) which eclectically applied linguistic models to interpretive problems, and finally (by the 1980s), deconstructionist critiques of literary-linguistic projects.[5]

Thus disillusionment quickly followed romance, and suddenly those critics who were once the active promoters of linguistics- and speech-act-based literary theory were—and still are—among its most vocal opponents. The critical conversation, most critics would now say, has moved on to new issues and topics—to deconstruction, to new pragmatism, to literary history and cultural criticism. Many critics simply

---

of the Theory of Syntax (also published in 1965). It was not, however, until the mid-1970s that competence models dominated critical discussion.

The 1971 Ohmann essay is "Speech Acts and the Definition of Literature." I don't mean to call Ohmann a New Critic here; in this piece he rejects several New Critical positions, though he wishes in some way to preserve the distinctiveness of literary discourse. An early collection of speech-act criticism focusing on similar issues is Teun van Dijk, *Pragmatics of Language and Literature* (1976).

[5] Collections of structuralist criticism included Paul L. Garvin, *A Prague School Reader on Esthetics, Literary Structure, and Style* (1964); Ladislav Matejka and Krystyna Pomorska, *Readings in Russian Poetics* (1978); Matejka and Irwin Titunik, *Semiotics of Art* (1976); John Burbank and Peter Steiner's collections of Jan Mukařovský's work, *The Word and Verbal Art* (1977) and *Structure, Sign, and Function* (1978); Pomorska and Stephen Rudy's collection of Roman Jakobson's work, *Verbal Art, Verbal Sign, Verbal Time* (1985); and Steiner, *The Prague School* (1982). There appeared, in addition, many collections of later French structuralism outside the scope of this discussion (several works by Roland Barthes, for example, appeared in English translation in the late 1970s and early 1980s).

Other survey-critiques of structuralist criticism and collections of commentaries on structuralism as a movement included Richard Macksey and Eugenio Donato, *The Structuralist Controversy* (1970); David Robey, *Structuralism* (1973); Robert Scholes, *Structuralism in Literature* (1974); Philip Pettit, *The Concept of Structuralism* (1975), and Terence Hawkes, *Structuralism and Semiotics* (1977). (I exclude here texts that discussed nonliterary structuralism or poststructuralism exclusively, save for the Macksey and Donato collection, which addresses some linguistic topics.) Many critical works also devoted time to an evaluation of early literary structuralism: Culler, *Structuralist Poetics*, included a discussion of Jakobson, as did Pratt, *Toward a Speech Act Theory of Literary Discourse*. Critical handbooks continued to include chapters on Prague School critics—Ann Jefferson and David Robey, *Modern Literary Theory* (1982 and 1986), for example; and Terry Eagleton, *Literary Theory* (1983).

grew impatient with imported models that turned out not to solve literary problems in the way they had anticipated; their interdisciplinary interests have quite naturally, from this point of view, turned them toward other fields for suggestive paradigms and methods. Yet much of this later critical rhetoric increasingly tends to oppose the aims of linguistics and literary study and consequently retains in at least this sense some investment in broadly "linguistic" issues. Thus Stanley Fish ("Consequences") came to see generative grammar as the kind of theory criticism must not adopt, and it is now rather routine for a critic to remark on the opposing aims of linguistics and deconstruction or, say, on the "antilinguistics" of an ascendant critical figure such as Mikhail Bakhtin.[6] From this perspective, then, we have not left linguistic study behind; the implication is rather that current criticism refutes linguistics and responds directly to it.

This history suggests that it is perhaps not easy to move on from the interaction with linguistics which once so occupied the critical scene. The volume of linguistics-oriented material has ensured, first of all, a saturation of critical discourse with linguistic and speech-act concepts; like it or not, terms such as "interpretive grammar," "sign," and "performative act" have become a permanent part of our critical vocabulary. Second, linguistics-influenced works recur in paraphrased form; the arguments of *Structuralist Poetics* and *Is There a Text in This Class?*, that is, are the assumed background against which critical discourse functions. Finally, critical theories continue to position themselves in reference to specific linguistic or ordinary language models: deconstruction contrasts to Saussurean linguistics; pragmatists and cultural critics rediscover Austin or Searle. It is not so much that critics have lost interest in linguistics and speech-act theory as that linguistic notions have been so assimilated as to escape notice.

But it is precisely this assimilation of linguistics-derived notions into the terms of literary debate which has kept commentators from examining the connections between these fields in the way one might wish. Despite the volume of material on linguistic and speech-act topics, in neither stage of linguistic criticism—the first enthusiastic, the second dismissive and critical—has the perspective of the imported fields been taken much into account. That it has not need not be surprising. A critic can reject linguistic analysis on some general ground—because, for example, a tabulation of textual features yields no definitive interpretation—without considering in detail the linguis-

---

[6] See, for example, Fish, "Consequences"; Ronald Schleifer, "Deconstruction and Linguistic Analysis"; Susan Stewart, "Shouts on the Street"; and the essays in Nigel Fabb et al., *The Linguistics of Writing*. I return more specifically to this topic in the last chapter.

tic model that legitimated such activity. But even among critics initially committed to linguistic models, the necessary focus on the insights generated for *literary* theory has encouraged rather cursory attention to the nature of the imported linguistic notions. This is not to say that critics have never advanced linguistics-based arguments in literary criticism. On the contrary, speech-act theory has been promoted over generative grammar as a critical model on the strength of its attention to matters of discourse; structuralist classification procedures have been rejected for more psychologically relevant linguistic methods; and pragmatic components have been added to Chomskyan syntactic models to improve their critical value. Even so, many germane, even crucial questions can somehow remain unanswered—whether speech-act rules are akin to literary-interpretive rules, for example, whether the psychological considerations of a syntactic model are those most material to a poetics, whether it is possible, given the constraints of the original model, to attach pragmatic and literary-interpretive components to a generative grammar. So long have critics reworked linguistic paradigms in this fashion that we might also ask in this later stage of the interaction between criticism and linguistics whether critics are able any longer to distinguish the source models from their literary-critical incarnations.

My first goal, then, is to make such critical positions explicit, to bring a somewhat more dispassionate point of view to the relation between these fields by examining the criticism of an interdisciplinary period but with greater attention than before to the original linguistic and speech-act accounts. Concentrating on selected instances of interdisciplinary borrowing, I ask such questions as, How does the outline of a language theory change as it becomes a metaphor for criticism? Conversely, what unresolved problems attaching to linguistic and speech-act concepts in the original discipline affect the outcome of the literary theory that imports it? What factors in a given literary theory influence its selection of a particular linguistic notion? Finally, how may literary theories apparently antagonistic toward linguistics share some assumptions with linguistic criticism or a particular linguistic model? I aim, in other words, to test linguistics- and speech-act-derived critical paradigms against their function in the original accounts, to identify the unexamined baggage imported metaphors bring to literary theory, and to press the limits such analogies reach in a critical context.

The turnabout of critical attitude toward linguistics and speech-act theory, the current mixture of respect and disdain for these outside models, the existing tension between disciplines can be understood only from this perspective, the perspective of the small and local successes and failures in attempts at rapprochement. But this shift in critical position, documented in many of the specific topics here, suggests also a second, broader aim for the project, an interest in what Peter Brooks has called the "archeology of criticism," a look "back at the sources of the present traps, dilemmas, and debates" (Wortman 38).[7]

It is only since the renewed disciplinary interest in history that such projects have acquired a measure of dignity in literary studies, for scholars in few fields are so anxious as we are to be current; this is a worry that paradoxically allows us to reconsider literary texts but not our own last periods of literary criticism. It is precisely my aim to examine a passing, perhaps past, era of critical production, however, for I contend that only now can we find in this critical discourse what, under the professional positions and pressures of the time, we could not yet see (or say). At the very least, the criticism I examine here impressively teaches us that our own arguments are not linear. Sometimes we take as settled, arguments that instead deserve elaboration. Jacques Derrida's reading of Saussurean sign theory, no matter how assailable Derrida proves on other topics, is a case in point, largely because it involves an external field already exhausted for critical practice. And at the same time we actively reengage arguments that we could indeed find decided. My discussion assumes that the nature of the interaction between fields is as important as which accounts get refuted, that Derrida's partial reproduction of Saussurean notions—which with more distance from the deconstructionist era we can better apprehend—has as much import as his departures from Saussure. I thus take an interest in the circularity of critical discourse, in the way it repeatedly worries identical problems—for instance, the analogy between text and speech act. I want to claim, merely, that critical texts bear rereading as well as literary works do, and that from our present, more disinterested perspective we are better able to treat linguistic criticism as a product of the general mechanisms that govern the grounding of our discipline in another whose own grounds are far from certain. Such an analysis is surely necessary to a critical discourse that develops beyond a superficial interdisciplinary rhetoric to a real engagement with these and other outside fields.

---

[7] An example of such reassessment of earlier criticism is Culler, "Political Criticism," on William Empson. Note, however, that the critical climate is most hospitable to critical discussions treating the more distant scholarly past, less welcoming to dispassionate engagements of more recent criticism (in the era of deconstruction, for instance, it was virtually impossible to discuss generative grammar without immediately dismissing it).

LINGUISTIC METAPHORS, MODELS, PARADIGMS

It is a commonplace of current criticism that literary theory works in and through its models and metaphors. Here New Criticism's tropes of organic unity are the distant and therefore transparent example. When (in 1955) I. A. Richards criticized the "Linguistic Scientist," it was because the linguist "does not know how to respect the language," because, it develops, he does not rely on the correct metaphor: "He thinks of it [language] as a *code* and has not yet learned that it is an organ—the supreme organ of the mind's self-ordering growth" (*Speculative Instruments* 9).[8] Similarly, when Cleanth Brooks (1947) outlined goals for criticism, principally he cast about for the apt metaphor. Criticism, he said, must emphasize "not the special subject matter [of the poems of different historical periods], but the way in which the poem is built, or—to change the metaphor—the form which it has taken as it *grew* in the poet's mind"; these (preferable) metaphors, Brooks commented, will enable critics to "raise questions of formal structure and rhetorical organization," to discuss "meanings," "symbolizations," "paradoxes and ironies," which (in rather circular fashion) will bring readers closer to "the structure of the poem as an organism" (218). And when Tzvetan Todorov (1968) defended structuralist methods against New Critical attack, he focused on the underlying similarity of the critical schools' dominating metaphors. A "living organism" has its "part[s]" too, he maintained (*Introduction* 10), a structure that a New Critic no more refuses to outline and label than the structuralist hesitates to describe the "geography" (Todorov, quoting Henry James, 9) of his more abstract object.

As the title of this book suggests, my focus is on such critical language, on metaphors and models derived from linguistics or speech-act theory, but similar in the sense that they suggest and structure critical goals, methods, and debates. Those linguistic metaphors that recur in the following discussions are now familiar to criticism—the rule (sometimes "law" or "norm"), the phoneme (or similarly invoked "sign"), and the grammar (or "system"). These are attractive candidates for analysis in a number of respects. All these concepts are key to both structuralist and Chomskyan linguistic theory, the rule to speech-act accounts; they still occupy a central place in more specialized linguistic criticism; and such metaphors, once important to mainstream

---

[8] Of course Richards himself promoted a kind of "scientific" criticism (see *Principles of Literary Criticism*), but he was opposed to linguistic criticism until late in life. See Geoffrey Leech's comments (87n.1). (Richards's later position on linguistics is in "Linguistics into Poetics" and "Factors and Functions in Poetry.")

critics, continue to resurface, often in rather antagonistic and discipline-defining critical rhetoric. Yet a characterization of this book as primarily focused on critical metaphors of this sort is limiting, perhaps somewhat misleading, since an investigation of such concepts inevitably requires attention to the more general paradigms that embed them. In another, broader sense, then, I concentrate on what seem to me the most important or neglected points of connection between influential language theories—Saussurean linguistics, generative grammar, speech-act theory—and (mostly Anglo-American) literary criticism—literary structuralism, reader-oriented criticism, deconstruction.

Since the term "paradigm," as Thomas Kuhn uses it in *The Structure of Scientific Revolutions*—a discipline's "coherent traditions" of research, shared assumptions about central goals, problems, and investigative procedures (10)—would appear to describe what it is that literary critics import from linguistics, it seems tempting to apply his discussion further. Indeed, linguists themselves habitually recount the history of their field, particularly in connection with the "Chomskyan revolution," as a series of Kuhnian paradigm shifts, and this practice would suggest here an analysis tracing parallel developments in literary criticism. (See, for example, Frederick Newmeyer, "Has There Been a Chomskyan Revolution in Linguistics?") But changing critical interests—from historical study, to New Criticism, to reader-oriented approaches, to new historicism and cultural criticism—have been much analyzed, much remarked, and reference to Kuhn does not especially add to these observations. The kind of theoretical impasse Kuhn finds characteristic of the demise of scientific models does not precisely describe what happens to critical schools (see 66–76, 92–110), and there has never been the same sort of universal involvement that Kuhn assumes for science in a single critical paradigm (see 35–42, 52–65). Whereas parallels have often been drawn between the developing interests of linguists and critics, especially from text-based analysis to psychologically relevant models, I argue here that such concerns are often not genuinely analogous between the fields. More often, one observes, critical programs, shaped at the start by quite independent interests, absorb and reform linguistic models.

Yet it remains intuitively attractive to speak of critics importing linguistic models or paradigms—as opposed to linguistic metaphors—in this context, quite apart from Kuhn, simply because one tends to think of applied metaphors as brief and suggestive rather than extensive and explicitly theoretical. In this respect the analysis here is not entirely the sort that applies to New Critical tropes, since "organism" is simply a more culturally available notion than "linguistic rule"; the imported metaphor in the case of linguistic criticism always stands in relation to its version in the source account, and this contrast complicates its critical function. It is impossible, in other words, to separate an overarching metaphor, part of the structure of assumptions which is perhaps closer to Kuhn's sense of "paradigm" or Max Black's sense of "model" (236) (literary texts as microcosms of the language system, for example) from the lower-level metaphors it generates (texts as organized by rules or structured like sentences).

In fact this contrast between an original conceptual framework redesigned for criticism and less extensively applied metaphors illustrates the distinctiveness of this period of criticism. Of course elaborated metaphors are the very stuff of both critical discourse and any variety of interdisciplinary discussion; next to poems read as artifacts we can place historical texts read as literature (see, for example, Darnton 3–7). But such examples are instructive in that they constitute what have been called "root metaphors" (Pepper 91–92) or "conceptual archetypes" (Black 239–42), sustained and perhaps to some extent submerged reference to a productive source analogy but without the recourse to an involved apparatus or developed source account that would detail the connection. The case of linguistic criticism, on the other hand, at least sometimes approximates Black's sense of "theoretical models," the use of the "language" (or a series of principles) from a more familiar or more fully articulated domain extended or applied by analogy to a new field (229–33). In some sense, then, linguistic criticism is the example par excellence of interdisciplinary literary theory. Although such criticism clearly alternates between applied models and root metaphors (with looser metaphors the more recent norm), it represents a unique attempt to shape criticism more particularly along the lines suggested by an outside discipline.

Linguistics and speech-act theory, or so it once seemed, functioned as ideal sources for critical models. For advocates of linguistic criticism, these were theories more fully grounded in their specific analytical tools, contrasting at the time to a critical practice often characterized as haphazard and imprecise and, in their self-consciously argued overall descriptive goals, connecting with a frequently articulated desire for a new, more energized poetics. The fields were similar enough in focus—on the details of language structure, on knowledge of language—to suggest natural-seeming analogies. Yet they were far enough apart to offer productive, rather than threatening, heuristics; no linguist or ordinary language philosopher, after all, was going to prove better at literary problems, and such models, once in place, immediately raised a number of novel critical issues to address.

In linguistic criticism the applied paradigm takes two general forms. In one variety of criticism, usually the earliest linguistic applications and the later speech-act accounts, critics think of themselves as elaborating the original model. That is, the theory is not just fortuitously relevant in a new domain; the practioners maintain, rather, that the original domain itself is being expanded. The most famous example here is Roman Jakobson's call for a unified "linguistics" that would subsume both nonliterary linguistics and poetics ("Closing" 350–51, 359); for him, linguistics and criticism simply pose the same problems, since one can investigate literary and ordinary language only comparatively. Similarly, Levin (*Linguistic Structures*) unproblematically transports the apparatus of (American) structuralist linguistics or generative grammar into literary contexts, and (later) Ellen Schauber and Ellen Spolsky ("Stalking"; *Bounds*) elaborate an existing generative model for literary analysis. Again such work rests on the assumption that critics need only adjust or supplement—or merely apply—the linguistic or speech-act model. The quality of their attention to the original paradigm is often the strength of these approaches; typically such critics are well versed in the source discipline. But of course there are corresponding limitations: many such accounts fail to explore real differences between projects or to relate the new analysis to the pressing concerns of the importing field. Thus such linguistic criticism sometimes has in retrospect—Levin is the particular example here—a parochial flavor, and it often expresses considerable anxiety over the future of the linguistic model in which so much critical energy is now invested.

A second variety of linguistic criticism works more consciously by analogy, and in it critics often vacillate between conceptions of the source theory as a (theoretical) model (in the limited sense already defined) and as a root metaphor (or conceptual archetype). In her earlier work, Pratt, for example, explicitly articulates the two functions, signaling a contrast between extensions of sociolinguistics and ordinary language philosophy into literary speech situations (to analyze implicature and narrative structure) and more thoroughly metaphorical applications (to discuss the literary marketplace) (see *Toward*). Such accounts acknowledge at the start that the fit between the source and the literary context is at best inexact, and a crucial difference is that critics in this case do not mean for incongruities to motivate adjustments of the borrowed theory. Other examples are reader-oriented critics such as Culler and Fish, who early on assumed roles as *bricoleurs*, taking to hand whatever tools—linguistic or otherwise—might offer an escape from particular critical problems.[9] Using linguis-

---

[9] See Claude Lévi-Strauss, *Savage* 16–33; and Derrida, "Structure" 285–88.

tic and speech-act accounts as heuristics clearly results in a more flex-
ibile and inventive criticism, but insight into the imported theory is
more limited, and such accounts sometimes scapegoat the source
model when the literary problems prove intractable.

In both cases the applied models or root metaphors thrive or collapse
according to the fortunes of the lower-level metaphors they generate. A
variety of troubles may eventually befall them. Critics may simply
make an initially productive analogy account for literary facts too diverse; loosely applied at the outset, one notion (language as system, for
example, or *langue* opposed to *parole*) applies to so many problems that
it finally no longer provides enough resistance—a strong enough sense
either of the goals of the original theory or of a coherent framework
in which its various applications are articulated—to be usefully heuristic. The metaphor exhausts itself in local functions without pointing
strongly toward an overall theory that will direct further critical practice. Or a (more strictly applied) metaphor starts as more genuinely
parallel to a source concept (a literary rule analogous to a syntactic
rule) but in a literary context accounts for so much more than was
relevant in the linguistic theory that the literary version begins to collapse, and the literary facts the metaphor does not explain become increasingly obvious. In some instances the original notion inflates as it
metaphorizes (sentence-level concerns in the source become text-level
concerns in the criticism); in other cases it constricts (knowledge of
language becomes knowledge of textual norms). These processes, naturally enough, eventually limit such metaphors' explanatory power, for
much of the original attached explanatory apparatus will no longer apply. In still other instances, critics transfer a concept from the original
field to criticism in some way nonmetaphorically; the notion is simply
meant to retain, roughly speaking, its original significance in the importing field. But in Black's terms, the "rules of correlation" (230) from
one domain to another sometimes go awry in the translation between
contexts (a "constitutive rule" loses its distinctive character). Often
the language of the original account starts to apply in its everyday
rather than its linguistic or speech-act sense (the term "acceptability,"
for instance), and the once specialized vocabulary again becomes in
some way metaphorical in the literary context.[10]

This list of permuted tropes does not mean, however, that this book
is to be a catalog of the ways in which critics have misappropriated
linguistic theory. To be sure, misreadings do abound, and the unex-

[10] See also Culler's taxonomy of linguistic metaphors in literary criticism: literature as
a whole as analogous to language, an individual work or works of one author as analogous
to a language system, texts as semiotic projects, and the like (*Structuralist Poetics* 96–
109).

amined critical assumptions that often govern both the choice of a particular linguistic analogy and its operation within a literary theory are a central interest of this project. In some cases there are even serious questions to be asked about the rhetorical status linguistic paradigms ultimately assume in critical discussion. That is, some misleading characterizations of linguistic models are both understandable outcomes of a certain literary program and yet disturbingly convenient readings for the literary argument at hand. That they are raises a general question about the conduct of interdisciplinary criticism; in this respect this work is a specific case of the way in which literary critics rework notions from outside disciplines. Still, the point is emphatically not that linguistics-based analogies fail precisely because they are analogies, because they are too loosely metaphorical and therefore illegitimate. The occasional appeal to a linguistic-literary theory simply to shed its cumbersome linguistic apparatus is at best presumptuous. One cannot legitimately complain that a revealing narrative theory fails only in its debt to a grammatical paradigm when that model is the critic's central source of insight, for such arguments assume what the criticism of the 1970s and 1980s eloquently belies—that (linguistic) models and metaphors are trivial and decorative, not genuinely productive. The problem that should be explored, rather, is how and why an otherwise effective model eventually came to limit the critical project. It is not that imported linguistic and speech-act concepts did not function well in literary criticism, but they did not work in all respects, and critical discussion has not always shown us why.

In addition, one can certainly discuss the fit, the suitability, the undetected consequences of an analogical framework without implying that it is possible for criticism to escape metaphorical formulation. I believe, on the contrary, that literary objects are available to readers only through some such structure of assumptions; there is no natural, neutral, or inevitable means of analysis. To read literature simply "as literature" can mean, variously, to read it as historical document, as stable artifact, as self-resisting argument, as linguistic data. And these metaphors in turn are constituted by critical paradigms that determine which textual facts readers will find, particular notions about the nature of history, about the status of cultural artifacts, about the structure of language, which find only further metaphorical expression: history, like persons, reacts and revolts; artifacts speak to humankind or comment on one another; aesthetic discourse is dense and complex. Besides, the linguistic notions under analysis find similar metaphorical expression in the original discipline: language is a mechanical system, a computer program, a psychological theory. In testing the boundaries of linguistic metaphors, I would never wish to suggest that there exists some nonmetaphorical alternative. Instead, my focus is on the tension between linguistic model and critical purpose, between alternative paradigms. The contrasting implications of Brooks's "organism" and Todorov's "geography" or "structure" are the kind of problem at issue; it is surely not possible to ask either critic to cease metaphorizing.

TOPICS

The chapters that follow consider specific instances of interdisciplinary criticism. As a point of clarification I should explain that I discuss both linguistics and speech-act theory in this book not because I feel their aims are similar (I do not confuse ordinary language philosophy with structuralist linguistics or generative grammar) but because those literary critics most committed to linguistic models have tended to borrow as well from speech-act accounts. And it is the case that a few such theorists have misconstrued speech-act theory as in some sense related to generative grammar, despite its different history and purpose. Although this confusion is unfortunate, the mere combination of interests is neither illegitimate nor unprecedented, however, since linguists (especially sociolinguists) themselves often draw from ordinary language philosophy to address certain problems.[11] So I feel justified myself in discussing both linguistic and speech-act models and, in any case, will need to do so to examine the critical discourse that closely relates them. The terms "linguistic model" and "linguistic paradigm," then, may often, for the sake of convenience, refer also to speech-act notions without meaning to imply that linguistics and speech-act theory constitute a single discipline.

The book concentrates primarily on what I take to be the most influential linguistic and speech-act texts in literary criticism, those I mentioned at the outset—Ferdinand de Saussure's *Course in General Linguistics*, Chomsky's *Aspects of the Theory of Syntax* (and *Syntactic Structures*), Searle's *Speech Acts*, and Austin's *How to Do Things with Words*. These choices, I think, will be uncontroversial, for these are demonstrably the most cited accounts in literary contexts and those that have generated the most (positive and negative) critical response.

---

[11] See, for example, William Labov's analysis (with David Fanshel) of discourse conventions in *Therapeutic Discourse*; Penelope Brown and Stephen Levinson's examination of politeness conventions, "Universals in Language Use"; and Deborah Tannen's discussion of indirection, "Ethnic Style in Male-Female Conversation." See also textbook accounts: Ralph Fasold, *Sociolinguistics of Language* 119–79; Ronald Wardhaugh, *An Introduction to Sociolinguistics* 282–311.

Each chapter also focuses on a few representative or especially influential critical texts. Not surprisingly, this selection of critical topics and texts has been more problematic than the choice of linguistic accounts. I have elected at the start to concentrate principally on Anglo-American—as opposed to Czech or French—criticism. I do so in part to achieve more coherence between the issues raised in each chapter but also partly because a fuller account of linguistic models in Czech or French structuralism would imply a massive treatment. One exception is the discussion of Prague School criticism in the second chapter, which I bring to bear on a reading of Jakobson's work in an American context, but in which I also invest some independent critical energy. This discussion is not meant to be as complete an accounting of linguistic models in Prague School work as I attempt in readings of American reader-oriented texts, for this would require a look at several stages of Czech criticism. Chapter 2 is surely not intended as an evaluation of the entire Czech structuralist movement, or of its work with other interpretive models—phenomenology, for example, or Peircean sign theory. A second, more obviously natural exception to the general focus here is the inclusion of (French) deconstructionist texts that became central to Anglo-American critical practice. French structuralist criticism I have excluded more completely. Many critics consider French criticism closer to the (Saussurean) linguistic model than other varieties of structuralism; certainly it does not reflect as eclectic an investment in other models as does Prague School work. While French critics have continued to build on the Saussurean model, however, they have been more removed from linguistic acccounts in the sense that these developments of the paradigm often have had more to do with other literary versions of Saussure than with continued or elaborated reference to developments in linguistics. So in this way French structuralism has seemed to me to require a different mode of analysis from that I attempt here.[12]

On a more local level, I have generally excluded critical work some readers might consider somehow "linguistic" in orientation which does not specifically refer to a linguistic or speech-act account. Thus, I have not discussed critics who work primarily in a semiotic rather than linguistic tradition (critics whose work, that is, relies on Charles Sanders Peirce's sign theory or on Peirce's [literary] elaborators or who have derived from Saussure and Peirce a general theory of cultural signs); nor have I incorporated deconstructionist accounts that discuss

---

[12] For these reasons I do not examine Gérard Genette's or Tzvetan Todorov's work on narrative as fully as it otherwise deserves. (Their analyses of linguists and critics I discuss in greater detail.)

problems of language and interpretation without detailed recourse to linguistic or speech-act models.[13] This is not to say that such work is not interesting or important; it simply does not entail a close linguistics connection or discernible borrowed paradigm to explore in the specific manner I have in mind. Perhaps more important, I select for analysis texts that construct "global" models, accounts of the nature of criticism as a whole, rather than those that use linguistic criticism to interpret individual texts, and I focus on such broad issues as how critics define literary texts, describe literary language, and account for literary meaning and production.

I have also aimed to avoid issues that have already been treated extensively and, to my mind, adequately. For instance, I skip over many of the issues involved in linguistics-based stylistic analysis because some pertain to textual readings and because a number of critics— Michael Riffaterre, Fish, Culler—have previously debated such points.[14] On the other hand, I attend to the role of generative grammar in projects founding a general poetics, for contemporary treatments insufficiently understood the interaction between the imported model and the borrowing criticism. Similarly, I mention only briefly Ohmann's early speech-act criticism, which Pratt, in a well-known account, analyzes extensively (*Toward* 87–99); instead, I consider more loosely applied speech-act metaphors, sometimes submerged and undetected, in later criticism.

I should add here, finally, that in what follows I have without exception chosen to focus on critics whose work I very much admire, those who drew me in the first place to the topic of interdisciplinary criticism. Never do I aim to analyze an entire critical career or to evaluate whole movements or theories; I intend simply to contribute to ongoing critical debate by examining the gaps, mismatches, connections, and inconsistencies between linguistic and speech-act models and their literary versions. The topics of the following chapters, then, do not pretend to exhaust the connections among linguistics, speech-act theory, and literary theory. They do address what I see as the central critical

[13] As an example of the first case, I mention just briefly Umberto Eco's *Role of the Reader*, despite its eclectic references to varieties of structuralism and speech-act theory, because it does not sustain these last connections as fully as alternative texts. As an example of the second case, I consider relevant only Paul de Man's direct engagements with speech-act theory.

[14] On stylistic analysis, see Riffaterre, "Describing Poetic Structures"; the last section of Fish, "Literature in the Reader"; Fish, "What Is Stylistics and Why Are They Saying Such Terrible Things about It?"; Fish, "What Is Stylistics and Why Are They Saying Such Terrible Things about It? Part II"; and Culler's chapter on Jakobson in *Structuralist Poetics* 55–74.

successes and limitations of the borrowed linguistic and speech-act models, first in Jakobsonian structuralism (or Prague School criticism as rewritten for the American context) (Chapter 2), in reader-oriented theory (Chapters 3 and 4), then in deconstruction and deconstruction-influenced criticism (Chapters 5 and 6).

CONTEXTS

I alluded at the outset to the two distinct phases of linguistic criticism on which this book primarily focuses—an initial optimistic period of varied, model-building interdisciplinary work and a slightly later deconstruction-influenced effort to dismantle linguistic and speech-act paradigms. In the interest of accuracy, however, I should stress, too, that linguistics tools were not entirely new to the critical scene in my so-titled initial phase and in fact had coexisted more-or-less happily for a time with mainstream New Criticism. This stylistic criticism, which employed linguistic analysis in more narrow, text-based projects, over-lapped and then contrasted, as I have also indicated, with linguistic and speech-act models as they were developing in the kind of general reader-oriented poetics with which we are now more familiar.[15] As a lesson in the cycling and recycling of interdisciplinary models, it is worth asking how this contrast in linguistic projects arose and also, simply, how it is that linguistic and speech-act models could partici-pate both in a formalist critical practice and in projects that explicitly rejected formalist precepts.

The answer is both that the pressures of critical practice are such that almost any critical program can absorb nearly any linguistic model and, paradoxically, that the models in question ultimately exert a certain resistance. What (in the 1960s) linguistics-oriented stylisti-cians shared with New Critics was a passion, largely inaccessible to us now, for all matters pertaining to style—style as it might explain a particular aesthetic effect, the distinctive syntactic habits of a prose writer, the habitual lexicon of a poet, or the syntactic preferences of a

---

[15] I am characterizing stylistics as akin to New Criticism in the sense that the assumed, shared critical goal was a close textual analysis without major recourse to readers' judg-ments, writers' authority, or the historical or political context of the work. There are, as always, exceptions and caveats to be made. Stylisticians, even in the Anglo-American context, departed from New Critical practice in several respects, as I note shortly. And some stylistics projects (Levin, *Linguistic Structures in Poetry* [1962], for example) were, like early narratology (Gerald Prince, *A Grammar of Stories* [1973]), more structuralist in flavor despite the incorporation of American (as opposed to Saussurean) linguistic con-cepts. See Fowler, "Linguistics, Stylistics" 169, for remarks on affinities between stylistics projects and New Criticism.

literary period.[16] Examples are instructive. Participants representing a range of critical perspectives at a 1958 conference on style enthusiastically took up the question of whether or not the repetition of Sam Cooke's line "You send me" was aesthetically pleasing, and they argued also over what prosodic facts accounted for listeners' preference for the poem title "Harvard Yard in April/April in Harvard Yard" over "April in Harvard Yard/Harvard Yard in April" (Sebeok 100, 24).[17] In this context linguistic critics claimed that they were merely answering more precisely, with more developed linguistic methods natural to the purpose, questions that any critic might voice.

But such critics really attended only to some issues of general interest, and for several of them linguistic analysis at the same time offered competing critical goals. This state of affairs is difficult to capture from a usual summary of this criticism, first, because it is often read as unproblematically invested in New Critical organicism and, second, because typical linguistics-based stylistic analyses are indeed likely to strike current readers as unredeemably formalist, exercises in mining texts for elements relevant to standard interpretations. The genuinely elegant readings that did emerge (for instance, Freeman's analysis of Keats's "To Autumn" or M. A. K. Halliday's of Golding's *Inheritors*) demonstrated how specific linguistic features contributed to local aesthetic or interpretive effects. This was an impressive enough achievement, but not one that would seem in retrospect likely to shake up then-prevailing critical norms. And yet such work did indeed generate a measure of antagonism from mainstream New Critics, with whom not all stylisticians willingly identified. In other words, (linguistic) stylisticians were formalists, but in importantly different respects.[18]

From this perspective one can begin to sympathize with some of these critics' impulses. Detractors, for example, steeped in the discipline-defining language of the period, often reacted to the sheer fact of stylisticians' interdisciplinary aims. Antagonistic critics responded,

---

[16] For a discussion of projects in stylistics, see Ohmann, "Generative Grammars."

[17] As Culler comments, perhaps more remarkable than the topic itself is the fact that Jakobson is quite capable of explaining precisely why it is that English speakers prefer the first title (*Poetics* 69).

[18] M. A. K. Halliday, whom I mention briefly here, introduced European text linguistics to this criticism.

Useful historical overviews of the relation between linguistics and literary study are Fabb and Durant, "Ten Years on in the Linguistics of Writing"; and Culler, "Literature and Linguistics." See also Fowler's insightful comments in "Linguistics and, and Versus, Poetics."

For an early example of an especially antagonistic account of linguistic criticism, see Peter Barry.

too, to the technical vocabulary and knowledge stylisticians displayed, which did not accord with a sense that critics should bring to texts principally a broad education and delicate sensibilities. Opponents rightly charged that stylisticians' obsession with textual description sometimes rendered them insensitive readers, overwhelmed by apparatus. Nevertheless, the project of detailed textual analysis, as an end in itself, at least displaced the paraphrase reading as the primary critical project (see Bierwisch; Freeman, "Approaches"; Ohmann, "Literature as Sentences").[19] The stylisticians' habit of conducting analysis in two stages—one descriptive and one interpretive—failed to account for the (interpretive) initial selection of elements to be analyzed. Yet this same practice foregrounded the critic's choice of interpretive perspective rather than naturalizing and suppressing it (see Bierwisch 110–14; Fowler, "Linguistic Theory" 28; Ohmann, "Generative Grammars" 143; Saporta 86; Stankiewicz 71). The linguistic critics' preoccupation with lexical patterning and deviance involved assumed—at times explicit—reference to the interpretive position of readers (see Bierwisch 108–9; Ohmann, "Generative Grammars" 139; Ohmann, "Literature as Sentences" 154–56; Sinclair 70; Thorne 195).[20] And the demystifying impulse of stylistic criticism (which Ohmann's title "Literature as Sentences" neatly exemplifies) worked to problematize the distinction between literary and nonliterary language (see Bierwisch 113; Fowler, "Linguistic Theory" 10–11; Levin, *Linguistic* 30). For all their high-drive formalism, then, linguistic stylisticians, in contrast to mainstream contemporaries, emerged with more interdisciplinary interests, more investment in nonliterary prose, and a budding attachment to general explanatory models, though perhaps with more memorable theoretical accounts than literary readings. Linguistic models themselves were thus positioned for a contrasting critical practice.

In early (1970s) speech-act criticism—as opposed to linguistic stylistics—a tension between the New Critical context and the imported paradigm was more obviously operative at the start.[21] An already shifting critical climate for this somewhat later criticism partly accounts

[19] I include Bierwisch even though he is a German scholar, because his discussion appeared in translation in Freeman's standard collection. I note that the deemphasis in stylistics on interpretation sometimes led to reflections on a rudimentary reader-based literary theory. However, textual description—as opposed to either a literary reading or a general model—was for some critics a sufficient critical aim in itself (Levin, for example, and Sinclair).

[20] Fowler maintained early on (1966) that the very selection of textual features for analysis was necessarily an interpretive choice ("Linguistics, Stylistics" 172–73).

[21] For a useful historical overview of the relation between speech-act theory and literary study, see Barrie Ruth Strauss, "Influencing Theory."

for this tension, but so do the sheer constraints of the model, for speech-act theory applied to literary readings necessarily assumed that extraliterary discourse norms were at play. And the particular insight of speech-act critics, principally Ohmann, an especially honest and engaging interpreter of the model, determined a somewhat different direction for this criticism. Although Ohmann dissociated himself from New Critics and detailed the changing relationships among text, writer, and reader, at the outset he again conformed speech-act notions to formalist principles ("Speech Acts" [1971]; see also Levin, "Concerning"). That is, while he defined literary works as mentally realized entities (3) and noted the referential properties of speech acts within literary language (4–5), he ultimately found illocutionary acts in literature mimetic (14) and autonomous, unproblematically distinct from other kinds of discourse (15–16, 18). Yet it is also the case that "literature" quickly became a much less stable category in Ohmann's later essays (see "Speech, Literature" [1974]). In fact, he soon began to argue through speech-act accounts for the political power of literature and for a politicized approach to teaching it (see "Literature as Act" [1973]).

Linguistic and speech-act models thus both served and disrupted existing critical norms. Formalist projects certainly accommodate linguistic and speech-act concepts. But the fact that even in early linguistic criticism one can find such (albeit buried and occasional) claims as that literary categories are selected and not given, that textual analysis pertains to readers' perceptions, that interpretive readings are no longer central, that literary acts are also acts in the extraliterary world suggests these models are more naturally assimilated into more broadly theoretical—rather than locally interpretive—critical programs. Just such projects are the topic of the next chapters. As history dictates, I begin with Roman Jakobson, the acknowledged source of linguistic criticism.

Chapter 2

Roman Jakobson's "Closing Statement"

> We can say that what is natural to mankind is not oral speech but the faculty of constructing a language.
> —FERDINAND DE SAUSSURE, *Course in General Linguistics*

No essay more aptly illustrates that critical texts—as much as philosophical or literary ones—bear rereading in the context of their own history of reception than Roman Jakobson's famous paper on the goals of a linguistics-based poetics. Titled "Closing Statement: Linguistics and Poetics," it was, as critics have wryly observed, more an opportunity for elaboration or engagement than it was a summation statement for the 1958 Indiana conference on style. "Closing Statement" has remained synonymous, in Anglo-American discussions, with the notion of linguistic criticism, so much so that any account of linguistics and literary theory would seem remiss not to address it. And the figure of Jakobson himself, always an authoritative presence and a major promulgator of structuralist methods in this country, has come, largely though not exclusively through this essay, so to embody principles central to linguistics-based formalist practice that no metacritical account can fail to acknowledge him.[1] Although many of the arguments of "Closing Statement" are summaries of Jakobson's conclusions elsewhere, the sheer density of its suggestions—for semiotics, stylistics, prosody, the analysis of extraliterary and aesthetic language— has ensured its critical force; it informs projects as varied as James

---

[1] For brief accounts of Jakobson's central role, see Derek Attridge, "Closing Statement" 15–16; Terry Eagleton 98; and René Wellek, "Foreword" ix. In my remarks on Jakobson's contrasting critical positions I am indebted to Wallace Martin.

Kinneavy's study of nonfictional discourse and Roger Fowler's functional linguistic criticism. In 1986 when critics met to assess the interdisciplinary exchange between linguistics and literary studies which the earlier conference in Indiana had helped to promote, many papers attempted finally to close the text of "Closing Statement" (see Fabb et al.). Yet Jakobson's essay has consistently proved difficult to exhaust. As an ambitious and complex paradigm text, it remains both compelling and intractable, and it is thus a natural starting point for this book.

If "Closing Statement" is a source text still, in its historical moment, a 1958 American conference on style, it was nothing less than seminal, a controversial statement of new—even radical—alternatives to existing (New Critical) practice. Since this sense of the essay is difficult to recapture, it is worth emphasizing how sharply Jakobson's perspective would have contrasted to that of the critics in his audience. First and perhaps most important, Jakobson repositioned the autonomous literary work within a rhetorical framework. In his communication model, that is, literary discourse was one subcode among others, shaped by its rhetorical aims like nonliterary language. One cannot productively study poetic language, Jakobson claimed, without attending to the "general problems of language" (356). Second, to critics accustomed to according a special status to literary discourse, Jakobson's scheme proposed functional connections between literary and ordinary language. Literary language in Jakobson's account defined itself against existing nonliterary codes, but it also shared with them features of any speech context. Third, Jakobson introduced an alternative critical focus in "literariness," the linguistic features marking literature as a functional language. The literary work in Jakobson's conception became less reified object than text, since literary devices were to be found in a variety of discourse contexts. Finally, "Closing Statement" foregrounded functional and pragmatic issues that had not yet begun to concern even those linguists invested in matters of style, anticipating by several years new directions in both linguistics and criticism. We will hardly wonder then that "Closing Statement" failed to close discussion or that we have yet to consume such a crucial text.

Of course to some extent Jakobson's essay meshed with the existing interests and needs briefly described in the last chapter. That is, it shared with other papers at the conference a concern with such matters as definitively locating aesthetic effects in particular elements of a literary text, arguing only, from this point of view, for more rigorous linguistic description. The essay thus accompanied—and further motivated—work on stylistic issues, and the well-known volume generated at the Indiana conference, *Style and Language* (Sebeok), was followed by many similar collections focusing on such issues as accounting for syntactic differences among prose writers, the function of deixis in poetry, and problems of prosodic description. In returning to literary issues after a long absence, moreover, Jakobson cast his program at the American conference in comfortingly familiar New Critical terms: he affirmed in his remarks the organic integrity of literary works (366).[2] But the paper was finally an unabashed polemic for the applicability of linguistic models, proposing even that a more broadly conceived linguistics would subsume both the investigation of ordinary language, linguistics as it is usually and more narrowly construed, and also poetics, the study of literary language, since for Jakobson it was only from a comparative perspective that the distinction could be apprehended (350). This less soothing message was embedded in other arguments distinctively European in flavor, clearly deriving from Russian Formalist and Prague School sources, arguments for the scientific study of literature, for the differential nature of literary language, and for the productivity of a Saussurean linguistic model.

Such contrasting rhetorical strategies in the essay naturally suggest two perspectives from which to treat it, either as a culmination of Russian Formalist and Prague School principles or as a more idiosyncratic expression of Jakobson's views re-formed and altered by the American context and his own intellectual distance from his earlier literary passions. My sense is that at least in mainstream survey-handbooks "Closing Statement" is too easily read through the lens of Anglo-American critical preoccupations, and a much different view of Jakobsonian principles, not unsupported by this later text, emerges from a glance at his earlier pieces.[3] A more productive approach would attend to Jakobson's earlier context and to reassessments of Prague School work—notably F. W. Galan's *Historic Structures* and Jurij Striedter's *Literary Structure, Evolution, and Value*—which effectively argue that Prague criti-

---

[2] I assume a general familiarity with Jakobson's history as a critic; he was a member of the Moscow Linguistic Circle from 1915 to 1920 and of the Prague Linguistic Circle from 1926 to 1939. Through the 1940s and 1950s (in Scandinavia and the United States), Jakobson wrote mostly on linguistic topics. See Linda Waugh and Monique Monville-Burston's account of Jakobson's career, "Introduction."

[3] For a brief account of the essay's critical contexts, see David Robey, "Modern Linguistics" 52–53, 56–62. For a history and evaluation of Russian Formalism, see Victor Erlich, *Russian Formalism*; Peter Steiner, *Russian Formalism*. On the Prague School, see F. W. Galan, *Historic Structures*; Jurij Striedter, *Literary Structure, Evolution, and Value*. See also shorter overviews of the Prague School: Wellek, "Literary Theory"; Thomas Winner, "Aesthetics and Poetics of the Prague Linguistic Circle." Lubomír Doležel discusses both movements in *Occidental Poetics*.

cism has been incompletely assimilated and largely misunderstood in this country (see Galan 1–4; Striedter 1–6). Nevertheless, as any account must admit, Jakobson simply did not write "Closing Statement" during either his Russian Formalist or Prague School period, and the essay quite clearly does not articulate many of the latter's most advanced and attractive theories, notably on literary history and reception; from the perspective of Jakobson's earlier literary criticism, the later essay often appears to disadvantage. A reasonable compromise, which I attempt here, is simply to treat "Closing Statement" as distinct from Jakobson's other criticism yet inevitably informed by certain of his earlier positions. Thus I count it sometimes appropriate to compare Jakobson's essay to Prague School statements of similar scope and purpose, particularly to Jan Mukařovský's important essays "On Poetic Language" and "Two Studies of Poetic Designation."[4] But reference here to Jakobson's Russian Formalist and Prague School roots, whether in the form of his own or others' work, does not constitute a claim that "Closing Statement" is essentially Slavic criticism; it merely acknowledges that neither can one assimilate the essay to New Critical precept or practice.

From the perspective of its metacritical history, these distinctions have not mattered as much as they might, which is to say that mainstream critics have found in "Closing Statement" essentially the same limitations as in any formalist enterprise, whether European or New Critical. This reaction is perhaps heightened by a sense that Jakobson's (more European) empiricist claims, far from distinguishing his from other formalist projects, merely render his critical position more dogmatic. For the text of "Closing Statement," the result has been an ambivalently successful body of metacritical discussion. While one would not wish to quarrel with many of the well-known objections to the critical tasks the essay outlines, to some extent the piece remains embedded in an unsatisfactorily general critical conversation. Thus, if one identifies Jakobson either as a diehard formalist or a naive and recalcitrant empiricist, then the project tends to fail on the grounds that all such projects fail. And if Jakobson is deeply conflicted in his critical aims, as several more sensitive analyses demonstrate, then his program

---

[4] By "similar scope and purpose" I mean only that Mukařovský's essays, written in 1940, 1938, and 1946, discuss such broad issues as the nature of literary language, the goals of criticism, and linguistic functionalism, much as Jakobson's "Closing Statement" does, and that certain of Mukařovský's positions correspond to Jakobson's. Obviously the critics contrast in several respects, and Jakobson wrote at a literal and historical distance from the Prague School context. (Mukařovský wrote his essays during and after the Prague School's so-called "classical period" [1929–39]; Jakobson left Prague in 1939. Detailed histories are in Galan and Vachek.)

ultimately collapses because the wrong formalist impulses, for whatever reason, finally win the day. What I offer here as something of a corrective is a more detailed examination of the specifics of Jakobson's linguistics, for emerging more pressingly from this significant history of metacritical discussion are some basic questions not about what Jakobson's limitations and blindnesses are but rather about their source. In particular, it is revealing to explore what the simple reality that Jakobson was principally a phonologist, proceeding from and elaborating a Saussurean phonological model, meant to the arguments of "Closing Statement"; for a bias toward phonological—even as opposed to his so-called phonocentric impulses—it develops, defines Jakobson's conception of aesthetic experience, complicates structuralist analytical procedure, and limits the functionalism of both his linguistics and his criticism.

THE LINGUISTICS OF "CLOSING STATEMENT"

Jakobson's writings on linguistics are voluminous and varied, and I will explore just a few issues in greater detail shortly, but many of his general linguistic principles emerge as he applies them to literary matters in the narrower context of "Closing Statement." His overall perspective is, as critics routinely note, Saussurean.[5] That is, he accepts doctrines now familiar to literary discussion through Saussure's *Course in General Linguistics*, principally the arbitrariness of the linguistic sign (that there exists no necessary connection between concepts and the sounds used to represent them), and the analogy between language and system (that the elements of language are differentially and interactively defined, that a change in one part of the system results in a fundamental change to the whole). Further, the language-as-system paradigm suggests to Jakobson, as it does to Saussure, that concepts exist because of, rather than independent of, the languages that describe them. The socially shared, abstract principles of a language or cultural practice, *la langue*, contrast for both Saussure and Jakobson with *la parole*, the individual and specific expression of the semiotic system. And Jakobson adopts as a sometimes useful fiction Saussure's well-known distinction between synchronic and diachronic linguistics,

---

[5] The essay has sometimes been read through the assumptions of generative grammar, toward which Jakobson briefly gestures, but such an approach is not compatible with his linguistics. Because Saussure's linguistics has been so widely discussed in literary contexts, I give less detail here than I do on other linguistic theories.

along with Saussure's contrast between the associative (or paradigmatic) and syntagmatic dimensions of language.[6]

But it is also clear that Jakobson sees himself—indeed, correctly—as an important reviser of Saussure's model. Although the program of "Closing Statement" is often read as pointedly text focused, Jakobson, at least, defines his literary and linguistic interests as more generally semiotic. His opening gambit, the call for a "linguistics" that would contain both a linguistics of ordinary language and a comparatively defined linguistic poetics, from Jakobson's perspective merely announces a semiotic critical practice (see 350–51, 359). It invokes his earlier work on folklore and on film, recalling Jakobson's explicit (Prague School) claim that he was expanding the semiotic possibilities of the Saussurean model as Saussure never had; and it gestures toward his later essays on music and painting.[7] The initial rhetoric of the essay itself echoes the language of the Prague School semiotic period, as in Mukařovský's optimistic announcement in "On Poetic Language": "A comparative theory of art is beginning to take shape on a semiotic basis" (63, and see 10). And Jakobson's essay alludes as well to his own elaborations of Saussurean sign theory, necessary to an analysis of visual and auditory signs, elaborations that added to the notion of arbitrariness important remarks on iconic, indexical, and partially motivated (partially arbitrary) signs (see "Shifters" and the later "Quest").

Although the important Saussurean language-as-system analogy is productive for Jakobson, certainly in this essay it, too, undergoes revision, and it would actually be more correct to say that the subcode or subsystem is for him the central metaphor. Jakobson repeatedly faults Saussure for his monolithic language system, preferring the more pressing linguistic problems posed by variant codes, by language as a "system of systems" ("Sign" 30). In the text of "Closing Statement," literary language is one such subcode, a kind of dialect of the national language, functioning in binary opposition to its nonliterary uses (356, 395; see also Mukařovský, "On Poetic" 7–11; "Two Studies" 68–69).

[6] The contrast is between categories of like, exchangeable elements (all nouns, for example) and elements linearly sequenced (the article-adjective-noun order in English noun phrases). Jakobson creatively exploits the distinction in a number of ways: to explain an opposition between metaphor (paradigmatic) and metonymy (syntagmatic), categories of aphasic disturbance, and the contrast between indexical and iconic signs. See "Closing" 358; "Two Aspects"; "Quest" 417.

[7] For examples, see the essays collected in the first and last sections of *Language in Literature*. Especially interesting in connection with this chapter are (the Russian Formalist) "Futurism" and "Dada" and (the much later) "A Glance at the Development of Semiotics."

Or subcodes are rhetorically defined categories of discourse—persuasive, emotive, referential, poetic (352; see also Mukařovský, "On Poetic" 1, 5; "Two Studies" 67–69). As Mukařovský elaborates, the subsystem of poetic discourse is sometimes literally a dialect in a language with a specifically literary subcode, but presumably, literary language may cut across dialect boundaries or exist as a subsystem of a regional variety ("On Poetic" 7). Further, Mukařovský imagines a hierarchy of subsystems; genre-specific language conventions and, finally, individual literary works are in turn somewhat "self-sufficient" subsystems (or, more accurately, subsystems within subsystems) of literary language ("On Poetic" 13–14). Thus in both Prague School work and in the text of "Closing Statement" an interest in language diversity and interaction begins to compete with arguments for the systematic (Saussurean) integrity of the subcode.

If language is a system of "interconnected subcodes," then, according to Jakobson, one investigates the nature of literary language by comparing it to other existing subsystems, particularly to referential language, from which it must defamiliarize itself (352).[8] And if this is a synchronic task of literary analysis, one might also recast the project historically. Literary history requires a strictly Saussurean methodology in the language of "Closing Statement": it is "built on a series of successive synchronic descriptions" (352) to which the critic applies the same contrastive analysis. But Jakobson's earlier conception of literary history is much richer and less static, and it derives very specifically from his pointed—often vehement—critiques of Saussure's separation of diachronic from synchronic linguistic study, some of which he developed as a response to problems in historical phonology ("Problems" [with Tynjanov]; "Efforts"; Galan 11–12). In his (and Mukařovský's) Prague School work, historical change is motivated, not accidental or random as it is for Saussure. That is, to accomplish its aesthetic effects, literary language must somehow distinguish itself not just from an existing everyday language deadened to perception ("automatized") by habitual use but also from an earlier poetic discourse that has been assimilated into the general language and consciousness (Jakobson, "What Is"). Both subcodes become inherently unstable. The

---

[8] I assume familiarity with this term. In Russian Formalist accounts, new literary devices achieve aesthetic effects as they deform or "defamiliarize" existing linguistic conventions (see Jakobson, "On Realism"). In Prague School criticism, subcodes or functional languages define themselves against one another; especially literary language renews perception of the "automatized" or habitualized elements of ordinary language (see Mukařovský, "Standard"). Innovative works deform the general aesthetic norms of an earlier era, resulting in an altered conception of the canon, and textual devices foreground themselves against a background of automatized elements (see Jakobson, "The Dominant").

absorption of a new (literary) device into ordinary language necessitates a compensating innovation in poetic language. This effective rewriting of "defamiliarization" results in a fluid, deforming relationship between functional languages (Mukařovský, "On Poetic"). As Jakobson says, evolution is itself a system ("Problems" [with Tynjanov] 26–27); that is, eventually explains to him such matters as changes in the literary canon, the revival of archaic poetic devices, and the altered effect of an earlier text read in a later era ("The Dominant" 85–87; "Problems" [with Tynjanov] 26; see also Mukařovský, "On Poetic" 12–13; "Two Studies" 79).

Jakobson is sometimes accused of unknowingly creating a separate *langue* and *parole* for literary and ordinary language (Pratt, *Toward* 10–11); yet here and elsewhere he simply appropriates the distinction for both larger system and subsystem. He declares both the realm of shared norms and particular instantiations of those norms—whether literary or nonliterary, whether of the language system or of the subcode—open to linguistic investigation (352–53; "Problems" [with Tynjanov] 26–27; see also Mukařovský, "On Poetic" 20). The result in "Closing Statement" is a series of loose and wide-ranging applications of the Saussurean opposition. Indeed, a kind of *langue-parole* metaphor applies variously to oppose any fixed or predetermined elements to areas of variation and choice.[9] Thus Jakobson contrasts the phonological patterns of a poem to the varied possibilities of its oral performance (365–66; see also Mukařovský, "On Poetic" 18, 31–33), the predetermined requirements of a verse form with its generic realizations (364), the limitations of a particular meter with the possibilities of violation and departure (364), a metrical tradition with its embodiment in a single (idiosyncratic) poem (365), and any text with its realizations for various readers at particular moments (365; see also Mukařovský, "On Poetic" 29).

The most famous passages of "Closing Statement," Jakobson's elaboration (after Mukařovský) of Karl Bühler's schematic of the speech situation, not only represent a further foray into the realm of *parole* but illustrate as well Jakobson's strong sense of himself (contra Saussure) as a functional linguist. In "Closing Statement," the functionalist position, that language structure can be understood only in reference to its communicative function, explains the origin of subcodes. Jakobson had argued early on for the importance of means-end or functionally motivated language change, and here (and elsewhere) the func-

---

[9] Philip Davis examines this distinction in Prague School discussions of nonliterary issues (228).

tional principle explains synchronic variation as well ("Problems" [with Tynjanov] 25). That is, he outlines kinds of discourse according to a rhetorical conception of the speech context.

In his own schematic of the speech event, Jakobson sketches first a relationship between an addresser (an encoder or sender of the message) and an addressee (a decoder or receiver), necessary elements of any speech exchange, along with a shared linguistic code, a context or referent of the message, and the message itself. Put in other terms, a speech event consists of a speaker, a hearer, a shared language, something talked about, and (presumably, since Jakobson is not explicit) a set of propositions transmitted, something said. To this outline Jakobson finally adds "contact," a "physical channel and psychological connection" operative between speaker and hearer (353). The scheme neatly explains for Jakobson varieties of discourse, which derive their distinctive character from their predominating rhetorical functions. Thus an orientation or "set" toward the addresser defines emotive language, whereas persuasive discourse focuses on the addressee. Similarly, an orientation toward the context generates descriptive or referential language; toward the contact, empty channel-opening or phatic language; and toward the code alone, metalinguistic discourse (353–57; see also Mukařovský, "Two Studies" 67–68). Poetic language Jakobson finally defines as message oriented: the poetic function derives from a "focus on the message for its own sake" (356). Subcodes, then, are motivated by a variety of communicative needs, not simply the competing needs of referential and literary language. Since an orientation toward one function does not obliterate others, literature is multifunctional, sometimes even strongly referential (357); poeticality is finally, then, not a fixed property.

Now critics have sometimes characterized this discussion as superficially functionalist, given Jakobson's focus in "Closing Statement" on literary tropes and devices. But in Jakobson's earlier intellectual context, the functionalist approach extended to all textual and syntactic phenomena. As Vilém Mathesius, who was instrumental in developing Prague School functionalism maintains, syntactic analysis requires constant reference to the immediate context of an utterance; thus in his work even elementary syntactic units gain rhetorical labels— "rheme," for example, not "predicate" (Mathesius 127; Vachek 6–7). As both Jakobson and Mukařovský repeatedly state, language defined as multifunctional accounts both for a nonessentialist definition of literary language (literariness is simply not unique to literature) and for the historical instability of texts (succeeding literary movements rank differently the nonaesthetic functions of works) (Jakobson, "Closing"

357; Mukařovský, "Two Studies" 69, 73–76, 79). If the aesthetic function of the literary work is, as in Prague School theory, "dominant," then the literary object is in part self-focused, not transparently mimetic (Jakobson, "Closing" 351, 356; Mukařovský, "On Poetic" 6, 68); and yet the still-present referential function enacts a (problematized) connection with the outside world ("Closing" 371; "Two Studies" 71–72; "On Poetic" 55).[10]

Although the functionalist position defines subcodes by rhetorical functions, as opposed to kinds of devices, such an approach is, for Jakobson, fully compatible with empirical projects. Indeed, in earlier Prague School work literary language deforms the automatized general language not just in the sense that it invents new tropes and devices; the literary subcode additionally defamiliarizes ordinary language in its contrasting "relative representation" or "average frequency" of particular speech sounds or syntactic features (see Mukařovský, "On Poetic" 20, 21; "Standard" 19–22). Rhetorical function, then, implies a preponderance of certain language structures—of personal pronouns in emotive language, for example—which can be comparatively tabulated. Literary language, in the text of "Closing Statement," particularly signals its difference from referential language in its density of "equivalence[s]" (358), in its "super-average accumulation" of related linguistic elements (373). In Jakobson's famous formulation, "The poetic function projects the principle of equivalence from the axis of selection into the axis of combination" (358, emphasis deleted). Literary language, in other words, duplicates the like elements of the paradigmatic dimension syntagmatically. As several critics remark of later essays, this principle of syntagmatic duplication means that Jakobson's consistent but apparently undirected enumeration of equivalent and contrasting textual features demonstrates for him the literariness of his object (Culler, *Structuralist Poetics* 63; Todorov, "Jakobson's Poetics" 279).

But Jakobson claims here that the principle of accumulation extends

---

10 The "dominant" function organizes the devices of a work. A literary work is thus a multifunctional text with a predominating aesthetic function, although the referential function may also be more or less prevalent. Dominant functions and norms are also historical, describing local aesthetic norms (an era in which the referential function is as important as the aesthetic function, versus another in which referentiality recedes), a dominant genre (a period in which other arts emulate musical norms), or the values of a particular genre (a genre that evaluates metrical regularity above other poetic values). See Jakobson, "The Dominant"; Mukařovský, "Art as Semiotic Fact"; Felix Vodička, "Response to Verbal Art." Prague School critics differ as to whether the dominant is a textual property (Jakobson's emphasis) or whether it derives from habits of reading (as Mukařovský implies and Vodička explicitly claims).

from phonology and syntax to semantic issues as well, despite the supposed conflict between texts as data and texts as meaningful. Thus the critic must note such phenomena as the repetition of items from similar or opposed semantic categories, the meaning effects generated by sound similarities which disappoint the expectation of semantic similarity, or interpretive operations prompted by equivalences and departures (368–73; see also Mukařovský, "On Poetic" 33–64). Since the semantics involved is relational, Jakobson sees himself as resisting textual closure. And since the "meanings" defined by his method are both local and nonevaluative, Jakobson eschews overall interpretive readings, seeking instead the source of immediate aesthetic effects.

From a sympathetic glance at the linguistic program of "Closing Statement," then, it would seem that Jakobson has in fact anticipated many of the objections routinely raised about structuralist theory. While he contrasts ordinary and poetic language, he defines this contrast as a functional difference as opposed to a difference in kind, and the theory itself would actually require, not limit, attention both to the nature of everyday discourse and to earlier aesthetic norms. While Jakobson's notion of poetic language preoccupies him with phonological and syntactic patterns, he never claims that exhaustive textual description predicts interpretation or that it corresponds to readers' conscious perceptions. And while texts relate ambiguously to the "real" for Jakobson, he does not entirely obliterate their connection to the outside world. But of course it is precisely the difficulty of maintaining these fine distinctions that attracts for Jakobson's work and for "Closing Statement" such continuing critical interest.

THE RECEPTION OF "CLOSING STATEMENT"

The metacritical history of "Closing Statement" (and of the essay in the context of Jakobson's other work) is quite naturally an outline of criticism itself, as variously invested critics have responded to one or another of the text's competing impulses. Despite its occasional gesture toward New Critical assumptions, early critics recognized in the empirical program of "Closing Statement" a largely antithetical critical practice (see Scholes, *Structuralism* 22–23). Reader-oriented critics, focusing on its self-described functionality, read the essay rather as a quintessential formalist program for its textual—as opposed to reader-centered—conception of aesthetic discourse. Later critical conversation focused on "Closing Statement" as a classic site of conflict between the formalist emphasis on literary language as contingent and constructed and Romantic conceptions of literary experience.[11]

My aim here is not to rehearse this entire history but merely to elaborate a context for a selection of issues that criticism has not fully explained or resolved, largely because the evidence of Jakobson's linguistic theory considerably complicates them. In the era of reader-oriented criticism, Mary Louise Pratt, in particular, focused on the Jakobsonian and Prague School distinction between ordinary language and literary language, which, since many of the more sophisticated Prague School documents had not yet been translated, she took as hard-and-fast (see *Toward* 3–37). The result, she claimed, was an essentializing conception of literary language and an impoverished account of ordinary discourse (*Toward* xv–xix, 38–39; see also Fish, *Text* 104–6). More important, Pratt pointed to problems involving Jakobson's functionalism. Jakobson's "orientation" of the subcode toward an aspect of the speech event obscures the construction and reception of texts; the "set" or orientation in question, she argued, is really the reader's or speaker's disposition toward persons and objects in the world (*Toward* 31–32; see also Attridge, "Closing"). And the asymmetrically defined literary language (self-oriented, as opposed to outward focused) ultimately detaches literature from its context, neutralizing its potential political power (*Toward* xviii–xix; see also Fowler, *Literature* 163–66, 182–84). In the same period, several critics—Jonathan Culler, Michael Riffaterre, David Robey—attacked Jakobson's empirical methods on similar, that is, reader-based, grounds. Jakobson's scientific claims lead him in stylistic analyses to locate linguistic elements with no clear end in mind. Such a method implies that texts are objectively existing, stable artifacts; but since readers actualize texts, it is only from their perspective that the theorist can decide which structures are interpretively important and, given the constraints of ordinary perception, when the analysis should end (see Culler, *Structuralist Poetics* 55–74; Riffaterre 206–13; Robey, "Modern" 49–53; see also Attridge, "Closing" 18–19).[12]

[11] The critical term "formalist" has several active meanings. In one sense, a formalist is any critic whose interpretive practice is text based or who considers texts interpretively stable or objectively meaningful. Thus the designation often includes in a single category Russian Formalists, Prague School structuralists, stylisticians, and New Critics. In another sense of the term, a formalist is an early proponent—hence a Russian Formalist or Prague structuralist—of the conventionalist position that literary language has no natural, reflective relation to the real. Such critics would here reject New Critical and Romantic conceptions of literary language.

[12] Pratt's objections extended to the inconsistency of the "orientation" of functional codes toward aspects of the speech event. She noted that the term sometimes specifies

But the best entry into these problems is through later analysis of Jakobson's autotelic definition of literary language, on which I wish to focus more particularly, partly because this criticism is especially attuned to the subtleties of Jakobson's position, but also because Jakobson's linguistic theory illuminates such issues. Briefly, the discussion, as Derek Attridge, Gérard Genette, and Tzvetan Todorov develop it, points to a conflict between Jakobson's formalist position, which stresses the arbitrariness of linguistic signs and hence the utter conventionality of literary language and device, and his sense that literary language is language for its own sake or language oriented toward itself (Attridge, "Literature" 132–35; Genette, "Modern Mimology" 208–10; Todorov, "Jakobson's Poetics" 272–75). The first position derives from general Russian Formalist doctrine and generates skepticism about representation; and I might add here that Jakobson early on elaborated this position into a compelling critique of assumptions about realistic literature and the relation between art and life ("On Realism"; "What Is"). In this account of literary language, foregrounded aesthetic elements are palpable and opaque, promoting recognition of the gap between signifier and signified, of the contingency of form. Since it unmasks the process of signification itself, poetic discourse is, as opposed to ordinary language, nonreferential (Attridge, "Literature" 129) and, as opposed to prose, nonmimetic (Genette, "Modern Mimology" 208). The second position, as these critics note, interacted early on with antithetical formalist precepts; it derives from Romantic theories of the symbol and depicts literary language as somehow communicating itself directly. If poetic language is nonreferential in this account, it is because it dispenses with representation altogether. In these moments, the palpability of literary language provokes an enhanced sense of the signifier as an apt expression of its signified; poetic language, now also somehow transparent, fuses with its object. In this way Jakobson eventually—certainly by the time of "Closing Statement"—participates in an aesthetics of natural signs. His lifelong interest in sound symbolism, these critics observe, and his later focus on essentially mimetic devices, on repetition, parallelism, and again on onomatopoeia, is symptomatic of Jakobson's search for a romantic moment of intransitivity in which language ceases to be arbitrary (Attridge, "Literature" 131–36; Genette, "Modern Mimology" 202, 209–12; Todorov, "Poetic Language" 14; "Jakobson's Poetics" 272–80).[13]

---

speaker intention, sometimes message content, sometimes truth value; none of these criteria applies, in any case, to the poetic function (*Toward* 31–32).

Jakobson's analysis of "Les Chats" with Claude Lévi-Strauss was a particular target for Michael Riffaterre. Jakobson's reply to such objections is in "Retrospect" (1962).

[13] Most critics note that the two positions appear in Jakobson's work at the start, al-

All three critics praise Jakobson's original, though attenuated, break with a pervasive mimetic tradition. Genette notes that Jakobson's work is an advance over romantic doctrine for its interest in nonliterary language ("Modern Mimology" 209); Todorov praises its relational accounts of literary device and literary meaning ("Jakobson's Poetics" 275–84). And both Attridge ("Literature" 135) and Todorov ("Jakobson's Poetics" 283) are sympathetic to Jakobson's attempts to reconcile what they agree are intuitively correct but theoretically contradictory experiences of literature, of literary language as overtly conventional and communicating extraconventionally. But as Genette stresses, Jakobson's formalism finally does not escape the seductive notion of a poetic language that "challenge[s] . . . the arbitrariness of the sign" ("Modern Mimology" 212).

I do not dispute the general outline of these arguments; neither are such theoretical inconsistencies surprising, given Jakobson's extended and complex career. My question, rather, concerns Jakobson's means of alternately suppressing and justifying certain difficulties in his treatment of literary language, for he was clearly more invested in—and at times more conscious of—counterarguments than the preceding accounts would suggest. To take some impressive examples, at the time he most analyzed literary texts as empirical objects, specifically within four years of "Closing Statement," in his work in semantics Jakobson stopped believing in a world—or in a grounded scientific system—outside language ("Retrospect" [1962] 632; *Main Trends* 62).[14] And in later semiotic studies he explicitly linked praise of romantic accounts of literary meaning to (only partly modified) formalist arguments for the conventionality of language ("Quest" 410–12).[15] We have, then, a curious series of incongruent positions: Jakobson's functionalism is such that it erases readers; yet Prague School criticism invested in theories of literary reception. His stylistic criticism suggests a naive sense of literary texts as fixed and delimited, but Jakobson consistently doubted the perspective-independent existence of the objects of lin-

---

though Genette in particular sees Jakobson as increasingly conservative. As Genette notes ("Modern Mimology" 208–10), early on in Jakobson's thinking, prose, not poetic language, is mimetic; later formulations valorize the iconicity of poetic device. Early on, the palpability of literary language promotes contemplation of the contingency of signifiers, later of their reflective qualities. See also Attridge, "Literature" 134.

[14] The last chapter of Jakobson, *Main Trends in the Science of Language*, is superseded by the more complete "Linguistics in Relation to Other Sciences," but I cite the earlier version when the date of Jakobson's position is relevant.

[15] In "Quest for the Essence of Language," Jakobson argues for partially mimetic linguistic features and devices, but within an overall doctrine of the arbitrariness of signs. He is thus a conventionalist who indulges in what Genette terms "Cratylism" ("Modern Mimology" 202).

guistic analysis and in fact problematized the subject-object relation earlier and more systematically than almost any critic one could name; Jakobson cited Sartre and Mallarmé on the opacity of literary language, when earlier he had rigorously dismantled arguments for the noncontingency of literary device. What I want to point out here is merely that, given such puzzling contradictions, we might say more about the roots of such problems, after all, than that Jakobson was superficially functionalist, naively empiricist, or a final victim of the Romantic doctrine of his age.

JAKOBSON'S PHONOLOGISM

Before approaching the text of "Closing Statement" more directly, I begin by embedding that text in a somewhat broader context, simply by noticing again that in Jakobson's early work the devices that promote the contrasting perceptibility of literary over ordinary language are primarily figures of sound. In "Closing Statement" and earlier, repetition and parallelism are also syntactic, and importantly, along with alliteration, onomatopoeia, and the like, contribute to literary effects. But since the Saussurean theory that gave impetus to Prague School linguistics was phonological in emphasis and since Jakobson himself was much more of a phonologist and semiotician than a syntactician, it will be instructive to reexamine "Closing Statement" from the rather different perspective of Jakobson as a phonologist and as a linguist whose very semiotics rests on phonological concerns.[16] From such a viewpoint, we find strange moments indeed in the text of "Closing Statement." At one point, for example, as he discusses how literary language exploits the possibilities of sound, Jakobson borrows Mallarmé's remarks on synesthesia.[17] Hearers, he asserts, will readily associate a phonological contrast between grave and acute vowel sounds with the contrasting concepts of dark and light; at the very least, no one will call [i], in comparison with [u], the "darker" sound (373). At another moment he apparently believes in the unambiguous semantics

[16] That Saussure excludes syntax from linguistic study is well known. Prague School linguists did not follow suit, but both they and Jakobson made more dazzling advances in phonology and morphology. Jakobson's focus in his aesthetics on matters of sound patterning has, in addition, independent, nonlinguistic motivation deriving from his early Russian Formalist context. For discussion see Peter Steiner (*Russian* 140–71) and Todorov ("Poetic Language" 10–28).

[17] Genette, "Modern Mimology" 209; and Todorov, "Jakobson's Poetics" 272–73, also cite the Mallarmé passage to illustrate Jakobson's interest in nonarbitrary meaning. I focus here on the aesthetic experience nonarbitrary signification entails and also on its sources.

of emotively significant, nondistinctive intonational cues, citing an experiment in which an actor (in Konstantin Stanislavsky's theater) is told to deliver the same sentence with forty different emotional casts; according to Jakobson's anecdotal account, an audience unproblematically interprets each separate expressive function, simply by attending to the varying sound shape of each utterance (354). If, in both descriptive linguistics and formalist poetics, signifiers and literary devices are arbitrary, bearing no natural connection to objects or ideas in the world, from what source can such remarks derive? And do such cruxes in Jakobson's text reveal a phonocentrism of the sort attributed to Saussure, a belief, especially in the first example, that literary language evokes a heightened consciousness of self or experience of the real as opposed, as Jakobson says elsewhere, to an intensified *effect* of the real? Or as perhaps in the second case, do such comments stem solely from meaning-independent specifics of Jakobson's linguistic theory?

There are actually two senses, requiring somewhat contrasting analysis, in which Jakobson may "naturally" connect signifiers to signifieds. According to later critiques of Jakobson's work, as we have seen, his account of literary meaning sometimes grounds signification in a fused or transparent, hence natural, relation of sound (signifier) to some object, whether real or constructed. Alternatively, the Romantic moment of intransitivity implies the natural relation in question is between the signifier and some direct or primitive experience of self—a self delimited, unified, and fully present to consciousness. This "natural" connection is most familiarly problematized in literary discussion through arguments in deconstruction and cultural criticism. Of course such accounts may implicitly interact and so it is somewhat artificial, though useful, to sort them out: one can cast an experience outside signification as reflexively an experience of oneself. But it is this second, somewhat differently inflected theory of natural signification, a position generally more associated with Saussure than with Jakobson, that I wish to explore as a point of reentry into both Jakobsonian sign theory and the competing arguments of "Closing Statement."

Now it might seem odd to ascribe to the early Jakobson, at least, a doctrine of natural signs in that second sense, of signifiers as transparently self-revealing or self-expressive, given his rigorous interrogation of representation of any sort. But one of Jakobson's most engaging characteristics is his open attempt to square his scientific interests with his personal experience of poetry. This attempt might well lead to such a theoretical program, particularly in the suspect early connection he makes between emotive and poetic language, where both are defined as superior to ordinary language in perceptibility, impact, and expres-

sive power ("The Dominant" 84). But if the foregrounded consciousness in question is the speaker's or poet's, then Jakobson carefully
treads a fine theoretical line. From the perspective of his initial linguistic work, literary language and emotive language are simply two of
many subsystems. Literary and emotive subcodes, though not coextensive, interact in that they exploit many of the same devices ("The
Dominant" 84). Since this discussion is in the context of the arbitrariness of all signs, Jakobson's remarks draw a neat boundary: the inter-
section of subcodes explains the emotionally evocative power of literary discourse while preserving the arbitrariness of the emotionally
expressive device. It further follows from Jakobson's discussions of the
relation between art and life that any literary representation of an ar-
tist's psychological state is just that—representation. Jakobson doubts
both that literary realizations directly communicate such truths and indeed that "real" experience can be definitively located ("On Realism";
"What Is").

If, however, we readjust the question slightly and ask whether the
reader of poetry is, in Jakobson's aesthetics, one who experiences some
enhanced moment of self-identity, then the answer is less obvious.
Again it is difficult to imagine (the Russian Formalist) Jakobson articu-
lating an aesthetics related to such a position—a full-fledged aesthetics
of pleasure, of emotive release, or of personal insight or catharsis.[18] He
is already rightly associated with contradictory statements on autotelic literary language and the conventionality of literary device, but
we might go farther in this case. These are conflicting but for him
particulary entangled positions. Indeed, Jakobson explicitly relates the
two experiences of literature: the moment when literary language lays
bare its own devices, the very process of signification, is also the moment when the now-detached signifier finds newly—and presumably
natural—expressive power.[19] The paradox, perhaps, relates to Jakobson's early commitment to the nonreferentiality of literary language.[20]

[18] "Pleasure" as a topic does arise, but I would rather call Jakobson's Russian and Czech
position an aesthetics of disturbance.

[19] Both Attridge ("Literature" 134–36) and Genette ("Modern Mimology" 210) note that
these contradictory positions fuse in Jakobson's work, but I emphasize here their causal
relationship in his aesthetics. In the aesthetic moment recognition of contingency frees
consciousness.

[20] The referentiality of poetic language is a vexed issue in Jakobson's work. As Genette
points out, Jakobson initially defines poetic language—as opposed to prose—as nonreferential, but of course his autotelic conception of poetic language assumes a kind of
referentiality ("Modern Mimology" 208–9). Yet, as Attridge remarks, the semantic height-
ening literary language is supposed to accomplish really has no clear referential object
("Literature" 131). See Todorov, "Jakobson's Poetics" 274–75, and Attridge, "Literature"

If literary language does not mean by referring, it must mean in some other sense, though how or what it does escapes precise articulation. The result is that Jakobson implicitly pays surprising attention to perceivers' aesthetic reactions. In early formulations literary language variously evokes an intellectual recognition of alternative signifying possibilities, a heightened consciousness of a constructed reality, an intensified visceral experience of the world (see "What Is" 174–75; "The Dominant" 87; "On Realism" 44).

What is unexpected about such suggestions is not so much Jakobson's interest in aesthetic perception—Russian Formalists and Prague School critics were, after all, early reception theorists—but the way in which much of this experience exceeds recuperation into Jakobson's linguistics-based model. That is, in Prague School theory in general, aesthetic reactions are shared by speakers who know the same language, literary conventions, and traditions. But in earlier Russian Formalist discussions of transrational poetry (*zaum*), an experimental poetry akin to speaking in tongues, poetic sounds foreground signification simply by refusing to link sound and sense conventionally.[21] Sounds, then, communicate extralexically, as pure signifiers. Jakobson, as Peter Steiner notes, rethought many of the positions associated with *zaum*, normalizing such aesthetic effects in the shared sound system of everyday language (*Russian* 234); nonsense syllables are aesthetically recoverable not because they immediately signify but because they suggest, though they deform, phonological conventions. Thus in his (later) discussion of Ivan Turgenev's nonsensical outburst in a stuffy British restaurant, Jakobson ingeniously makes contextual sense of an otherwise incoherent string of words and sounds ("Supraconscious").

But Jakobson never entirely leaves behind Russian Formalist enthusiasm for the unstable, unpredictable—therefore unshared—effects of foregrounded poetic sound. Alongside his convention-based accounts

---

128–29, for remarks on the evolution of Jakobson's thinking. This problem is further complicated by Jakobson's Prague School position, in which the doctrine of multifunctionality allows him to view literary texts as mixed entities, consisting of referential and nonreferential features in some hierarchy (see "The Dominant").

My own comment is that we should distinguish between motivations for the doctrine of poetic referentiality. That is, one can more legitimately fault Jakobson for valorizing the mimetic capabilities of poetic language (where poetic language represents emotion or some higher reality or experience of the world) than for conceiving of literary works as enacting a problematized referential relation to a (constructed) reality (where Jakobson opens up a way to preserve the real-world political force of literature without resorting to a transparent mimeticism). In other words, I think the issue is just as troubled—and in parallel respects—in current criticism.

21 I am indebted here to Steiner's excellent discussion of transrational poetry (*Russian* 149–61). See also Todorov, "Poetic Language" 13–14.

of defamiliarized sound is the Jakobson who—now late in his career—explains Velimir Xlebnikov's five-part sound sequences as supraconscious imitation of the fivefold symmetry of the natural world ("Subliminal" 254) and who links Turgenev's utterance as well to the poet's unconscious and more direct connection to the underlying reality of the scene (Turgenev's experience is "beyond words," and only the disjointed utterance can fully express his irritation [265]). For the reader of poetry, Jakobson continues to associate a recognition of signifying practices, "the word . . . felt as a word" ("What Is" 174), with an intensified experience of extralinguistic reality and poetic sounds especially with a direct decoding of their semantic import (*Dialogues* [with Pomorska] 54–55). More explicitly in some accounts, a writer's moment of heightened consciousness, sometimes described as unconscious expressiveness, transforms an experience of or beyond reality into art (see also "Marginal Notes" 305), and a reader's experience of the associated distorted or repeated sounds and devices enlivens perception and consciousness. The moment of unveiled signification, then, often involves an enhanced experience of (self) awareness in a world of deceptive surface appearances. Of course, Jakobson's formulations throughout his career vary, and not all such aesthetic moments require a "self" suddenly more present to itself; but Jakobson gestures in this direction each time he attempts to describe in the same terms, through the suggestive power of literary language, both a personal experience of literature and the nature of literary signification.[22]

Jakobson's aesthetic principles are thus rooted in an assumed rather than examined experience of foregrounded poetic sound and structure. Yet much in this account remains compelling; one wants to deny neither Jakobson's appeal to the emotional force of literature nor his lively fascination with aesthetic perception. It is also worth considering what is distinctive in Jakobson's approach to these topics. His interest in sound as separated from sense—in the "word . . . felt as a word"—points to just how much his poetic theory depends at the start on ascribing to poetic language a visceral impact, an emphasis that contrasts markedly with most theories in a strictly Anglo-American critical tradition.[23] Such a focus reminds us that when reader-oriented critics were faulting Jakobson for failing to relate textual features to specific interpretive effects or readings, Jakobson was explaining literary experience of another sort. Defamiliarized devices in these accounts startle

[22] I think by now it should be clear that there is no easy distinction to be made on such points between Jakobson's position at early and late moments of his career; rather, such themes resurface.

[23] I. A. Richards is the obvious exception.

perceptions, not intellects, so that while one expects Jakobson the linguist to explore the phonological and morphological conventionality of onomatopoeia or poetic nonsense, Jakobson the reader of poetry often celebrates instead the sheer physicality of literary experience.

Such enthusiasms are interesting in themselves, but they seem misleadingly straightforward to critique outside the context of Jakobson's developing linguistic interests. For Jakobson's linguistic concerns mean that he assumed, especially in his late career, that he could explain a good deal about the psychophysical aspects of aesthetic effects. And this assumption, more than his personal celebration of poetic experience, helps explain the increasing role of mimesis and the particular forms it took by the time of "Closing Statement" and later. In this particular case, Jakobson's view of aesthetic experience would have been importantly shaped by the need to distinguish in his linguistics between conventionality and biology. Essentially this is a missing third term in later critical discussion, for "natural," as opposed to "conventional," would have operated for Jakobson in the distinct senses of nonsemiotic but nonbiological, on the one hand, and nonsemiotic but biologically motivated on the other. That is, in critical accounts "natural" normally means a nonarbitrary relationship between signifier and signified. But for a linguist there is a second active and important sense of the term: biological. "Natural" in the sense of biological simply involves a claim that there are constraints on human linguistic abilities which affect the sound units (phonemes) that meaningfully construct languages.

Note that this is a far different argument from one about a motivated relation between sound and sense: there is an important distinction here between phonologism and phonocentrism. What I want to call phonologism is simply an interest in the biological aspects of sound. Such an interest proceeds from basic observations about language acquisition and argues only that there are biologically based regularities governing the sounds that speakers use in language, constraints on which sounds are more linguistically available to children learning language and thus acquired (as meaningful elements) first, which phonemic distinctions they must learn later.[24] Arguments about these mat-

---

[24] More specifically, the argument is that all infants are born with linguistic abilities that predispose them to distinguish certain sounds. Psycholinguists theorize that these innate linguistic abilities speed the process of language acquisition. For example, both American and Japanese prelinguistic infants react to an opposition between the sounds /r/ and /l/. Not long before they reach the age of language acquisition, however, American babies continue to "hear" the opposition, but Japanese babies no longer do. The assumption is that exposure to the parents' language has already begun to influence and shape—

ters do not in the least require a theory of natural signs or of fixed meaning, as literary critics have sometimes claimed, nor do they entail a supression of unconscious meaning and motive; for whenever they are acquired in whatever language, sounds still signify arbitrarily, signs still exceed intentional meanings. Phonocentrism, in contrast, in the sense we have inherited from Derrida, involves an association of sound, word, or voice with a "metaphysics of presence," usually a submerged doctrine of natural signification or an implicit sense that speakers control their own conscious and unconscious linguistic intentions and the future meanings of their utterances.[25]

Of course, saying that an interest in the biological aspects of sound does not, strictly speaking, entail a belief in the semiotic nonarbitrariness of signs does not mean linguists never confuse such matters. In this Jakobson has a well-known predecessor in Saussure, who himself made perfectly reasonable observations about the natural (biological) human propensity to vocalize sign systems but who also—most famously in his study of anagrams—searched for a natural, immediate signification antithetical to his own larger theoretical program.[26] Jakobson, not so incidentally, admired this strain in Saussure's work ("Spell" [with Waugh] 224–25), but Jakobson's case is somewhat more complex, for he developed both a more complete semiotics than did Saussure and investigated a much broader range of biological issues. His persistent study of the biological aspects of sound, which historically frames "Closing Statement," illustrates the delicate interaction between his aesthetics and his linguistics. In fact, it is clearer from a glance at Jakobson's linguistics just what is at stake in his account of aesthetic experience. And one can eventually observe the tension between Jakobson's interest in sound as a phenomenon for science—as objectively

---

enhance and suppress—innately existing linguistic abilities. (The /r/ versus /l/ opposition is an active one for English, nonphonemic for Japanese.) Apparently other phonemic oppositions children are not so predisposed to acquire and thus must learn later (if necessary) in the language acquisition process; this explains why it is that there are cross-cultural regularities in the order of the acquisition of phonemes. See Steven Pinker, *The Language Instinct* for an accessible account of psycholinguistic issues.

[25] The term is most associated with Derrida, *Of Grammatology*.

[26] Saussure's biological interests are concentrated in the notion *faculté de langage*. This natural linguistic ability does not control the form of particular languages as such, but apparently does trigger language learning and determine a first connection between articulatory apparatus and language (*Course* 10). In other words, Saussure merely recognizes that sign making is a mental rather than physical activity, but that persons are biologically predisposed to articulate such systems and to acquire them at a biologically controlled pace. His sense of the "natural," clear here, is considerably more confused in his discussion of writing and also in his other texts. For discussion of Saussure on anagrams, see Culler, *Saussure* 123–34.

measurable, biological, textual—and sound as aesthetic and ungovernable, though Jakobson himself by no means wished to oppose the two sets of terms.

Consider, for instance, assumptions about consciousness and rationality in Jakobson's psycholinguistic work in the areas of child language acquisition and aphasia, begun before "Closing Statement."[27] Although Jakobson's major work on language acquisition does not mention the connection, one might well treat babbling, the random, experimental, presumably pleasurable play with articulated sound which children in all cultures begin before they speak or understand language, as the extraaesthetic equivalent of transrational poetry. That is, Jakobson could easily have connected babbling, as indeed early formalists did, with a theory of transparent self-expression (see Steiner, *Russian* 151). Jakobson, however, implies something quite different. He hypothesizes (somewhat incorrectly) that in babbling a child articulates all possible linguistic sounds, sounds found in the languages of the world, narrowing down this set of sounds as initiation into the parents' language begins (*Child* 21). Such a premise means that babbling is for Jakobson a play of signifiers before signification, and thus it is even more temptingly like transrational poetry than one might suspect. Yet Jakobson is surprisingly consistent here in not extending biological explanations for possible sounds into a doctrine of natural signification. A biologically shaped inventory of sounds remains essentially inexpressive until the moment of shared meaning, when the speaker assimilates a semiotic system. Babbling, according to Jakobson, is egocentric, but he associates it with neither self-awareness nor creative or aesthetic pleasure. Rather, experience before language is isolating, failing, non-Edenic (*Child* 24–25, 34).

Jakobson's treatment of babbling contrasts somewhat to his account of aphasia, defined as a process inverse to language acquisition ("Two Aspects" 117; *Child* 62).[28] Although he has no aesthetic interest in babbling, Jakobson does link aphasia with literary language. He defines aphasia, in fact, as essentially identical to literary language: aphasia regressively projects the axis of similarity onto the syntagmatic plane. In more concrete terms, aphasia erodes phonological, grammatical, or semantic categories, producing in the aphasic's language the substitutions and repetitions that Jakobson associates with literary language ("Two Aspects" 129–33; *Child* 36–37). Of course, aphasic speech is as

[27] His best-known text is *Child Language, Aphasia, and Phonological Universals* (1941); other articles on these topics (the publication dates ranging from 1949 to 1966) are collected in *Studies on Child Language and Aphasia.*

[28] The idea is that language categories first acquired are last erased in aphasia.

isolating as babbling, and Jakobson does not find its disruptions aesthetically apt. It is akin in effect to babbling but somehow exhibits literariness without being aesthetic. Although Jakobson does not explain, there are obvious reasons to treat it so: aphasia involves a deformation of the language system as the protolanguage of babbling does not, and thus one can systematically explain its disruptions; but its aesthetic effects are solely textual, unintentional, and so in terms of Jakobson's functionalist perspective, not fully literary.

More important, such remarks clarify late developments in Jakobson's aesthetic theory, particularly his broader treatment of issues of consciousness. His linguistic interests, set alongside his literary theory, explain why Jakobson is now much more likely to cast the palpability of literary language as consciousness of signifying alternatives and autotelism as extralinguistic recognition or unconscious expressiveness. Given his increasing interest in psycholinguistic topics, in prelanguage and unconsciously patterned linguistic disruption, it is not surprising that in his late semiotic phase Jakobson also wrote, as we have seen, on the literary aspects of semiconscious nonsense, on dream speech ("Anthony's"), and mused with Jacques Lacan, apparently, on the language of the unconscious (Waugh and Monville-Burston 521 n. 78). From the perspective of such issues, babblers and aphasics fail to produce literature not so much because they lack a global literary intention, which Jakobson seems not to require for literary language, but because they have no consciousness of signifying contingency (see "Two Aspects" 130). Of course in Jakobson's ambivalent aesthetic moment knowledge of contingency at the same time liberates consciousness—at least from the conventionalized association of sound and sense. Thus a competing aesthetic experience, now associated more emphatically with loss of cognitive control, altogether obviates signification. The regressive effects of aphasic speech, then, are also in some extratextual sense literary; like dream speech and semiconscious nonsense, aphasic speech hovers tantalizingly on the edge of sense. And that boundary straddling, for Jakobson, becomes an important part of poetic value.

This is not, of course, to claim that Jakobson ever confronted unconscious meaning head-on or, indeed, that he sorted out kinds of unconscious association.[29] In fact, the linguistic interests that help generate exploration in this area paradoxically kept him from doing so. Such matters as unconscious motives and intentions are submerged in

---

[29] Jakobson does not develop literary readings centering on unconscious motives or desires. He does discuss the role of the unconscious in language development ("On the Linguistic Approach" 123–30), the unconscious structuring of dreams ("Anthony's"), and the unconscious genius of literary structuring ("Subliminal").

Jakobson's work, and naturally enough, since he comments that they lie beyond the scope of a linguistics-based poetics. Nevertheless, even in early discussion of the relation between art and life, he assumes that Karel Hynek Mácha's poems sublimate desires more clearly revealed in the journals, while in the journals the poet reacts against idealizing poetic pressure ("What Is" 166–70). In his later discussion of the "supraconscious" Turgenev, unconscious motives and meanings of the sort familiar in Anglo-American criticism are again implicitly at issue; Turgenev reaches an "apogee" of alienation in the frigid context of the upper-class British restaurant, which his superficially nonsensical outburst counters, as Jakobson points out, with a Russian peasant vocabulary associating sex (or the feminine) and food. Jakobson thus clearly assumes the political and sexual thematics of the utterance are personally and contextually relevant, but he takes such matters up only as evidence of the unconscious genius of poetic structuring, not as issues of interest in themselves. Rather Jakobson calls such meanings semantic patterns, thereby relegating the larger implications of vocabulary choice to the level of the grammatical and phonological symmetries and repetitions that mark the literariness of this language. The early source of such curtailed analysis is Jakobson's consistent belief that psychological and political comments end in unscientific speculation, however such concerns may serve as background necessary to his own explication. Later he increasingly grafts issues of aesthetic perception onto phonological models and onto biological models of language learning and processing.

This movement in Jakobson's work is at once obvious and subtle. His late linguistic accounts contain even stronger statements of the autotelic position than his much-analyzed aesthetic writings. Yet, since Jakobson left no comprehensive attempt to integrate his research in both domains, it is easy to miss how intricately he inflects his linguistic theory to account for his aesthetic interests and, similarly, how deeply linguistic problems must have informed his late treatment of literary matters.[30] Jakobson's conception of aesthetic experience, implicitly composed now of both rational and nonintellective elements, generally developed into a two-pronged theory of signification, though his posi-

---

[30] Many of the studies I discuss were published before or in 1960, the publication date of "Closing Statement"; two studies with later publication dates Jakobson first delivered a bit later: "Quest" (1965) and "Linguistics" (1967). Two of the linguistic accounts I cite, however, represent Jakobson's last positions: with Waugh, "The Spell of the Speech Sounds" (1979); and "Brain and Language" (1980). But these clearly illustrate where Jakobson was headed; both essays, for example, clarify what explanation Jakobson had in mind for his Stanislavsky Theater anecdote.

tion was not always consistent. One set of arguments applied at the level of sound and naturally invoked phonological paradigms; the other applied to the higher levels of syntax and semantics and developed a significantly different but still phonologized theory of representation. Now Jakobson simply worked in the phonological tradition of Saussurean linguistics. But for aesthetic projects the phonological metaphor promised additional attractions: it directly addressed unconscious perception, and it suggested a biological account of aesthetic impact.

Jakobson's phonological theory involves two distinct treatments of sound, which he terms "mediate" and "immediate." Phonemes, the elementary sound units in a language, and the distinctive features that make them up, are mediate, "signs of signs," since they represent meaning only as parts of other signs (Waugh and Monville-Burston 11; see "Spell" [with Waugh]; "Brain"). In English, for instance, /b/ and /p/ are phonemes or discrete sound units because they are employed to signal higher-level meaning differences, that "pit" and "bit" are different words. Phonemes themselves are complexes of acoustically perceivable features; /b/ and /p/ are both articulated nonnasally at the lips with a quick constriction of air, and they contrast in that the vocal cords vibrate for /b/ but not /p/. These features are termed "distinctive" for English because altering such features produces a phonemic, potentially meaningful distinction (/m/ varies from /b/ in the feature nasality, just as /b/ contrasts with /p/ in voicing). Such phonemes, though bundles of distinctive features, are immediately processed as units, which speakers distinguish in the otherwise chaotic realm of sound. Any particular actual (phonetic) articulation of a phoneme, for example, may be accompanied by additional acoustic features that speakers do not process as relevant. (An example for English speakers of a "nondistinctive" feature is aspiration, which sometimes accompanies /p/ but does not signal a meaning difference as it does for speakers of Thai.)[31] Thus the phonemic structure of a language arbitrarily determines which acoustic elements speakers hear as linguistic.

Jakobson, then, elaborates the principle of conventionality at the phonemic level and below. Whereas phonemes and distinctive features are arbitrary, available for any signification, they are also biologically constrained in the sense I have already discussed. Jakobson finds universal (cross-language) phonemic and distinctive feature patterns; some sounds operate phonemically more often than others, just as children acquire some phonemes before others. Jakobson relates this phenome-

---

[31] Thus in Thai, aspiration is distinctive, and /p/ unaspirated (/p/) versus aspirated (/pʰ/) has the same force as voicing (/p/ versus /b/) in English.

non once again to the genetically defined limits and abilities of human linguistic apparatus, specifically to the capabilities of the left hemisphere of the brain (see *Child* 13–66; "Brain"). In Jakobson's semiotics, it is precisely the mediate nature of phonemes and distinctive features which corresponds to their status as biological universals; since such elements are not directly representational, in fact are so only at several removes, from a semiotic perspective they yet remain arbitrary ("Linguistics" 475).[32] In other words, genetically determined phonological abilities cannot constrain meaning if phonemes do not directly encode it. In contrast to Saussurean phonological theory, then, Jakobson developed a more complete account of the phoneme and—at least to this point—a clearer sense of the relation between signification and biology.

But Jakobson's phonemic theory at the same time suggests several problematic relationships to his aesthetics. First, that speakers perceive and process phonemes on some unconscious and automatic level tends to suggest to Jakobson, when he moves to literary problems, an aesthetic perception that is given, nonrational, and automatic, not developed or intellectualized in the course of a reading. This is one simple reason why reader-oriented critics—whose model is essentially syntactic—stay so at odds with Jakobson, despite efforts to understand him and despite a shared interest in problems of reception. Second, since phonemes and distinctive features constitute language at its most basic but, nevertheless, are not meaning-bearing or representational except at other levels of the system, the theory in aesthetic contexts paradoxically implies that sounds communicate in some other, more direct fashion. Indeed, while phonemic distinctions illustrate pure conventionality itself, for Jakobson their status as biologically conditioned elements and as not-quite signifiers significantly complicates their function in a theory of representation. Specifically, the more code dependent and mediate a linguistic element, the more Jakobson associates it with intellection, the less with emotionality ("Brain" 502–5); on the other hand, since it is so tempting somehow to motivate universally recurring elements, he also toys with the putative evocative and aesthetic power of (sometimes) phonemic sounds ("Spell" [with Waugh] 185, 234–38).[33] Finally, universal constraints on phonemes, when ex-

---

[32] Jakobson doubts the existence of syntactic universals, by contrast, because such a notion would conflict with his particular brand of functionalism. See "Linguistics" 473–75.

[33] Specifically, Jakobson maintains that poetic contexts cancel the mediate nature of distinctive features, and he then associates the immediate signification of poetic sounds with their status as universals ("Spell" [with Waugh] 185, 234–38). The aesthetic argu-

tended to Jakobson's continued association of aesthetic experience with sound value, normalizes aesthetic reactions. Again this problem helps explain some otherwise puzzling contradictions: Jakobson explicitly addresses asymmetries between the experiences of readers and writers (see Steiner, *Russian* 226) and between readers of different eras, but rarely between readers of the same period, whom he rather pictures as conditioned by the same given—as if phonological—aesthetic norms.

Such aesthetic consequences derive rather from Jakobson's phonologized aesthetics—from phonemic theory suggestively applied—than from any inevitabilities of the model itself. But this is less and less the case as Jakobson departs from phonemic theory in (late) idiosyncratic accounts of (in his terms) nonrepresentational sound, where aesthetic issues are a root motivation.[34] Such sounds, really nonphonemic sounds, which Jakobson calls "immediate," he contrastingly associates with right-brain functions: noise (traffic), nonphonemic but socially meaningful variation ("car" said with more or less [r]), nonphonemic stress patterns, including prosodic devices, and intonational contours (rising pitch to connote hesitation), emotionally expressive sound features (the elongation of vowels for emphasis, as in "This is good!"), and aspects of voice quality (for instance, pitch) which identify speakers' gender or age ("Brain" 502–8, 512–13). To such lists Jakobson adds aestheticized sound ("Brain" 508–9; "Spell" [with Waugh] 234–38). The most obvious problem, of course, is that it does not follow that even if these were, as his evidence apparently indicates, right-brain functions, they then are, as Jakobson implies, phenomena of the same order.

Whereas one might assume that the unstructured aspects of sound are precisely those least open to linguistic investigation, Jakobson instead takes these as central objects of linguistic study, especially in their revealing contrast to mediately representational sound. He has here two basic claims (although I have highly interpreted Jakobson's inexplicit account). First, since the interesting sounds on the list—intonation patterns and expressive features—are nonphonemic and nonbinary (that is, the presence or absence of an associated acoustic feature distinguishes no elements representational at some higher level of the language system), Jakobson takes them to be nonrepresentational,

---

ment thus reverses his general position. Jakobson actually developed the specifics of mediate sound after "Closing Statement" was published. Again, the point is that his position is strongly prefigured in the earlier essay, particularly as he refers to empirical tests for the emotive effects of sound.

[34] I call these idiosyncratic accounts because they do not represent positions familiar in mainstream linguistics (especially the conception of aestheticized sound as nonrepresentational).

essentially on the model of noise or, as in his last example, nondistinctive pitch ("Brain" 502–8). But since it is also obvious that such sounds "mean something" in some sense—an intonational difference can turn an assertion into a question, an expressive feature can direct focus or emphasis—they clearly deserve a place in a theory of signification. Jakobson's solution is to elaborate a theory of nonarbitrary signs (see "Quest for the Essence"). Aestheticized sound, in particular, Jakobson calls iconic. Like icons, and unlike phonemes articulated at higher levels, such sounds assert nothing ("Quest" 420); rather, according to Jakobson, they immediately and directly signify ("Quest"; see also "Spell" [with Waugh] 181–98; Waugh 47–53). Jakobson's second claim for right-brain sounds stresses the connection between expressive features and emotionality. Since he argues that these sounds, like phonemes, exhibit cross-language regularity, they also must be biologically conditioned ("Spell" [with Waugh] 192). Yet because they remain, unlike phonemes, nonrepresentational, Jakobson understands them as akin to cries of animals, that is, as once again directly and unmediately expressive ("Spell" [with Waugh] 182–85).

Because Jakobson's remarks on the iconicity of sound are much more muted in his criticism, it would be easy to rest with a critique of the "voice as natural" trope a la Derrida. But in his late linguistics, Jakobson returned emphatically to this visual metaphor, which somehow itself succeeds in supressing further reflection on the conventionality of nonphonemic but meaningful sound. Icons in the usual sense—the crude stick figure with a triangular skirt, say, to represent "woman"— are only partially motivated; they bear some physical (usually visual) resemblance to the objects they represent, but this resemblance is, of course, of a culturally constructed kind.[35] But the specular metaphor works differently for Jakobson in the realm of sound. Transferred to aural formlessness, the likeness is no longer between the visual construction and the conventional concept but between sound unformed, sound itself, and meaning; and Jakobson begins to remark instead the parallel between color, rather than visual form, and sound ("Spell"

[35] Jakobson follows Peirce in identifying three types of signs, the symbol, the index, and the icon. These are already familiar in literary study, but briefly, symbols are signifiers with no relation to the signified, as in the ordinary linguistic example of "chair," in which sounds have no relation to the concept. Indices and icons are partially motivated. An index represents some causal or contiguous relation, such as a representation of a plume of smoke denoting the concept "fire"; an icon represents some relation of (usually) visual similarity, such as the rough outline of a roof and cross denoting the concept "church." Jakobson's discussions are in "Quest for the Essence of Language," "A Glance at the Development of Semiotics," and "Shifters and Verbal Categories." (Brief historical comments on Peirce are in *Framework* 31–38.)

[with Waugh] 191–98, "Quest" 418; *Child* 82–84). Thus a metaphor that might have prompted further speculation on kinds of representation, indeed might have caused him to reflect on the binarism of his phonemic theory, instead suggests natural signification more strongly here than in his semiotics.[36] This is a direction prompted, of course, by Jakobson's long-standing interest in both the aesthetic impact of sound and the idiosyncratic nature of linguistic play, for such extraconventional phenomena would seem parallel to nonphonemic sound. Both the impetus and the context of Jakobson's phonemic theory are worth stressing here, for they explain the apparent naiveté of his remarks on synesthesia, on the "dark" or "light" value of vowel sounds in "Closing Statement." And they neatly illustrate a central Jakobsonian paradox—a scientific argument for aesthetic unpredictability.

This paradox surfaces again in "Closing Statement" in Jakobson's argument for the immediate emotive effect of expressive features, specifically in the Stanislavsky Theater anecdote (354–55). The narrative itself foregrounds issues of consciousness and conventionality—the actor must choose among intonational devices to convey the emotional shading of forty different deliveries of the line—but Jakobson focuses instead on the automatic decoding of emotive effect. On the one hand, while Jakobson once again suggests an autotelism at odds with his formalism, at least issues of creative possibility motivate his position; the especially expressive potential of aestheticized sound (here nondistinctive intonational patterns) seem to him connected to their nonphonemic, hence unconventional, status. On the other hand, casting such effects as emotionally immediate ultimately renders them once again predictable, for Jakobson imagines the listeners as an interpretively uniform group. The linguistic accounts that follow "Closing Statement" illustrate more dramatically the direction in which Jakobson was moving, for here he more explicitly universalizes emotive effect through phonological paradigms, choosing a solution that seriously forestalls local investigation either of unconscious creative motive or of idiosyncratic acts of recuperation. Specifically, Jakobson terms nonphonemic interpretive consistencies "biological" in a new sense: he simply comes to believe in biopsychological universals ("Spell" [with Waugh] 192; Waugh and Monville-Burston 23). Such an account is, interestingly enough, modeled on *phonemic* sound, despite Jakobson's initial arguments for the essential difference between mediate and immediate signification. Although phonemic distinctions are biologically

---

[36] I should say that this is not at all to denigrate Jakobson's monumental contributions to the study of phonology. For discussion, see Waugh and Monville-Burston.

conditioned, that they are does not constrain representational possibility. Once Jakobson postulates a biological account of sound defined as immediately representational, however, all aesthetic effect becomes as generalized and predictable as *potentially* representational phonemes. However much Jakobson's emphasis on the viscerally emotive impact of sound generates such an account, it dismantles his early clean distinction between the conventional-aesthetic and the biological components of language experience. Thus the temptations he consistently held at bay both in early accounts of transrational poetry and in later accounts of child language acquisition rather dominate his last linguistics; indeed, his arguments here are very like early Russian Formalist claims for *zaum*.

Jakobson's treatment of immediate sound, then, baldly recasts assumptions suppressed in his account of phonemic or mediate sound. He would simply like to account for a certain kind of aesthetic experience in the way one describes phonological elements. In defining phonemic elements, Jakobson's phonological model necessarily terms other sounds "nonlinguistic," which in his surprising conception of things is to say such sounds become nonsemiotically meaningful. These suggestions prove difficult to sort out, for phonemic and nonphonemic models both reasonably apply to aesthetic language. Eventually they compete. Thus, Jakobson claims both that aesthetic sound is unpredictable and unstructured, therefore more naturally expressive, and that aesthetic sounds, like phonemes, are automatically but conventionally structured and processed. From the perspective of aesthetic issues, one could say that Jakobson perhaps does not sort out varieties of aesthetic experience which might well require alternative models. From the perspective of linguistics, one might note that Jakobson does not distinguish suggestions of the term "universal"—as strictly and mundanely biological or as experientially shared. Simply put, by the end of his career, Jakobson romanticized his biology and biologized his psychology.

JAKOBSON ON REPRESENTATION

What might Jakobson's phonologism explain about his sign theory? Recall that I distinguished at the outset two rough senses of "natural" signification. I can now briefly reapproach issues of signifier-world relations, as opposed to the signifier-self relations I have been discussing, from this perspective. That is, the interplay both between Jakobson's phonology and his semiotics and, more generally, between his linguistics and his aesthetics on topics beyond the level of sound help explain one of those initial puzzles—why it is that Jakobson can consciously and unblushingly in his later semiotics announce competing positions on issues of representation.

The first question is how Jakobson's linguistic theory—independent of his Russian Formalism—allows him to hold conventionalist and mimeticist doctrines simultaneously. The answer in his late career is that through his linguistic model Jakobson imagines a limited scope for the expressive value of sound in itself and thus keeps from facing these positions in full conflict. Whereas in his criticism he valorizes (and equates) the mimetic value of onomatopoeia and figures of repetition, in his semiotics Jakobson sometimes contrasts sound symbolism and synesthesia to partially motivated signs or icons and onomatopoeia (see "Spell" [with Waugh] 181–203, 199; "Quest" 417; *Child* 25–27; Waugh 46). Although he consistently describes synesthesia as a core experience of sound, transparently meaningful, biologically conditioned, and nonrational (see also *Child* 82–84), for onomatopoeia Jakobson more intermittently suggests "natural" signification. Since onomatopoeia functions both at the phonemic level and above—in sounds, but also in vocabulary and imitative reduplication (as in "woof-woof")—Jakobson often reconventionalizes its reflective function. Sounds are culturally available for onomatopoeic expression (imitative truck noises, for example), only if they are not already in conventional linguistic use (*Child* 25–27); and imitative reduplication works in violation of general lexical rules ("Spell" [with Waugh] 199). By this logic, an onomatopoeic word, like any partially nonarbitrary sign, relies on the language system already in place, indirectly depends on conventions. This conventionality, Jakobson claims, is more important to onomatopoeia than imitative faithfulness (*Child* 26).[37] As we have seen, Jakobson does not

---

[37] Jakobson develops involved accounts of nonarbitrariness and partial motivation. An element can be (partially) nonarbitrary in two senses. First, it may be motivated within an existing system, as in morphology or morpheme-phoneme relations; for example, a new term, "gluckful," is partially motivated in its morpheme "-ful," already in active use ("Quest" 415). Or an element may be nonarbitrary in the sense that it takes up elements not in the linguistic system (as expressive features must in order not to be confused with words) (Waugh 51) or in that its sound shape somehow matches its meaning (when morphemes reduplicate to indicate extra size or importance) ("Quest" 412–17). Jakobson defines onomatopoeia as both internally and externally motivated (Waugh 46). His most ingenious elaborations of this sort are applied to morphology (where he opens up such issues as the greater systematicity of grammatical morphemes compared to derivational morphemes, the consistent [cross-language] use of bare-stem forms for imperatives, the regular use of more morphemes for larger or greater meanings ["Quest" 413–17]) and to deixis (where he invents an extremely useful functional scheme derived from Peirce's sign theory) ("Shifters").

entirely sort out the biological and aesthetic implications of universal principles at the level of sound. He does, however, distinguish between genetically encoded phonemic universals, which he ultimately connects with synesthesia, and morphological and syntactic regularities deriving from the "logic of the system," from the specific adaptive needs and arbitrary self-governing principles of particular languages ("Linguistics" 473–75; *Main Trends* 19–20). Such a solution explains not only how Jakobson reconciles his position on aesthetic signification but also why in his linguistics he opposes generativist claims for syntactic universals even as he finds aesthetic sound iconic.[38]

A second question is more difficult: How can even some such constrained notion of natural signification survive Jakobson's serious and well-known doubts about reality? Of course, this problem generally arises from competing Russian Formalist and Prague School premises—a radicalizing of objects, on the one hand, and an object-focused empiricism, on the other. The usual view of Jakobson's late aesthetics is that the first, mostly early impulse gave way to the late one in the context of more conservative American New Criticism. Yet Jakobson is actually quite consistent throughout his career on the topic of a culturally or linguistically constructed world. "I do not believe in things," he says, quoting Georges Braque not long after "Closing Statement," a document which is usually read as naively empirical and is strikingly at odds with Jakobson's more expansive remarks on phenomenology and relativity (Waugh 54; Jakobson, "Retrospect" [1962] 632; see also Holenstein 87–89; Jakobson, *Main Trends* 57).[39]

Here moving between accounts on related topics is most revealing. Initially, Jakobson invokes a meaning-reference distinction in order to account both for consistency of (word) meaning and for the meaning-

---

[38] Despite his productive investment in phonological universals—and also despite his wrongheaded arguments for the iconicity of sound—Jakobson objects in his late work to the innateness hypothesis as generativists had developed it. Basically, Jakobson rejects the notion of syntactic universals. Syntactic regularities across languages, unlike phonological regularities, he argues, derive both from the exigencies of the world which speakers of all languages share—that is, from similar functional problems—and from the logic of language systems in themselves, from general principles underlying the structure of languages rather than of the brain ("Linguistics" 474, and see 464–65). Jakobson essentially follows Saussurean tradition here in believing (wrongly, I think) that the notion of syntactic universals would severely constrain linguistic invention and play ("Linguistics" 474–75).

[39] My reservation about Genette's impressive analysis is that I think he does not enough credit Jakobson's skepticism about reality. Even early on, Jakobon's reference is to a constructed world, and his semantics, as Todorov ("Jakobson's Poetics" 278) and Waugh (29–30) note, is consistently relational. His discussions increasingly interrogate the subject-object distinction—an issue that applies especially to scientific discourse (*Main Trends* 62; or "Linguistics" 488).

producing role of (discourse) context; two elements may refer to the same object but in different contexts mean differently ("On Linguistic Aspects" 260). This solution means essentially that to accommodate the functionalist perspective Jakobson must reintroduce (into a formalist scheme) extralinguistic experience as the necessary interpretive context ("Linguistic Glosses" 286; "Shifters" 386–89). At the same time, Jakobson's conventionalist position generates important precepts about the relation of form to meaning. Specifically, Jakobson argues (in almost Derridean fashion) that meaning and form require each other. Since meanings are relational and system derived, there exist no form-independent or directly communicated meanings; variations in form, conversely, must encode some difference in meaning (Waugh 40–44). This is not a necessary conclusion, I think, but a claim that allows Jakobson to argue (contra early generativists) for the meaningfulness of surface stylistic variation, to doubt the principle of synonymy, and to problematize translation ("On Linguistic Aspects"; "Boas'"). But as Jakobson reflects further on a relational conception of meaning, his meaning-reference distinction collapses, for it insufficiently captures the context-bound nature of all meaning and the contingency of objects of reference (see *Main Trends*; or "Linguistics"; Waugh 29–30).[40] However radical this move is, I think in Jakobson's case it unfortunately boomerangs into a surprisingly conservative position on the meaning of form, for Jakobson tends at this point not just, as in earlier accounts, to complicate the referential value of signifiers but to dispense with it altogether. It is then possible for him to emphasize form in itself, as meaningful not in relation to a constructed notion of the world but merely in relation to other forms. If such a theory does strongly inform Jakobson's late aesthetics, then, repetition and variation do not reflect a world outside the text so much as enact their own transcendent meaning; aesthetic variation for Jakobson, you will notice, necessarily—rather than possibly—means. Once again I suspect that literary needs motivate theoretical inconsistencies, for the primacy of form as a critical heuristic serves Jakobson well.

If I now retrace Jakobson's movement between his linguistic and aesthetic interests, I can highlight the resulting interdisciplinary tensions.

---

[40] Attridge perceptively notes that the breakdown of the meaning-reference distinction also complicates Jakobson's use of "message" in "Closing Statement." If the formulation of literary language as a "set toward the message" embraces this theoretical collapse, literary language must involve all semantic concerns, since reference is system-internal. This position, however, minimizes Jakobson's distinction between literary and ordinary language; there is then nothing distinctive left for referential language to do (Attridge, "Literature" 128–29).

When Jakobson works on specifically phonological matters, his linguistics, which adequately models only conventionalized sound, raises questions that Jakobson the critic would like to address in his aesthetics. As a phonologist, however, Jakobson applies just the kind of explanatory apparatus the aesthetic phenomena exceed. The solutions he derives in this way, principally the concept of iconicity for sound, eventually compromise his psycholinguistic theory when he returns to linguistics. Similarly, when Jakobson develops a semiotics, his phonologized conception of basic problems of signification generates two competing theories of signification operating at different levels. And when Jakobson reinserts literary issues into his sign theory, he unexpectedly stabilizes the meaningfulness of signifiers even as he destabilizes the world and the reality to which they (apparently) refer; "arbitrariness" is thus a notion that for him intermittently requires an internal or external object of reference. In short, Jakobson's method is productive, inasmuch as problems in one field suggest solutions in another, but his multiple interests are also limiting, for his piecemeal approach to a comprehensive model—a general ordinary and literary linguistics—suppresses and masks ways in which such projects simply do not coincide.

THE PHONOLOGISM OF "CLOSING STATEMENT"

If we turn now more directly to the essay, granting the faults so often imputed to it—its stubborn confidence in the concrete literary object, its ambivalent functionalism—but reading it here through Jakobson's linguistics, the document no longer seems so straightforwardly "empiricist" as it has been characterized. Rather, we might better describe it as the site of an extended and impressive conflict between competing linguistic aims. Specifically, "Closing Statement" is even more vexed than, say, a transformational-generative account over the relation of mental experience to data, in this case to literary texts.

We might, for instance, ask how it is that Jakobson selects the elements of literary analysis in the kinds of projects "Closing Statement" describes. Certainly questions about proper linguistic procedure trouble the Saussurean linguistic tradition in which Jakobson works. By "procedure" I simply mean the practical process by which the linguist delimits the objects of analysis—in this case phonemes, morphemes, and the like. If one assumes, as in Saussure, that linguistic objects are not given in advance, that speakers instead impose language conventions on the otherwise confused and accidental realm of sound (112), then one must decide just how linguists are to identify such immaterial objects, either in their own or in a new, perhaps undocumented language.

Saussure himself (instructively) vacillates between two solutions. One relies on his essentially mentalist position, associated with his *faculté de langage*, a distinctively human sign-making ability. If language is a system constructed from any given material, then its true elements are abstractions, units that have psychological relevance and reality for speakers (see 102, 109–10, 127, 137–38). Saussure is inexplicit, but such an account assumes linguistic analysis corresponds in some way with speakers' phonological or morphological judgments. In a second approach, however, Saussure describes linguistic analysis as a set of procedures performed on collected data. By this account, the linguist delimits relevant units by observing recurring sequences: the series "painful," "delightful," "fruitful," for instance, illustrates that "ful" is a meaningful unit in English and that it is governed by recognizable rules of combination (104–6, 129). The question, then, is whether synchronic linguistic description moves forward by consulting speakers or by applying operations that dissect utterances or texts. To generalize the distinction, is semiotics to be a branch of social psychology, its object the psychologically real elements of all sign systems, as Saussure claims at one point (16)? Or as he implies elsewhere, will it base itself on generalizations of observed behavior, as one infers principles of politeness and the like (68)?[41]

Structuralisms of all sorts, whether literary or linguistic, have argued for an emphasis on one position over the other.[42] A later linguistic approach—as in early generative grammar—asks rather for a systematic account of the relationship *between* mental experience and observed data. Actual data provide a check on sometimes unreliable speaker intuitions, and tests on speakers constrain the otherwise limitless possibilities of data analysis. The problem is that Saussure does not successfully relate the two concerns. The most dramatic result is that he excludes syntax from linguistics proper. Saussure does this for a variety of reasons, including the understandable focus of the historical linguistics of his day on phonological concerns, but also because he associates syntax with the unpredictable realm of *parole* (124–25) and because he invests in a particularly strong form of mentalism requiring that linguistic elements be "real" objects in the minds of speakers

[41] Philip Davis finds this same ambivalence in the *Course in General Linguistics* but sees Saussure as quickly rejecting the strictly procedural solution (20–22).

[42] Contrast, for example, corpus-based projects (Vladimir Propp on wonder tales) to explicitly mentalist ones (Culler's generative poetics).

(102). Such a position, as Philip Davis points out, leads him to suspect syntactic categories invented by grammarians, which seem to him to have "doubtful" "psychological reality" (106, 109–11, 127, 138–39; see also Davis 19–21).[43]

Prague School linguistics, Jakobson's more particular, though early, context, did not define syntax as an area of idiosyncratic and unpatterned variation, but procedural concerns nevertheless remain ambiguous. A requirement of psychological relevance, as in Jakobson's claim for the unconscious and subliminal significance of textual elements, is broadly compatible with a functionalist linguistics; yet Jakobson's exhaustive analyses of literary texts themselves, generated by the autotelic definition of poetic language, obviously rely on data-focused operational procedures. Such problems emerge particularly in Jakobson's— and in Mukařovský's—extensive applications of the *langue-parole* metaphor. While this model is obviously productive, one could just as well view its many (Jakobsonian and Prague School) permutations— canon or corpus to literary work, verse design to verse instance, meter to metrical violation, text to text read or realized—as symptoms of confusion over the proper object of linguistic analysis, for *langue* simply defines the scope of the linguist's task, whatever is regular or constant and therefore worthy of description.

Several moments in the text of "Closing Statement," for example, imply a criterion of speaker awareness for the *langue-parole* metaphor. Verse forms, versions of *langue*, are sets of "enchained probabilities" (361) ultimately expressed in the *parole* of the actual poem. While such a characterization focuses on texts as data—the critic finds (apparently in poems of a type) features "compulsory for any line composed in a given meter," along with those that occur with "high probability" (361)—the surrounding discussion increasingly focuses on issues of psychological relevance. If conventions of verse form state "probabilities," then texts do not uniformly and inevitably map generic norms; Jakobson in fact interests himself in writers' assimilation of and resistance to general metrical laws (363). If readers absorb some "inkling" of metrical probabilities, then the perception of variation and departure—not of the isolated device—is the source of aesthetic effect (362–68; see also Mukařovský, "On Poetic" 8). For Jakobson, and also for Mukařovský, my comparative (Prague) example, aesthetic norms

---

[43] Davis has called this Saussure's "condition of realism"; since Saussure admits into linguistic analysis only those elements that have psychological reality for speakers (as opposed to operationally defined categories), he must exclude syntax (21–25). Of course, Saussure has other reasons as well: his association of syntax with choice, randomness, and diachrony (*Course* 19, 124).

thus start as generalizations of textual features but end as sets of established and shared expectations.

Ironically, however, a competing impulse arises from Jakobson's wish to avoid an essentialist definition of literature. If one admits that literary devices appear in both ordinary and literary discourse, then one can simply define literary works as texts in which the sheer abundance of such devices serves to foreground them. This quantitative solution, which focuses on differential frequencies of elements among functional languages, unfortunately erodes the *langue-parole* metaphor, for it is no longer necessary to distinguish between an underlying principle and the possibilities of its expression. Far from ignoring *parole*, as his critics would have it, Jakobson in these moments takes the arena of variation as his sole interest. Or one could simply say that particular literary texts are realizations of a much more abstract conception of *langue*. The *langue* of poetic language, that is, now consists of its definition, the orientation of the signifier toward itself. But if literary language, as Jakobson and Mukařovský both claim, is a super-average accumulation of features, as opposed to an expression of distinctive relations between elements, then the critic can only repetitively discover this sole fixed principle (see Jakobson, "Closing" 358, 373; Mukařovský, "On Poetic" 21). If no grammar or system of laws is to emerge for literary discourse analogous to the *langue* of the general language, then we have lost much of the initial promise of the Saussurean metaphor. In contrast to the *langue-parole* metaphor cast as probability and expectation, this inflection of the Saussurean model is in the tradition of the less dominant object-focused strain in Saussure's *Course in General Linguistics*. Such an account is finally also incompatible with Prague School functionalism, with literary discourse conceived as a total reorientation of the sign, as opposed to a concatenation of surface features (Mukařovský, "Art" 6, "On Poetic" 4; Jakobson, "The Dominant" 84; see also the later "Closing" 377).

Yet Jakobson is often close to a solution here. In a discussion of metrics, he notes the variety of rhythmic binaries poetry may exploit, depending on the language and genre—stressed and unstressed syllables, contrasts in syllabic intonation, long versus short syllabic nuclei. These, according to Jakobson, exist independently in texts, but are meaningful only as they are functional in the native poetic tradition and as hearers may thus hear them (359, 363–66; see also Mukařovský, "On Poetic" 22). Such statements not only constrain the critic's task—analysis must locate only those devices aesthetically relevant to perceiving subjects—but also suggest that hearers verify results. A native poet, Jakobson comments, may not articulate poetic norms but "nevertheless notices and repudiates even the slightest infringement of these rules" (364). The real issue, however, is that rather than systematically relate texts to mental experience, Jakobson more often assumes that these correspond in some transparent way; an (unbounded) analysis of data reveals precisely what the reader in some sense knows indistinctly. Just why Jakobson should assume a statement of one unproblematically outlines the other is not at all obvious, given both his earlier complex approach to the reception of texts and especially the earlier Prague School conception—which Mukařovský forcefully articulates—of literary objects as abstractions realized in the collective consciousness ("Art").

Now I have already said that Jakobson's approach to aesthetic perception was shaped both by the independent suggestions of the phonological model and by his particular focus on a kind of low-level, visceral aesthetic experience. But such statements do not entirely explain how Jakobson's position developed in response to specific critical problems. If we look at Jakobson's rule statements, however, we can observe the *langue-parole* metaphor strain under its explanatory burden. The rules of *langue*, that is, naturally reflect the problem I have been discussing; some are generalizations of data, and others are in some way predictive either of more data (other works of a genre) or of readers' and hearers' responses. Genre rules, for example, are summaries of data, whereas metrical rules (termed "optional" and "cumpulsory") characterize both form and patterns of expectation (363; see also Mukařovský, "On Poetic" 8, 22). In a weak form, rules that model responses account for "literary gratification," the pleasure invoked by rhythmic and phonological repetition and variation, the musical or immediate sensory effect of literary language (Jakobson, "Closing" 363, 358; Mukařovský, "On Poetic" 17–18). In a stronger form, textual elements "prompt" regular but more consciously interpretive actions; for Jakobson a reader's comparison of devices for similarity and difference (368–69), for Mukařovský a reader's assignment of intentional significance ("On Poetic" 50–51). Because the *langue-parole* metaphor accounts for so much, the rules of *langue* express confused perspectives—on the data side both actualized and potential texts, on the reception side both the unconscious, automatic experience of meter and sound and conscious interpretive choices.

Certain consequences follow. First, conflating such issues curtails exploration of the reading experience itself, despite Jakobson's and Mukařovský's clear interest in reader-associated effects—expectation, surprise, association, and appraisal. These remain effectively textualized phenomena as long as they automatically derive from (or are the same thing as) an empirical difference between the general and literary language or between ideal and real texts. One is tempted to construe in this approach similarities to later reader-oriented criticism; acts of readers become elements (in "motion" or in "interaction") in texts (Mukařovský, "On Poetic" 14; Jakobson, "Closing" 369). Yet here, I think, there is simply not faith enough in texts as entities outside perception to motivate an account of prolonged, and essentially syntactic, interaction between the independently existing text and reader. (Thus we can understand the later Jakobson who bridles at the suggestion he is phenomenologically naive.) Second, since Jakobson and Mukařovský subsume both textual and extratextual norms under the rubric of textual semantics, the otherwise suggestive *langue-parole* metaphor suppresses questions about the interpretive significance of nonlinguistic norms. If conscious interpretive acts are among the patterned responses the critic describes, if the theory is now semiotic in this new sense, the critic must then ask how interpretive decisions relate to extraliterary conventions. This is the kind of question that occurs to Mukařovský elsewhere (see *Aesthetic*) and in later Prague School criticism but remains at best implicit in Jakobson's work, in, for example, his remarks on folklore (see "On the Boundary" [with Bogatyrev] 92, *Dialogues* [with Pomorska] 14).[44]

The problem is that the notion of defamiliarization rather pressingly suggests psychological explication, reference to perceivers for whom an experience of language or the world is renewed. To keep quantitative, text-focused projects, therefore, the theory must connect textual facts to readers, something that certain assumptions about proper scientific procedure will not allow Jakobson and Mukařovský to do. Specifically, a phonologized conception of the relation of language to perceiving subjects suggests that historically variable elements in texts nevertheless synchronically invoke stable responses; and the scientific proscription of unnecessary psychologizing means that such assumptions remain in place. Similarly, if norms of *langue* model conscious interpretive behavior, no longer unconscious, purely linguistic rules, the theory must explain how individuals acquire group norms. And here—at least for Jakobson—a conception of the shared literary norms of the collective

---

[44] Mukařovský and Felix Vodička are the Prague critics who most concern themselves with social questions. Mukařovský discusses at length the extra-aesthetic functions of art, the relation of class to aesthetic reception, and the social movement of aesthetic norms. See *Aesthetic Function, Norm, and Value as Social Facts*. Vodička touches on such topics as the development of public reading tastes, the impact of prevailing ideological attitudes on aesthetic perception, and the integration of new works into the established canon. See "Response to Verbal Art."

consciousness as like lower-level linguistic rules masks the relation between broader social norms and aesthetic interpretive practice. When late Prague School critics (Mukařovský and Felix Vodička) seized on such topics, I might note, they were often more complete on diachronic than on synchronic variation among readerships.

Such issues naturally affect Jakobson's functionalism, since functional approaches ordinarily claim linguistic objects are produced through intentional acts in specific circumstances; if Jakobson ambivalently locates the literary object, he is understandably uncertain about its relation to speakers and outside contexts. Jakobson's (and again the earlier Mukařovský's) functionalism does attempt to mediate between undesirable positions, on both the topics of intentionality and reference. Were they to rely on a too narrowly intentional account of textual meaning, they would run afoul of the early structuralist proscription of needless speculation about authorial intentions, and of course they would fix a historically permuting object (see Mukařovský, "On Poetic" 10). Both critics are quite clear that texts escape creative intentions (Jakobson, "Closing" 371; Mukařovský, "Two Studies" 72). On the other hand, dismissing speaker intention diminishes texts as communicative acts. Although Jakobson's explanatory perspective is often the writer's, he is not satisfying on this point; often he assumes the (generalized) agency of creative genius. Mukařovský, in contrast, calls construing intent an important, though neither attainable nor constraining, interpretive strategy ("On Poetic" 50–51). Similarly, as conventionalists, Jakobson and Mukařovský overtly reject a simple mimetic conception of literature; yet to preserve its real-world impact, they allow literature multifunctional properties. Again this move perserves the category of literature without obliterating its referential and social function (Jakobson, "Closing" 356; Mukařovský, "Two Studies" 71–72).

Given such reasonable positions, then, how, as various critics observe, do the functionalist concepts "mode" and "orientation" come to be fixed properties of texts? Nothing in the theoretical program I have just outlined requires a text-focused critical practice; whereas both Jakobson and Mukařovský reject naively intentional and mimetic approaches, a functionalist linguistics might well imply some more complete treatment of aesthetic contexts. Yet recall that Jakobson's functionalism positions referential and persuasive discourse in the speech context but orients aesthetic language toward itself. We can explain this generalized orientation in part through the particulars of Prague School functionalism, which somehow fails to pressure the limitations of the theory's general phonologism enough. Prague School lin-

guists rejected Saussure's focus on the passive association of concept
and sound image as the only speech event of legitimate concern (11–
13). Rather, they claimed an interest in the entire speech chain, from
the intentional act of choosing a speech form, to the available category
or fund of speech forms, to the verbal or written expression of the
speaker's linguistic choices (see Davis 218). In this scheme, however,
the speaker or writer makes a linguistic choice not from among sentence or utterance specific intentional modes as later pragmatic theories would have it. Instead, the intentional gesture is essentially a selection from among subcodes or functional languages, and it becomes a
kind of global intention or mode that then characterizes the resulting
text. Thus the theory emphasizes this "dominant" function, despite
protestations about the mixed nature of discourse, especially of aesthetic language. An intentional gesture, then, determines in part the
aesthetic nature of the literary object, but when this act may be assumed, literariness becomes its general defining feature. Recourse to a
speaker's intentions is no longer necessary, and one may then focus on
details in the text, the remaining record of the linguistic choice.

Such assumptions are the source of those much-remarked critical
contradictions. For Jakobson the poetic function is a "total re-evalua-
tion of discourse" ("Closing" 377); yet its inevitable hallmark is dense
language, a projection of linearity on the paradigmatic plane (358). For
Mukařovský the poetic function is both a *"mode,"* a way of using language, and a permanent feature of texts ("On Poetic" 3, 4). When they
wish to eschew essentialist definitions of literature, both critics invoke
a fluctuating functionalism in which poetic elements are utterance or
sentence specific, appearing in various discourses. When they wish to
examine texts, Jakobson and Mukařovský resort to a global functionalism that characterizes every textual element as aesthetic and undercuts the doctrine of multifunctionality. Functionalism itself, then, becomes a textually expressed reflex of a speaker's or writer's choices, a
solution that remains satisfactory only if one assumes uniformity in
hearers' and readers' responses; otherwise, texts, as intentionally realized objects, become too unstable for empirical analysis. To complete
such a project one must believe, too, that critics can access their own
linguistic and aesthetic judgments. In short, Jakobson and Mukařovský
are both free of the doubts that plague later transformationalists,
doubts over such issues as the psychological relevance of grammatical
facts, the consciousness of linguistic behavior, and the judgments of
ideal speakers or hearers.

For Jakobson this confidence once again makes sense in the context
of his phonologism, his remarks about the immediate and universal

impact of aestheticized sound in his otherwise eccentric analysis of the Stanislavsky Theater and Mallarmé anecdotes in the text of "Closing Statement." And again Mukařovský serves as an interesting contrast, for here the problem arises not so much from his empirical interests as from a certain view of the text's relation to society. Since Mukařovský frequently discusses the evolution of interpretive norms and the interpretive effects of an evolving language, it is all the more surprising that he does not (at this point) much consider different realizations of a text at one moment. In fact, he explicitly dismisses the problem; the individual reader is "a member of a collective," and his "conception of reality," hence of the elements of a literary text, will coincide with that of the other members of his group ("Two Studies" 72). It follows both from Saussure and from Mukařovský's own interest in the problem of a national language that aesthetic objects are synchronic and shared social realities. Because his own social context leads him to assume a small and homogeneous reading community, and because, like Jakobson, he often defines a felt, rather than intellectualized aesthetic experience, Mukařovský does not fully explore such topics as contradictory readings rooted in divergent social experiences. It is not obviously contradictory for him that a text set in "motion," its semantic elements in continual interaction, should yet "impose" ("Two Studies" 67) an immediate, automatic, and generally uniform aesthetic experience.[45]

Although one can charge these accounts with intractable empiricism, it is rather more accurate to say that such contradictions derive precisely from decisions meant to anticipate the considerable difficulties of defining aesthetic objects. The nonuniqueness of the literary device motivates the functional approach; yet this functionalism in turn generates a textual definition of the aesthetic object. Since Jakobson and Mukařovský claim no special status for the literary device, they define literary discourse instead as a concentration of interrelating or self-focusing devices, choosing a solution that implies a discrete system within which such an interaction of elements can take place. "Literariness" is thus both a functional or intentional gesture and an empirical property of texts. Similarly, since their phonological orienta-

---

[45] Galan also comments (after an earlier version of this chapter) that in "On Poetic Language" Mukařovský does not explain how the collective consciousness is constituted, nor does he connect it to a relevant psychosociological or sociological theory (122). I hesitate to fault Mukařovský too harshly, since he does associate differences in aesthetic norms with differences in social class. But I agree that the mechanisms for transmitting such norms, and their relation to extra-aesthetic norms, remain general. See *Aesthetic Function*.

tion means they assume tabulated textual features are psychologically relevant, Jakobson and Mukařovský argue for contradictory investigative procedures. On the one hand, they need not limit description to readers' reports of their own perceptions, since aesthetic effect is largely unconscious. Thus the principle of "unconscious awareness" (with the emphasis on "unconscious") anticipates the most obvious objection to the investigative procedure; if one assumes a stable relation between text and perception, then descriptions of texts will unveil the patterned source of unconscious awareness. On the other hand, this same interest in psychological relevance develops at the semantic level into a discussion of meaning-effects significantly different from the earlier analysis of unconscious sensory impressions; the account thus requires stronger reference to readers' judgments (the emphasis now on "awareness"), changing the nature of the scientific procedure considerably. It seems, then, the reader is largely incidental in Jakobson's and Mukařovský's accounts, not so much because they rely absolutely on texts as objects as because they believe that only nonidiosyncratic and universal responses to literary works are of interest. Since any reader's perception of textual elements reflects a shared social reality, the text itself is finally a record of its own meaning.

REREADING "CLOSING STATEMENT"

Reassessing "Closing Statement" is clearly an exercise in reading a difficult, layered critical background. Obviously the author of the document himself emerges from a complex history: a Russian Formalist become a Prague School structuralist, at the same time a practicing linguist, who much later formulated the essay's arguments in the context of an American conference of New Critics. For this reason I believe it important to resist assimilating Jakobson's late criticism into a simple binary scheme, where one casts his text-based analyses as essentially like New Critical textualism, his metacriticism as never seriously functionalist, opposing such positions to American reader-oriented critical practice. Instead, Jakobson's Russian Formalist and Prague School background, to which he intermittently refers, offers important lessons on literary reference and on defining literary objects. Essentially, later criticism rehearses similar conundrums: how to reject a conception of literature as mimetic, yet preserve its discursive power, how to destabilize texts, yet save the objects of analysis. Of course Jakobson in this context also offers instructive negative lessons; set alongside the earlier Mukařovský, in "Closing Statement" we see Jakobson select a linguistic model informed by his expanding biological interests, whereas Mukařovský chooses a social model informed by a linguistics that more effectively structures shared aesthetic norms.

Jakobson's linguistic model raises additional questions about the broader context of his work and the delicate balancing act he almost accomplished between disciplines. Here also Jakobson is difficult to approach, if only because he did indeed succeed in finely discriminating among issues and topics. Just as he ranged impressively, if somewhat chaotically, in his criticism among textual, perceptual, and cultural issues, in his (independent) linguistics he addressed such then-unpopular topics as the social meaningfulness of phonological variation and the interaction of intonation and sentence meaning. We must, too, credit to Jakobson's multiple interests his often novel solutions to problems in several fields. An impressive illustration is his work on morphology and deixis, to which Jakobson brilliantly applied the same semiotic theory he developed for literary texts (see "Shifters"). Todorov sees a Jakobson who consistently aimed to reconcile a personal experience of poetry with a scientific account of language ("Jakobson's Poetics" 283). But we could also remark the Jakobson who integrated specific (even phonological) linguistic problems into a broader functionalism, who tried to sort out biological components of aesthetic experience, and who worked his theory of literary language in the context of a general theory of signification.

As we have seen, however, Jakobson's multiple interests, his aesthetics and his linguistics, also and perhaps inevitably conflict, even as they suggestively interact. Jakobson has sometimes been accused of a totalizing perspective, but I prefer to think of his as a synthesizing intellect; he wished to account for all linguistic facts, literary and otherwise.[46] His work thus illustrates a classic problem: one applies an approach productive in several domains, but crucial mistakes attach to the project of a general mission. It simply becomes more difficult to distinguish between problems in the now-related disciplines. Jakobson's work is an especially revealing example of this process. We have seen several such instances, and others are not difficult to unearth. A revision of the Saussurean metaphor, for example, in early Prague School work recast as systematic evolution, was especially productive both for phonology and for a dynamic conception of literary history. Yet its literary version ultimately constrains analysis; the source and contexts of literary evolution—as opposed to phonological change— prove more elusive.

But we have come a long way since the first enthusiastic reception of

---

[46] Note, for example, the thrust of most essays from that second conference on linguistics and literature (Fabb et al.).

linguistic models, and later criticism has sometimes collapsed such issues as these into a basic commentary on the inevitable clash of linguistics and criticism or on the predictable (empirical) search for stable and nonarbitrary meaning (see Seamon). A block to investigation of the variety of linguistic projects and paradigms has been Jakobson's own iconicity. Jakobson, that is, has simply come to stand in literary contexts for the general problem of science in literature. It is unfortunate that he has, inasmuch as there are many kinds of empirical impulses we might name, all potentially affecting literary theory in different ways; and critical interest might center instead on the range and ambition of such projects, on kinds of science. In his insightful remarks on Jakobson, Todorov cites the critic's problematic invocation of both science and semantics; Jakobson simultaneously seeks objective and subjective knowledge ("Jakobson's Poetics" 277). Yet the source of trouble is is not so much a necessary theoretical impasse at that general level as a specific problem with those concerns Jakobson calls "semantic," for these simply do not submit to biological, as opposed to semiotic, analysis. Similarly, while it is clear Jakobson invests in the now-familiar metaphor "voice as natural," we can identify contrasting sources of mimetic desire. Like Saussure, Jakobson indulges in both aural and specular metaphor, in occasional arguments for natural signification; however, unlike Saussure, Jakobson's self-expressive moments are both more clearly centered in private experience and more complicated by the purely animal, physiological tint he applies to aesthetic effects.

Having said this, we might then search for the important particulars of Jakobson's account. His biological approach to literary response may at first seem outmoded. Certainly biological claims are not new, nor, though I am not especially attracted to them, should one reject them out of hand. My objection is that an account of aesthetic experience must reconcile its biological claims with its conventionalism, with a broader theory of signification. As we have seen, Jakobson does not manage to do so; that is why his phonologism—even beyond his phonocentrism—causes him so much trouble, even when it begins as a legitimate linguistic investigation. Although he is never altogether free of the (Russian Formalist) romanticizing impulse, Jakobson early on locates the conventionality of emotionally expressive language more consistently. He does so until his (limited) version of the innateness hypothesis necessitates a distinction between programmed and learned, biological and cultural, linguistic regularities. Here we might sympathize, for most critics need not account for linguistic facts so diverse. Jakobson's thinking about the automatic and nonintellective aspects of language processing unfortunately tempts him finally to reintroduce a means of self-expression beyond form and device. Such issues are not about to go away, as the growing critical interest in cognitive linguistics will soon prove; and we may once again discover a (literary) biology that diverts or complicates cultural accounts of literary experience.[47] Here again Jakobson is an invaluable model, if only because his mistakes on this head are especially subtle ones.

[47] Joseph Bizup and Eugene Kintgen review this work; Ellen Spolsky, *Gaps in Nature,* is a further example. I do not dismiss such projects, but I do want to be cautious about leaping from innate structures of the mind to mechanisms of literary processing.

Chapter 3

Transformational-Generative Grammar as Literary Metaphor

In the technical sense, linguistic theory is mentalistic, since it is concerned with discovering a mental reality underlying actual behavior.

—NOAM CHOMSKY, *Aspects of the Theory of Syntax*

If we ask who is the best-known linguistic critic, we will get the name Roman Jakobson; but if we ask which is the most familiar linguistic theory, we will surely hear something about Noam Chomsky and generative grammar. It really was not so long ago, after all, that mainstream Anglo-American critics anticipated the reorganization of critical theory according to the precepts of generative grammar, often in some eclectic mix with speech-act theory or sociolinguistics.[1] Many of these reader-oriented texts are still familiar—among them Jonathan Culler's *Structuralist Poetics*, the early essays collected in Stanley Fish's *Is There a Text in This Class?*, Mary Louise Pratt's *Toward a Speech Act Theory of Literary Discourse*, Roger Fowler's *Linguistics and the Novel*, and Ellen Schauber and Ellen Spolsky's *Bounds of Interpretation*. Since these works succeeded a protracted debate on the relation of linguistics to stylistics and coincided with enthusiasm for French structuralism, they emerged during that brief but intense critical moment I described earlier, in which critical discourse suddenly absorbed the terminology of linguistics and linguistic philosophy.

This was a time, I think, not of mere linguistic faddism but of opti-

[1] The texts mentioned appeared in the 1970s and 1980s. Others of the period are: Culler, *Pursuit of Signs* (1981); Fowler, *Literature as Social Discourse* (1981) and *Linguistic Criticism* (1986); Susan Sniader Lanser, *Narrative Act* (1981).

mistic, not to say idealistic, interdisciplinary work that naturally accompanied a major change in the critical climate; for as I have already
suggested, linguistic models were particularly well positioned to par-
ticipate in the revolt from formalism. If protest arose from more conservative quarters, still the general notion prevailed that literary theory
had much to learn from outside disciplines. As readers became more
and texts less the focus of critical discussion, nothing could seem more
natural than the analogy between this development and linguistics'
earlier shift in descriptive focus from language data to native speakers'
linguistic knowledge. Similarly, the resulting emphasis on the institutional nature of interpretive activity appeared perfectly consonant with
an institutional, context-bound analysis of speech acts (the focus of the
next chapter). Apparently literary critics were just discovering later
what linguists and ordinary language philosophers already knew.[2]

We can productively contrast such critical goals to Jakobson's linguistic practice. Here, instead, we had nonlinguists importing linguistic paradigms; the advantage was a linguistic model applied to problems of more pressing and general critical interest. In this case, too, we
had a variety of applications as opposed to a dominating and comprehensive vision; naturally the payoff was a creative and sensitive poetics. Such projects also complicated the process of interdisciplinary
borrowing, however, since the borrowers in question (understandably)
retained little investment in the outside field—a fact we might bring to
bear on later critical pronouncements on generative grammar.

Simply put, times have changed, so much so that I would guess that
those critics who once themselves developed linguistics-based reading
theories secretly suspect that critics now have more to teach philosophers and linguists.[3] In some cases, to be fair—I am thinking, for instance, of Mary Louise Pratt's "Interpretive Strategies/Strategic Interpretations"—this later discussion has really taken the form of sober
and intelligent reflection on all that such critical programs might entail.[4] Elsewhere, the language of the new engagement with linguistics
has been less constrained. Thus Stanley Fish, in one well-known liter-

[2] As noted in the first chapter, I combine some discussion of speech-act theory with
generative grammar not because I confuse their aims but simply because the linguistics-
oriented critics of this period tended to incorporate speech-act accounts. The critics I
discuss here have all demonstrated some interest in speech-act theory. Others are Steven
Mailloux, *Interpretive Conventions* (1982), and (briefly) Wolfgang Iser (1978).

[3] This attitude is, perhaps, not so secret. See Culler, "Towards a Linguistics" 176–77;
Pratt, "Linguistic Utopias" 60; Fabb and Durant, "Introduction" 2; Christopher Norris,
"Theory" 91, 95–96; Ronald Schleifer, "Deconstruction" 394; Colin MacCabe, "Lan-
guage, Linguistics" 443–44. I return to this topic in the last chapter.

[4] See also Pratt's analysis of speech-act models ("Ideology").

ary debate (see Mitchell, *Against Theory*), unkindly associates Noam
Chomsky with literary critics who would impose one valid interpretation on literary works; he rejects generative grammar because it somehow comes to symbolize the false authority of an interested political
program that pretends impartiality ("Consequences" 106–12). Exactly
how Chomskyan linguistics suggests this connection with Fish's opponents is an involved matter. My point for the moment is merely that
the terms of debate have undergone a radical transformation. Whereas
once linguistics provided applied metaphors for various critics' programs—the rules of generative grammar for Jonathan Culler, linguistic
"competence" for Fish, conversational implicature and narrative
models for Pratt—language theories themselves, and generative grammar in particular, now often function as whole, loose metaphors for
conservative interpretive positions.

It is clear that for most critics the project of a linguistic-literary theory has failed in some fundamental way; Fish merely articulates more
eloquently the generally waning interest in these earlier critical models.
And yet I think that the shift of critical attention away from linguistics-oriented theory represents something a little more interesting than
the usual lost enthusiasm for a critical experiment. That is, Fish defines his critical position very specifically in opposition to Chomskyan
linguistics, even to the point of characterizing the theory as politically
repressive ("Consequences" 110–11). That a usually fair-minded critic
such as Fish could come to describe the language theory of a well-
known political activist as essentially fascist should be enough to suggest that critical discussion has taken a rather remarkable turn. A new
linguistics-derived rhetoric has emerged, an antagonistic one, and it is
only by revisiting the earlier critical accounts that one can hope to
decode it. I begin such an analysis here by focusing on transformational-generative grammar as it has been used in a familiar type of
reader-oriented criticism. What I eventually wish to suggest from the
discussion is, first, that the initial source of attraction in this influential linguistic model—principally its attention to "internal," mental
concerns—was an inevitable point of frustration and disappointment,
given the nature of the original paradigm; and, second, that it is essentially generative grammar as recreated for literary theory which becomes the actual object of critical attack. Although the theoretical issues involved are necessarily specific and local, the ultimate point is
not. More than in Jakobson's project, critical discourse functions here
to reinvent, then reject, the imported paradigm; and we may thus ask
whether an authentic interdisciplinary criticism is any longer possible.

LITERARY GRAMMARS

I do not, of course, claim that the impetus for reader-focused literary theory has derived solely from linguistic models; other sorts of reading theories, psychoanalytic and phenomenological, abound. Indeed, I think it is rather the case that linguistic paradigms served to justify literary programs of largely independent history and purpose. Yet certainly one group of influential writers, those whom Steven Mailloux has termed "social critics" (*Conventions* 19–65)—including Culler, Fish, Pratt, to some extent Wolfgang Iser, and Mailloux himself—can be identified in their earlier work both by common general aims and by an interest in linguistic or speech-act models. One shared notion is that the literary work is created and interpreted not in reference to a private code but according to a set of rulelike principles held within some group and assimilated by the individual; a second is the variously demonstrated interest in the political character of criticism. Initially, both these concerns were developed largely in connection with generative grammar or by analogy with speech acts. Yet given the current critical climate, it is easy to forget just how thoroughly such theorists once embraced these language theories. For this reason it will be useful to review briefly the role of generative grammar (enmeshed to some extent with notions drawn from speech-act accounts) in two central texts—Culler's *Structuralist Poetics* and Fish's collection of essays *Is There a Text in This Class?* I choose these works because they are still very much with us—much cited, recommended reading for newcomers to the field—and because they set the stage for much of the later focus on criticism as an institutional practice.[5] While they proceed from rather different interests (Culler saw Chomsky through literary structuralism; Fish read him alongside ordinary language philosophy), these texts are elegant examples of generative grammar brought to the service of a general poetics.

Both works begin by posing reader-oriented critical theory as the solution to the deficiencies of previous stylistic analysis. For Culler, this problem pertains especially to structuralist criticism (he of course includes Jakobson's work here), which has developed ever more "elaborate and complex analytic procedures" while failing to explain adequately what the classification and tabulation of linguistic structures really means (21, 53–54). In particular, he notes, such a linguistic practice is theoretically limitless, since there is nothing to indicate when

[5] I do not represent in this section either critic's current position.

the identification of textual elements should cease; it is clear neither that analysis is logically limited to the features readers normally perceive nor that descriptions of texts are related in a regular way to critical interpretation (71–74, but generally 31–95). Fish similarly cites the case of (mostly British and American) stylisticians whose work he finds disturbingly "arbitrary" and "unconstrained" (8); the usual result of such analysis is, he says, an enumeration of textual features from which any conclusion can be drawn (71–83). Clearly, what criticism needs, then, is a theory relating textual elements to interpretive processes, to readers.

The new reader-oriented theory, according to Culler, would take the form of a general poetics analogous to generative grammar. That is, just as Chomskyan linguistics shifted the focus of linguistic study from describing sentences, a corpus of data, to determining the internalized rules, the linguistic knowledge or competence that makes the production of all such sentences possible, so too should criticism turn from specifying textual features to consider the "underlying system" of "internalized" mental principles (118, 120), the "literary competence" (114, 121–22) by which readers generate all literary meanings (117–18, 121–22). Although he invokes generative grammar less exclusively, Fish similarly comes to describe the overall goals of literary theory in Chomskyan terms. Readers' minds, he explains, can be described as "repositor[ies] of the (potential) responses a given text might call out" (49), just as speakers in linguistics are said to hold all the productive semantic, syntactic, and phonological principles of their native language (44–45); a critic's task, then, is to construct a model of "literary competence" (48), a literary grammar that describes the "properties of literary discourses" a reader will have "internalized" (44).[6] To each critic linguistic theory thus suggests an important source of interpretive consistency and stability—a common set of literary norms. Literary meaning is finally freed from dependence on the text alone and yet saved from interpretive chaos (see *Poetics* 113–22; *Text* 292).

As Fish later argues, often by way of John Searle's speech-act model (the analogy he increasingly prefers and sometimes contrasts to generative grammar), such a critical program not merely aims to relate textual elements to the interpretive efforts of readers but must insist also that the putative textual "facts" themselves be seen as products of interpretive processes. Since, as Searle explains, brute facts can acquire

---

[6] Culler cites Chomsky's *Syntactic Structures* and *Aspects of the Theory of Syntax*. Fish obviously has in mind here the *Aspects* model.

meaning only within the context of an institution, there exists no such thing as a textual fact prior to interpretation. Just as, in Searle's own analogy, the characterization "he scored a touchdown" requires the institution of football, knowledge of its rules and goals, likewise, critical readings rely on the institution of criticism to identify in the first place the textual units it defines as relevant to its operation (*Text* 84–91; compare Searle, *Speech Acts* 33–42). Culler, too (though he does not cite Searle directly), departs momentarily from his linguistic model to echo *Speech Acts* on literary interpretation as a cultural practice: "The cultural meaning of any particular act or object is determined by a whole system of constitutive rules which . . . create the possibility of various forms of behavior" (*Poetics* 9; from Searle, *Speech Acts* 33).[7] For both critics the proper object of attention is necessarily the institution from within which a literary work is read (*Text* 106–10), for it is this institution, not the objective features of artifacts, that accounts for our "shared ways of seeing" aesthetic objects (*Text* 332). Thus the legislation of correct readings falls outside the critic's descriptive task (*Poetics* 117–22; *Text* 50).

Generative grammar also provides the methodological example for building the "literary grammar" (*Poetics* 122–23; *Text* 48–50), now not only a model of literary-reading activity but a description as well of the institution of criticism. Here the new poetics would rely on the intuitive responses of an idealized reader akin to the ideal "speaker-listener" or "native speaker" of Chomsky's similarly ideal "homogeneous speech-community" (see *Poetics* 124; *Text* 45–49; Chomsky, *Aspects* 3). The literary theorist, analogous to the linguist who begins outlining the syntactic rules for sentences a native speaker identifies as grammatical, describes the system of literary norms by asking what interpretive operations an ideal (Culler) or informed (Fish) reader must bring to texts in order to make sense of them as literary works (*Poetics* 114, 123–24; *Text* 44–45). As Culler and Fish discover, one way to highlight interpretive conventions is to apply them to (normally) nonliterary works (Culler sets out a newspaper report as a poem, Fish a blackboard reading assignment). Both critics are struck in the course of such analyses by the power of a basic, pervasive interpretive principle, the "rule of significance" (*Poetics* 115), the rule that "everything counts," by which readers construe a place in some overall pattern for every

[7] The animosity between Culler and Searle notwithstanding (Culler, *On Deconstruction* 110–12, 117–22; Searle, "Word"; "Exchange"), in *Structuralist Poetics* Culler does briefly draw from Searle to discuss interpretation as an institutionalized activity. There he derives from Searle the term "constitutive rule" (compare *Poetics* 5, 9 to Searle, *Speech Acts* 33–37).

aspect of a literary text (*Text* 330). Other conventions include rules
peculiar to fiction or poetry (genre conventions, sometimes also lik-
ened to speech-act rules), conventions governing the assumed relation
between author or narrator and text, and general expectations of coherence and thematic unity (see *Poetics* 115–16, 131–238; Culler, *Pursuit*
66–79; *Text* 322–30).

To test the reliability of a model so constructed, Culler suggests an
adaptation of Chomsky's notion of "acceptability" or "grammaticality." Just as syntactic models are tested against speakers' judgments
about the grammaticality or deviance of the sentences they generate,
so can the critic check hypotheses about interpretive operations against
a variety of literary works (*Poetics* 117–18), considering in each case
what it is the "ideal reader must know implicitly in order to read and
interpret works in ways we consider acceptable, in accordance with the
institution of literature" (123–24). The notion of a "well-formed" or
"intelligible" literary work analogous to a grammatical sentence is
"notoriously problematic," Culler admits (122), but systematic check-
ing and manipulation of postulated interpretive norms will clarify
their relation to specific literary effects (31, 117–18). Fish, too, finds a
parallel between positive reception of an interpretation within a critical community and judgments of linguistic acceptability (*Text* 357) or
perhaps speech-act notions of "felicity." The practice of criticism, he
notes, echoing Searle, includes in its "rules of the game" some "stipu-
lations as to what counts as a successful performance," and even novel
or challenging readings must be produced within its general confines
in order to be accepted and recognized (358; compare 356–58 with
Searle, *Speech Acts* 33–42, 54–56). Critical disagreements pose no ultimate problem for the theory, for both Culler and Fish find such arguments regular and predictable. In Culler's scheme they are coherent
productions of alternative textual facts according to different but acceptable interpretive principles (116–20; see also *Pursuit* 47–79). In
Fish's they are the result of critics' membership in various interpretive
communities analogous to unified language communities, institutions
that legitimate consistent but opposing sets of interpretive norms
(338–55).

Of course, there are significant differences between the two works.
In later essays, for instance, Fish stresses the structuralist notion that
readers, as well as aesthetic objects, are composed of rules or codes in a
way that Culler, though he considers the matter briefly, does not (*Text*
335–36; *Poetics* 28–31). From this premise Fish eventually concludes
that he has effectively dissolved the distinction between subject (reader)

and object (text), something with which Culler later takes issue.[8] Chomsky and Roland Barthes figure importantly in *Structuralist Poetics*, whereas J. L. Austin and Searle hover in the background of *Is There a Text in This Class?* And in contrast to Fish, who continues, despite his own theoretical interests, to conceive of the critic's business as the interpretation of individual texts, Culler concentrates on the analogy between critic and linguist. Yet the two accounts produce many nearly identical results: a redefinition of the literary canon (as variable, as dependent on general agreement among readers); an awareness of the changing conventions and proprieties of literary interpretation; an acceptance of multiple readings for any one text; a collapse of a distinction between literary and ordinary language (as dependent on readers' local attitudes toward the text); an identification of all reading acts as immediately interpretive rather than innocent or neutral; and most important for the analysis here, a reformulation of the literary work as a mental object accompanied by some linguistics-based account of its consistent production.

GENERATIVE GRAMMARS

The now-habitual reference to "competence models" or "institutional theories" testifies to the initial persuasiveness of such accounts of literary experience. We have become familiar, too, with the succeeding objections (some voiced by Culler and Fish themselves), in particular, that the notion of a specifically literary competence tends rather to underscore than undermine the independence of literary from ordinary experience, that readers in some such theories function as disappointing stand-ins for textual authority, that whatever their declared interests, many reader-oriented theorists have had surprisingly little to say about the political nature of critical practice. Later discussion has reminded us, in short, of the essential indebtedness of various reading theories to the formalist criticism they apparently repudiate. But as important as it is to place the linguistic apparatus of works such as Culler's and Fish's in this perspective—that is, in the context of ongoing critical debate—this focus on questions internal to criticism has necessarily obscured the matter of the theories' relation to the original

---

[8] Compare Fish's discussion of this point (*Text* 335–37) with Culler's response (*On Deconstruction* 74–75). See also their similar positions on the mutability of literary rules (*Text* 336; *Poetics* 30, 130) and on the nature of critical norms (*Poetics* 161–68 and *Text* 322–37; *Pursuit* 47–79 and *Text* 338–55).

linguistic models, and it is this rather different angle I wish to pursue further. This line of investigation will ultimately return us to some of these same critical issues, but with a clearer understanding both of how generative models have functioned to shape and limit the critical programs that borrow them and, conversely, of how criticism has reworked generative grammar in its own image.

As the preceding summary will have indicated, the mentalism of generative grammar (and also the intentionalism of speech-act theory) provided for criticism apparent solutions to the problem of stabilizing literary works now defined as abstract rather than concrete objects. From the point of view of linguistic study, the borrowed model suggests two, related problems. We might ask, first, whether the "internal," mental concerns of the different fields of inquiry are at all consonant and, second, whether sentence-level models may be properly adapted to longer texts. In the case of transformational-generative grammar, the answers to these questions are related. That is, the psychological claims of generative grammars are clearly distinct from those postulated for literary "grammars," and these troublesome differences derive from attempts to draw an analogy between sentence-level and textual concerns. To demonstrate these problems will require some discussion of the linguistic accounts Culler and Fish draw on, Chomsky's *Syntactic Structures* and the later *Aspects of the Theory of Syntax*. Since the currently accepted grammatical model is now rather different, I should add that this is a retrospective account of the linguistic issues, but it will serve to illustrate the original source of (literary) confusion.[9]

A look at the early generative grammar of *Syntactic Structures* is revealing in this context, for the account lacks dramatic psychological import.[10] The basic model for the grammar is drawn from logic and mathematics; it consists of phrase-structure and transformational rules that together "generate," in exactly the same sense that a mathematical formula generates a (possibly infinite) set of numbers, all the sentences of a language (13, 15, 48).[11] At the same time, this productive

[9] In this brief account I focus on overall goals rather than on more technical innovations, and I discuss just those linguistic issues that have concerned literary critics. Detailed summaries are in John Lyons 35–70; and Frederick J. Newmeyer, *Grammatical* 34–72; *Linguistic Theory*, 1st, 19–92, or 2d, 17–80. For later developments see Henk van Riemsdijk and Edwin Williams 80–88, 157–92; and Newmeyer, *Linguistic Theory*, 2d, 197–229. Newmeyer's two editions of *Linguistic Theory in America* differ slightly. I am particularly indebted in this discussion to Newmeyer's clear treatment of the issues.

[10] There are disagreements on this point not crucial to the discussion here.

[11] See Jerrold Katz 34; Lyons 69. I borrow the mathematical analogy from Lyons 44–45.

capacity is limited to only the sentences of the language, so that the grammar functions to separate grammatical sentences (possible syntactic arrangements) from nonsentences (13–14). Since a grammar so defined is "simply a description of a set of utterances," it is "neutral as between speaker and hearer" (48); its rules describe neither the "synthesis" nor the "analysis" of actual sentences by native speakers (48) but rather the syntactic principles compatible with the notion "grammatical in English" (13). Grammaticality itself Chomsky terms "an intuitive concept" and equates it with "acceptable to a native speaker" (13), but he requires in this context only that the speaker recognize a sentence as a sentence in the language (15, 98–99). Chomsky advances the notion of "let[ting] the grammar itself decide" the grammaticality of borderline sentences; that is, formal considerations (the simplicity of the grammar) determine the grammaticality of uncertain cases (14). Speaker judgments, then, are merely a check on the success of the model, on what syntactic arrangements it must define. Even the grammar's productive capacity is said here to reflect native speakers' "behavior," not their tacit knowledge of creative principles (15).[12]

The role of semantic concerns in the text of *Syntactic Structures* is somewhat unclear, and on such issues it presents arguments that have become grounds for literary-critical attack. On the one hand, the model's ability to assign multiple structural descriptions to an ambiguous sentence is advanced as a point in its favor (28, 33, 85–88). On the other hand, certain passages argue strongly for the independence of syntax and semantics (93–105). Syntactic and semantic principles interact, Chomsky observes, so that transformations often capture synonymous relations (101–3), but such correspondences are not reliable, as in the case of nonsynonymous active/passive sentence pairs (101).[13] Since they summarize relations between sentence types, transformations simplify the grammar, and they are rather to be justified by such nonsemantic, "purely formal" criteria (102). Grammaticality, he notes, is not equivalent to "meaningful[ness]" (15); the nonsensical sentence

---

An example of an infinite yet defined set is the set of even numbers. Chomsky now stresses that while two grammars may be extensionally equivalent, only one may correctly describe the form of the internal grammar (*Knowledge* 24–36). James McCawley notes that he must no longer take the generated sentences as including their structural descriptions; thus a string of unanalyzed sentences is opposed to internalized linguistic rules (355).

[12] See Newmeyer, *Linguistic Theory*, 1st, 28–31; Katz 40–42; Lyons 46–47, 67.

[13] The example Chomsky gives is "Everyone in the room knows at least two languages" (which languages unspecified) versus "At least two languages are known by everyone in the room" (everyone knows the same two) (*Syntactic Structures* 100–101).

"Colorless green ideas sleep furiously" is more nearly grammatical than an otherwise meaningful sentence that violates English syntactic order ("Read you a book?") (15).[14]

By the time of the more familiar *Aspects of the Theory of Syntax* model, Chomsky's conception of the grammar had become overtly psychologized, and it was largely the language of this account that critical discourse absorbed.[15] Here formulation of specific grammars is to accord with information about linguistic universals, defined as innate initial constraints on the form grammars can assume (27–30). The goal of linguistic description, still ultimately a model that produces or generates the sentences of the language, is "the underlying system of rules that has been mastered by the speaker-hearer" (4), the "internalized" grammar "that expresses his knowledge of his language" (8). This linguistic knowledge is again distinguished from the corpus-based generalizations of previous linguistic practice; "competence" or knowledge of the abstract predictive principles of the language is opposed to linguistic "performance," to language use or a finite body of recorded utterances (4). While the model now explicitly mirrors speakers' creative abilities, their ability to produce an infinite number and variety of sentences (15–16), it does so only by generating as its output the potential sentences of the language (9) and by assigning them revealing structural descriptions (24). A grammar relates and disambiguates sentences, predicts possible syntactic arrangements, but does not imitate a step-by-step production of sentences by native speakers (9). Sentence-

[14] There is confusion about Chomsky's position here. One problem is that *Syntactic Structures* was a shortened version of a then-unpublished manuscript (*The Logical Structure of Linguistic Theory*). As Newmeyer notes (*Linguistic Theory*, 1st, 28–33), most readers took Chomsky to say that syntactic rules were independent of semantic rules and to argue for a broad definition of grammaticality (for the "green ideas" sentence as grammatical). Chomsky has since clarified the first point; by "independence of syntax" he meant merely that semantic considerations cannot wholly motivate grammatical notions (*Logical* 19, 96–97). On the second point, Newmeyer comments that a careful reading of *Syntactic Structures* reveals that Chomsky then considered the "green ideas" sentence less than grammatical and wished to account for its anomaly (*Linguistic Theory*, 1st, 30–31). *Logical Structure* (144–55) confirms that he did, but this reading is difficult to derive from the text of *Syntactic Structures*, since Chomsky flatly terms the nonsense sentence grammatical (15); a note suggesting a ranking of sentences by "levels of grammaticalness" (16n.2, 42–43n.7, 78) does not mitigate the text's main thrust.

[15] Chomsky does not now present his position as shifting between *Syntactic Structures* and *Aspects*; he says that he was merely hesitant to introduce psychological considerations in the earlier work, but he also notes that the implications were evident to reviewers (*Logical* 35–36; also Newmeyer, *Linguistic Theory*, 1st, 42, or 2d, 51). Others have doubted this claim (Katz 40–41). But the important point is that the *Syntactic Structures* text has often been read as contrasting with *Aspects* on the topics of semantics and psychology.

processing questions are of interest, but they fall outside the scope of competence; they require a complementary but separate theory of performance (1–15).[16]

The competence/performance distinction also allows Chomsky to clarify and limit the role of native speakers' linguistic intuitions, despite the increased investment in psychological explanation. "Grammaticality," he explains, pertains to linguistic competence and to the formal exigencies of the model (the simplicity of the account). "Acceptability," in contrast, relates to the realm of performance, to speaker intuitions about sentences beyond their grammaticality (11). It is, for example, the task of the grammar to describe the structure of relative clauses, but a study of performance is required to investigate the processing limitations on multiply embedded clauses. That is, the linguist might define a given sentence as grammatical inasmuch as it fits the known syntactic patterns of English, but this same sentence might nevertheless seem unacceptable to native speakers for its difficulty, awkwardness, or length (10–14).

Yet militating to some extent against this broad and technical treatment of grammaticality is increasing attention elsewhere in *Aspects* to speaker perceptions, a potentially misleading topic for literary critics. Certain speaker intuitions—of the deviance or ambiguity of sentences—are no longer peripheral to the grammar, and borderline cases, problems involving "degrees of grammaticalness," are more explicitly at issue (77). To account for such perceptions involves a narrower definition of grammaticality, for it is only in terms of its violation of grammatical rules that an anomalous sentence can be identified as such. Thus "Colorless green ideas sleep furiously" is here clearly deviant in its disruption of the usual selectional restrictions ("sleep" ordinarily takes an animate subject); its deviance explains why the sentence requires metaphorical interpretation (149). (An earlier account mentions resulting literary effects [*Logical* 149].) Such observations lead to detailed discussion of subcategorization rules and rankings of deviant sentences (violations involving "count" nouns, for instance, are more disruptive than for nouns specified "human") (*Aspects* 149–53).[17]

If relations of synonymy and ambiguity no longer merely coincide in interesting ways with the grammar but are central to it (21–24), if semantically anomalous sentences require this elaborate explanatory apparatus, then Chomsky would appear to have changed his position on

---

[16] Chomsky himself researched some language-processing questions, but at this point he believed the results could not be effectively incorporated into a competence model.

[17] Such issues appeared only cryptically in *Syntactic Structures*.

the relevance of meaning to syntactic description.[18] But he continues to speculate on this point, first embracing the Jerrold Katz–Jerry Fodor–Paul Postal semantic component (154), then considering divergent solutions—incorporating selectional rules into a semantic component (153) or allowing the syntactic component to absorb the semantic (158–59). The position of the later account thus has an understandable literary appeal: Chomsky ultimately finds the boundary between syntax and semantics difficult to draw (154, 159–60).[19]

Now whatever one might believe about the incorporation of semantic concerns into the generative model, the relation of Chomsky's psychological claims to its formal apparatus is clearly a source of confusion in literary studies. It is not that Culler and Fish are cavalier readers of Chomsky's works; both critics, in fact, allude to Chomsky's own remarks about popular misreadings of the generative model (*Poetics* 24–26; *Text* 75). But the constraints of the literary project are such that they inevitably undermine attempts to apply a "literal" linguistic analogy. The language attached to the components of the grammar (which "interpret" and "read" merely in the sense that the output of one feeds into another) becomes associated with actions of the speaker/hearer, and the terminology of native-speaker intuition and judgment becomes a part of the rule apparatus of the literary model.

Initially, that is, Culler carefully describes literary grammars as lists of principles defining a set of all possible literary interpretations; literary rules do not outline reading events so much as predict or extrapolate readings (*Poetics* 118–21). More often, however, he simply associates syntactic rules with the choices and decisions of readers. This shift of explanatory emphasis is particularly striking when we compare Culler's appropriation of the Chomskyan terminology with the original passages. In *Aspects*, Chomsky describes a generative grammar as "a system of rules" that "assigns structural descriptions to sentences" (8), consisting of a syntactic component that "specifies an infinite set of objects" (sentences); a phonological component that "determines the phonetic form of a sentence generated by syntactic rules"; and finally a semantic component that "relates a structure generated by the syntactic component" to a certain semantic representation" (16). In *Structuralist Poetics*, however, the formal components of the grammar no longer interact with one another; rather it is the hearer/reader who

---

[18] Violations of selectional restrictions Chomsky termed syntactic rather than semantic in nature (*Aspects* 153), but whether they should be so described was an open question.

[19] See Newmeyer, *Linguistic Theory*, 1st, 91–92, or 2d, 79–80, for discussion. Newmeyer notes that Chomsky could not have been strongly committed at this point to the independence of grammar (1st, 92, or 2d, 80).

"convert[s] the sounds [of the language] into discrete units," "recognize[s] words," and "assign[s] a structural description and interpretation to the sentence, even though it be quite new to him" (113; see also *Pursuit* 50, 53; "Towards" 174). The literary grammar as a whole "permit[s] [the reader] to convert linguistic sequences into literary structures and meanings" (*Poetics* 114). Similarly, in *Is There a Text in This Class?* Fish briefly describes the Chomskyan model as neutral on matters of production and reception (75). But elsewhere the analogous literary grammar is a "spatial model" "corresponding more or less to the internal mechanisms which allow us to process (understand) and produce sentences" (44); it "monitor[s] and structure[s]" the "temporal flow" (46), the reader's "uncovering of the deep structure and extraction of deep meaning" (47).

The Chomskyan model is explicated, then, in two different ways. In the first, the new paradigm is in some sense analogous to the general outline of the *Syntactic Structures* and the conservatively interpreted *Aspects* grammar: it consists of a theory or set of principles that defines the range of conceivable readings. In a second version, the suggested model is unique to literary studies, a heavily psychologized model unrecognizable in the original context.

The problem begins with the initial analogy between sentence and text, which dramatically inflates the semantic facts accounted for. One does not, after all, speak of the ambiguity of sentences within literary works without some larger question of textual meaning in mind. But since the borrowed model is essentially a syntactic one, its semantic concerns remain, even in the *Aspects* version, too limited for this purpose—limited, that is, to sentence-level ambiguity, synonymy, analycity, and the like. In any case, the analogies central to literary grammars are all drawn from the *syntactic* apparatus of the generative model; no principles are derived, as one might anticipate, from the Katz and Fodor or Katz and Postal proposals for the semantic component.[20] Additionally, once critics expand the notion "intuition" to accommodate larger problems of textual meaning, the literary grammar inevitably becomes a temporal model, since the knowledge accounted for must include meaning produced by textual structure. Again the revised model contrasts to the original grammar, which has no motive to outline coding or decoding events if the ultimate explanatory goal is a set of sentences, not a conversation or text.

While the impact of Chomsky's psychological speculations on language-acquisition and language-processing research is well known, his

---

[20] This choice signifies the collapse of semantic and syntactic concerns.

major innovation in linguistics proper was to turn grammatical description into a model-building enterprise. The comparison between *Syntactic Structures* and *Aspects of the Theory of Syntax* is instructive, since the formal apparatus of the generative grammar is demonstrably separable from both its semantic and psychological claims, such descriptive goals having been added to some extent in a later version. (Notice that literary critics essentially read *Syntactic Structures* through *Aspects*.) Similarly, while grammatical models now retain many of Chomsky's initial explanatory goals (see van Riemsdijk and Williams 3–13), the associated semantic claims are comparatively reduced.[21] In contrast, every aspect of the literary grammar has been so intensively psychologized that there is no longer a distinction to be made between what the model is (in some formal sense) and what it is meant to account for. Once the descriptive goal is so broadly construed as to render "competence" a very general "knowing how" in exactly the sense Chomsky wishes to exclude, the model becomes a theory of textual production, and we are finally in the realm of the kind of performance the original theory has stated it does not have the means to analyze.

While the Chomskyan metaphor now better suits the demands of the reading theory, the other terms of the models naturally begin to break down. It is worth noting, as one example, that it is even more difficult to defend idealized readers than idealized native speakers. Since ideal readers are not just necessary to test and validate the grammar but essential for its operation, much previously irrelevant behavior becomes crucial. That is, at times such reader constructs merely stand for the collection of rules all readers have internalized, but elsewhere they react, choose among possible actualizing strategies, or discard one interpretive approach for a better one in a way that the literary grammar does not provide for. They represent not only what all readers know but some succession of events, some application as well as knowledge of rule-defined principles. Clearly this activity is not explained by mere reference to the analogy with native speakers, for the judgments in question involve high-level, purposive behavior as opposed to decisions on the well-formedness of sentences.

More interesting, perhaps, is the erosion of the notion of well-formedness itself. We have already seen that the concept becomes more problematic the more semantic considerations are added to the gram-

---

[21] There are other major differences—an emphasis on universal grammar, a simplified transformational component, an enriched surface structure. But these have emerged as elaborations (though substantial ones) of the *Aspects* model. See van Riemsdijk and Williams 170–75; Newmeyer, *Linguistic Theory*, 2d, 197–229.

mar (from *Syntactic Structures* to *Aspects*). Once the grammar is called upon to account for semantic anomaly, for a variety of speaker intuitions, the status of the "colorless green idea" sentence becomes questionable and the explanatory apparatus correspondingly intricate. At the discourse level the analogy of the grammatical sentence understandably collapses altogether (Culler, in fact, consistently equates "grammaticality" with "acceptability"). There is, after all, no recognizable formal component against which to define deviance; a concept originally used to distinguish intelligible sentences from those that fall completely outside the scope of the language becomes hopelessly broad when finally identified with the acceptability or plausibility of literary readings. Applied to texts, well-formedness inevitably runs afoul of that central feature of literary interpretation—that any text, no matter how "deviant," can be made coherent, made to mean. But this is a minor point since Culler and Fish apply "acceptability" to particular interpretations, the reader-actualized literary objects, texts having no independent existence. Yet this project, too, is doomed to contradiction. If a literary grammar is said to outline the principles by which readers do read texts, how can particular readings be judged unacceptable for violating principles of literary production? Of course there is a sense in which we would like to say that some readings are more plausible and coherent than others, but such judgments are once again at a great distance from yes/no decisions on morpheme strings; the linguistic model takes us no farther in this case than our everyday sense of what good, bad, or better readings of texts are.

It seems obvious that the rules of the two "grammars" differ in kind. The rules of a generative grammar are akin to what Max Black has termed "principle rules" (113–14); they are statements of lawlike universals, atemporal principles of the form "X is Y" ("Verbs follow subjects") or "X always does Y" ("relative clauses take the following form").[22] But the more a literary grammar becomes a model of textual processing, of speaker-hearer relations, the more these rules assume the status of heuristics and strategies. Thus many of the reading principles Culler and Fish describe are rather of the form "Do X"—involving either immediate recovery strategies ("Read for coherence") or calculations against some knowledge of an institution (a genre, a cultural practice). Chomsky speaks of the internal formulation of syntactic rules according to universal principles (of a very abstract kind); acquisition of rules is triggered by exposure to language data but not entirely determined

---

[22] These are constitutive rules in Searle (*Speech Acts* 33–41), but Black stresses the independence of such rules from their application (113–14).

by it. In contrast, acquisition of literary-interpretive principles is described as a process of generalization, the result of many encounters with texts. It is an axiom of Chomskyan linguistics that language is not learned by some such means as positive reinforcement; but institutions that legislate and authorize interpretive strategies are central to literary competence models. It is not necessary to say that one view is correct, the other not; it seems rather that the rules involved represent different kinds of knowledge.

Basic uncertainties about the exact nature of the language theory on which the literary grammar is based, then, ultimately result in unexpected skewing of its central terms. Production of a corpus is equated with production of meaning; the artificial levels of syntactic description are construed as real states in a psychological process; ideal readers become necessary not just to test and validate the grammar, but to operate it, once the generative output is mental, not mathematical; and notions of well-formedness apply no longer to data—to a set of possible sentences—but to a largely unavailable cultural and mental object. Now it can be reasonably argued, I think, that most of these permutations of the original model are inevitable within a literary context. How is it possible, after all, for a theory of reading to separate final definitions from the process of their application? And how is it possible to keep a discourse-involved theory from outlining heuristic rather than definitional rules? This is, however, exactly the problem. The generative model is appealing because it offers both rigor and some consideration of internal matters, but in the interests of this rigor it limits inquiry into just the sorts of nonconventional operations that might prove most useful for a description of reading activity.

NARRATIVE MODELS

Although I have focused thus far on the (literary) limitations of the generative paradigm, I do not at all dismiss its historical influence, and I want to acknowledge clearly its explanatory power as well. Among reader-focused theories, the generative approach particularly pressed issues of institutional meaning; that is, it suggested to critics such as Culler and Fish important questions about how we argue with one another or train our students, for it now seemed natural to ask how it is readers acquire the minutely constrained interpretive perspectives the linguistic model suggested. Since, as I have just argued, the language-learning issues of the generative model are of a significantly different order, it has little, analogously, to say to us about these matters; nevertheless, it was instrumental in bringing critical discussion to this point.

If the generative model could take us no farther, then just how productively did reader-oriented critics exploit it? Consider a brief but instructive contrast between the generative model imported into narrative theory as opposed to a poetics of the sort I have been discussing; for we can also outline its limits and merits from that perspective. Narratologists, unlike Culler or Fish, were already deeply invested in linguistic theories, whether from Saussure, by way of Russian Formalism or French structuralism, or from American linguistics, by way of stylistics. Any new related development—naturally including generative grammar—was therefore an almost automatic source of narrative metaphor. In fact the generative paradigm applied in the context of an already predominating linguistic analogy: narratives are structured like sentences.[23]

While many narratologists casually absorbed the notion of a specifically narrative competence (see Eco, *Role* 7; Rimmon-Kenan 8), the broadest narrative programs of this sort, notably Gerald Prince's and A. J. Greimas's, outline overall generative goals in now-expected terms. Here the literary grammar generates not possible readings but a set of potential narrative structures, all and only the sentence sequences readers accept as narrative (Prince, *Grammar* 10; *Narratology* 79–80; Greimas, "Narrative" 794). The apparatus of the narrative model thus identifies elementary units (minimal narratives, *énoncés*), rules for combination and expansion (sometimes modeled on phrase-structure rules), and transformations (a means of varying the emphasis or chrononolgy of basic stories) (Prince, *Grammar* 38–83; "Aspects"; *Narratology* 79–102; Greimas, "Narrative" 796–801).[24] Whatever objections one might raise—the descriptive technical details weary some readers—two concrete accomplishments recommend such projects. First, narratologists' investment in linguistic theory means they seriously contribute to it, not in elaborating the generative model itself, but in successfully relating syntactic to discourse concerns. While we may dispute, for example, Prince's specific judgments on the accep-

[23] Excellent overviews of issues in narratology (with special attention to linguistic models) are Shlomith Rimmon-Kenan, *Narrative Fiction*; Michael Toolan, *Narrative*; and Wallace Martin, *Recent Theories of Narrative*. For debates see W. J. T. Mitchell, *On Narrative*.

[24] I draw here on those of Prince's and Greimas's accounts most explicitly influenced by generative grammar: Prince, *A Grammar of Stories*, the third chapter of *Narratology*, and "Aspects of a Grammar of Narrative"; Greimas, "Narrative Grammar" and "Elements of a Narrative Grammar." See also the framing assumptions of Prince, "On Narrative Studies and Narrative Genres."

tability of various sample narratives (see *Grammar* 19–21), or question the narrative role he assigns causation (26), his analysis nevertheless locates probable constraints, both grammatical and pragmatic, on narrative structure—the minimum number of events, necessary temporal ordering, and conjunction of stative and active statements essential for interpretation as narrative.[25] Second, and perhaps of more moment to critics, such narrative schemes prove flexible as heuristics; again in Prince's case the generative project doubtless informs his later elegant analyses of narrative as theme (see *Grammar* 48–49; *Narrative*).

Tension between narratology's formalist concerns and the temporality of its descriptive object remains the persistent problem, however. Like reader-based competence theories, narratology wrestles with processing issues in the generative paradigm. Prince and Greimas, my examples here, initially build successful set-defining machines; the narrative project—extracting an ordered but textually given logic of events—seems less problematically descriptive and atemporal than an account of a developing interpretation. Yet reading concerns do not disappear. Prince, for instance, posits a necessary causal link between two events in a minimal story, but as he himself observes, readers may impute causality not textually given; such actions explain how readers make sense of postmodern fiction (*Grammar* 24–28). We might also ask how causal and logical relations shift between first and second readings of texts.[26] Thus, as soon as the narrative grammar moves beyond locating sentence-associated propositions to larger discursive patterns, narrative analysis implies a reading perspective that naturally alters its fundamental units.[27]

Narratologists also imported a second set of "generative" issues into prevailing practice: they superimposed the surface-structure–deep-structure distinction of generative grammar onto the familiar opposition between story and discourse (or *fabula-syuzhet*), the natural or logical chronology of events contrasted to actions ordered and shaped in narration. In various formulations, "story" is a logic of events stripped of style or elaboration, an extractable underlying narrative that different media or languages may express (Chatman, *Story* 19–22; Greimas, "Narrative" 793–94; Prince, *Grammar* 13; Rimmon-Kenan 7). The distinction is again heuristically productive; it opens discussion not only

---

[25] On the matter of sequencing and causal relation, see also Prince, "Aspects" 50–51 (he seems here to change his position); Rimmon-Kenan 18; Todorov, "Two Principles" 28–38.

[26] The problem forces Seymour Chatman, for example, to decide which reading the narrative grammar will describe ("New Ways" 18–19).

[27] Prince does acknowledge many of the model's explanatory limits (see *Narratology* 101–2).

of narrative options and orders but also of narrative space and time, departures and iterations (see Genette, *Narrative Discourse*). In the generative version, given "surface" narratives, again like sentences, contrast with their "deep" or basic form. They derive from deep structure through narrative transformations—negation, repetition, transposition—which characterize habitual modes of narrative presentation just as grammatical transformations define particular writing styles (see Fowler, *Linguistics* 20–22).[28]

But the generative account now also foregrounds alternative conceptions of "story." Seizing on the suggestive language of "deep structure," narratologists began to elaborate a more fully analogous narrative level. Although earlier critics (Russian Formalists such as Vladimir Propp) also identified functions and transformations throughout a corpus of tales, later critics argued these consist of mere surface descriptions, not "deep" or motivating narrative principles. Such a practice contrasts with, for example, that of Claude Lévi-Strauss. His approach one might term (after the fact) a deep-structure analysis, since it distills semantic oppositions that underlie all narrative (Greimas, "Narrative" 795–96; Rimmon–Kenan 11).[29]

If one styles the deep-structure approach as a critique of linearity, as paradigmatic rather than syntagmatic, the interesting question then is what narrative deep structures consist of if neither natural chronology nor an inventory of textual elements (see Brooks 16–17; Pavel, "Narrative" 352; Todorov, "Two Principles" 30). For narratologists who employ the term, deep structures are usually a kind of modal logic, a sequence of events causally, rather than chronologically, ordered (Greimas, "Narrative" 797; Rimmon-Kenan 10–11), or they consist of more abstract achronic semantic primitives (Fowler, *Linguistics* 12, 30).[30] Some narratologists initially invoked universal narrative principles, on

---

[28] Since structuralists also use the term "transformation" in reference to Propp, one must hesitate before ascribing the generative model to all such language. Todorov and even Greimas do not always, for instance, derive discussion of transformations and derivations from generative grammar. See Todorov, "Two Principles" 30–38; Greimas, *Structural* 76–106.

In generative-grammar–influenced accounts, transformations variously reorder and style basic propositional content according to the author's perspective (Fowler, *Linguistic* 12–16, 20–22); rearrange relationships within the narrative—passivize actions, and the like (Chatman, "New Ways" 27); expand and condense—temporally and spatially organize—deep-structure events (Greimas, "Narrative" 797); or combine and embed minimal narratives (Prince, *Grammar* 56–83; *Narratology* 88–92).

[29] The reference is especially to Lévi-Strauss, "The Structural Study of Myth."

[30] See Martin for a discussion of arguments about deep structure (99–103); David Lodge also gives a brief overview. Again, deep structures vary: they are the variously realized "overriding" structures of the text (Chatman, *Coming* 29) or underlying basic functions and actants (Greimas, "Narrative" 799).

the suggestion of both Lévi-Strauss and universal grammar (see Todorov, *Grammaire* 14–17). Later most critics agreed that underlying primitives are local and culturally specific. Thus for Roger Fowler, narrative deep structure is necessarily political, encoding shared cultural values (16, 30, 41–44); for Susan Sniader Lanser it represents a more personal (authorial) ideology, which then generates value-laden textual structures (226–45; see also Eco, *Role* 5–8).[31]

However unobjectionable its later political positions, the generative narrative project—indeed, narratology in general—has provoked considerable antipathy. Critics complain that it assumes a natural order of events in the world, valorizes a Platonically ideal causal structure, and invests in some notion of an authentic original story (see Smith).[32] Narratologists in turn contend that the paradigmatic approach itself interrogates "natural" chronology, that the chronology in question is an identifiable, textually given one rather than real in some extratextual sense. They also respond that underlying forms are convenient fictions, not seriously ideal, merely ways of asking about alternative, not authoritative, narrative versions (Chatman, "What" 310–13; "Reply"; Goodman). And such critics finally point to their own disillusion with universalist claims by applying narratological methods to historical analysis (Genette, "Fictional" 756–57; Pavel, "Narrative" 362; Prince, "On Narrative" 280–82). Although I believe that certain of the formalist practices of narratology remain problematic, I think narratologists have answered these particular attacks well enough. My own reservation aims rather at the form of the linguistic model. That is, in this application the metaphor is perhaps not apt enough. While "deep structure" begins as a critique of faith in overt or surface narrative form, the project of specifying underlying semes is at once a significant problem. And yet if the critic rejects the anthropological, universalizing impulse, the project no longer requires the linguistic metaphor: one might as well specify outright, without apparatus, the suspected ideological motives for discursive practices.

This is not to say that this discussion has not been useful or that it should or could have been apparatus free. But if we return to my initial question about contrasting appropriations of generative grammar, I

---

[31] The focus on universal narrative principles derives primarily from anthropology and from narrative analyses of folklore and is not especially associated with interest in generative grammar.

[32] Barbara Herrnstein Smith most forcefully lodges such arguments. Perhaps her best points are that these narrative models privilege scrambled chronologies (223) and focus on texts at the expense of narrative acts (222). Chatman ("What We Can Learn"; "Reply"), Genette ("Fictional" 757–60), and Goodman are among those who reply to her several objections.

would want to claim that reader-oriented critics—and I mean especially Culler and Fish—gained from it more distinctive mileage, more resistance to given critical practice, a more oppositional discourse. And this gain, whatever its further fortunes, defines the generative model's literary value. Much of the narrative project might have been cast in other terms—almost any spatial model works as well—whereas the linguistic terms of reader-oriented criticism are for good reason more persistently with us. Of course I should also suggest one further contrast. Narratology invented eclectic and suggestive applications of generative grammar, and its practitioners had independently developed goals. Despite a longer history of linguistic interest, therefore, narratologists expressed less idealism about the generative model, and as we will see, they perhaps came more naturally than reader-oriented critics to address its shortcomings.

LATER POSITIONS

It is hardly surprising that critics should now focus on the limitations of a linguistic model not initially suited for literary projects. The general dissatisfaction with generative grammar has been variously demonstrated—from more moderate arguments for the revision of linguistic theory along lines suggested by literary problems (Culler, "Towards" 176–77; Pratt, "Linguistic Utopias" 59–64; Hopper 22–23), to full postmortems on linguistic study (Fish, "Consequences"; Norris, "Theory"; Schleifer, "Deconstruction" [on linguistics in general]).[33] In part the new orientation derives from deconstruction; references to Jacques Derrida associate his critique of Saussurean sign theory (*Of Grammatology* 27–73) with the limitations of generative grammar as a social model or theory of meaning (see Fabb and Durant, "Introduction" [citing general attitudes] 2, 8–10; Pratt, "Linguistic Utopias" 60; Hopper 21). But in good measure the new mood bespeaks past critical failures; such accounts suggest that the resources of linguistics have been explored but found wanting, maybe even that critical theory does better what linguistics itself attempts to do. I choose Fish's contribution ("Consequences") to the debate collected in *Against Theory* (Mitchell) as the central example here, simply because his is an extended and dramatic articulation of this attitude. (And I should at the same time add that I wish my comments on this particular essay to be

---

[33] A problem is that critics are (understandably) unaware of specific developments in linguistics. Comments here on phonological and syntactic study are often off the mark. See Henkel, "Comment" for further discussion.

taken in the context of my general regard for Fish's criticism.) In the rhetoric of his position he is perhaps idiosyncratic—he parts company with Culler at this point. But he is not at all alone in several of his key notions, that at best generative grammar is a failed model of discourse (see Fish, "Consequences" 109–11; Pratt, "Linguistic Utopias" 51; Schleifer, "Responds" 332–33; Morson 5–6), at worst an authoritarian interpretive scheme (see Fish, "Consequences" 108, 110, 124–25; Norris, "Theory" 92; Mitchell, "Introduction" 4; Stewart 44; Fabb and Durant, "Introduction" 2).[34]

As I noted at the outset, generative grammar is Fish's example par excellence of "foundationalist theory" ("Consequences" 112; see also "Anti-foundationalism" 66–67). Briefly, it is a theory illustrating the impossibility of theorizing activity in general. Chomskyan linguistics—like New Criticism, with which Fish compares it—is a theory that attempts to guarantee right results for its practitioners, to exclude less than ideal information or practical considerations, to ignore even local empirical facts bearing on the theory, anything that would revise the nature of a model conceived beforehand as perfect and complete (107–12). Just as New Critical methodology legitimated only the readings generated by correct application of its major precepts, so Chomskyan linguistics acknowledges only nonpoetic, nondeviant, well-formed sentence meanings (109; see also Norris, "Theory" 91, 93; Stewart 44, 45). Since it apparently relies on mindless and unvarying procedures, generative grammar becomes associated with the evils of a computerized world, and since the theory in this version requires a rule follower (107–11, 124–25; see also Norris, "Theory" 92) who "surrenders his judgment" to a "theoretical machine" (110), it participates in a repressive, police-state politics.

The logic of this elaborate vilification is of special interest not only because generative grammar is in fact nothing like this characterization but also because it represents such an about-face. Of course Fish's focus here is his antifoundationalist argument, and linguistic theory provides only one rhetorical example. Even so, the question is how generative grammar can come to serve this function. And in the context of the earlier critical work on linguistics-based models, this rhetoric does finally make sense. An initial problem is that Fish and the writers of the linguistic literature he cites simply proceed from entirely different understandings of the word "language," so that Fish assumes that generative grammar is a theory of knowledge and mean-

---

[34] Chomsky finds readings of his work as authoritarian "unintentionally comical" (*Knowledge* 47n.4).

ing in its broadest possible sense—that is, in the sense required for a literary theory. Any claims about language at all, therefore, are viewed in relation to overall interpretive issues. Indeed, Fish has said that he is not interested in any theory of "language" that proposes more modest goals ("Consequences" 130n.12); and I suspect he would fail to acknowledge the attractions of theoretical problems involving phonology or syntax alone. If, at the start, one mistakes the linguistic model for a text-processing mechanism (*Text* 44–47; "Consequences" 109), then it would seem perverse in failing to address questions of textual interpretation. Thus even linguistic studies that explicitly specify matters of world knowledge and theories of action as outside their intended scope are nevertheless at fault for not addressing them.

The situation is complicated further both by Chomsky's specialized use of terms such as "linguistic knowledge" and Fish's own competing though never fully articulated theory of language. Fish, I think, believes that language is weighted in its every part with its full significance; put more precisely, he does not share with linguists the notion of interacting but distinguishable levels of language. That he does not is reflected in pronouncements about the inseparability of syntax from semantics (*Text* 106–7, 266; "Consequences" 110; see also Norris, "Theory" 96), in the nonrole of lower-level semantic matters (word meaning, for example) in discussions of pragmatic constraints on speech acts (the last essays of *Text*), in the investment of the syntactic terminology of the *Aspects* model with more than its usual semantic import (see *Text* 5, 44–49, 246–47; "Consequences" 109–11). Despite a tendency elsewhere to treat linguistic theory as a monolithic entity, Fish here echoes arguments from well within linguistic study itself, citing generative semantics on the identification of syntax and semantics (*Text* 106, 266; see also Fabb and Durant, "Ten Years" 58), sociolinguistics on the importance of language use to basic linguistic theory, speech-act theory on the relation of utterances to their context.[35]

Once the semantic concerns of the generative model have been inflated beyond their initial scope, it would seem natural to announce the collapse of syntactic and semantic problems. Such rhetoric, however, is seductive in its generality. Of course there are interesting questions to be answered about the relation of syntax to semantics, but it is not correct to say that all syntactic facts admit semantic explanation. In the realm of language use, a choice among syntactic options (an assertion over a mitigating tag question) has identifiable pragmatic consequences, but the subject-verb-object arrangement of English has

---

[35] Many research problems befell generative semantics.

no such clear relation to the world, and it is thus at this point that one might want to appeal to universal constraints on language structure. Similarly, there are good arguments that case marking in ergative languages is in part semantically motivated; it operates generally according to identifiable semantic features of verbs. But there is in these systems a considerable element of arbitrariness, so that some verbs lacking the expected semantic associations nevertheless require the inflections of verbs that do fit the overall pattern (see Dixon). In this case we have grammatical facts (a case system) related to but not wholly predictable from semantic ones, and this unpredictability in turn raises questions about how such meaning considerations can be integrated into a formal syntactic description. A statement that grammatical notions are not consistently motivated by semantic ones does not amount to a claim that no relationship exists.[36]

Doubtless these are not the kinds of problems to excite a literary critic, but they are exactly the sort of issues alluded to in the linguistic literature Fish cites. To Chomsky's insistence on independent but interacting syntactic and semantic components (first articulated in *Syntactic Structures*), Fish has always responded that no such independence is possible, largely because for him all semantic problems are located at utterance level and beyond ("Consequences" 110; *Text* 107, 266). But "independence of grammar" Chomsky has said, is not a concept that implies sentence meaning is independent of "questions of fact and belief," merely a claim that formal grammar and world knowledge make distinct contributions to interpretation ("Questions" 38). Since there is no perfect correspondence between grammatical and notional categories ("On the Nature" 27), since a grammar cannot be consistently derived from semantics ("Questions" 43) or semantic notions from grammatical structure ("Questions" 35), it seems reasonable to posit semiautonomous systems that relate at the surface. At present the semantic component (closer now to the *Syntactic Structures* conception of semantic concerns than to *Aspects*) is very narrowly conceived as defining "structural meaning," so that only semantic information clearly related to syntax—anaphora, pronominal reference, the scope of quantifiers—is part of the formal linguistic description; tautology, analycity, and the like receive pragmatic explanation (see van Riemsdijk and Williams 80–88, 181–92).

Fish, of course, often moves from issues on the border of syntax and semantics to discussion of interpretive norms, and in this way linguis-

---

[36] I am not saying Chomsky is always right or consistent about where to draw the boundary, only remarking on the problem of identifying syntax and semantics.

tic and speech-act accounts become enmeshed in his criticism. To these arguments on the importance of the speech situation at the level of speech act or text I am more fully sympathetic. Much of his thinking on this topic derives from Searle, whom he tends to oppose to Chomsky, and we can assume that, like Searle, Fish believes many of the semantic issues once addressed in the semantic component of extended standard theory are better explained in reference to pragmatics. Searle himself attacks this fledgling (and now defunct) semantic component in an early essay on Chomsky ("Chomsky's Revolution"), and his analyses elsewhere of reference, of indirection, of the dubious status of "literal meaning," are elegant demonstrations of the necessarily central role of context in a theory of meaning (see *Speech Acts* 72–96; *Expression* 30–57, 76–136). But unlike Fish, Searle distinguishes between his own program and Chomsky's. It is significant that he detaches the goals and methods of generative grammar, in fact selects them for praise, from the more specific (and wrongheaded) claims for the (earlier) semantic component; we thus find in the opening pages of *Speech Acts* admiring allusions to *Aspects* (12–15). It is worth emphasizing in this connection that whereas Chomsky has viewed lower-level semantic concerns as inseparable from world knowledge—when he has, in effect, shared Fish's belief that few such concerns can be isolated—he has excluded them from formal description. Certainly this exclusion is evidence that the theory was never meant to answer the kinds of interpretive problems that concern Fish or Searle.[37]

But the earlier linguistics-oriented criticism also sheds light on the specific points of Fish's attack. It is only in the context of treating syntactic rules as primarily semantic in nature that one can begin to interpret generative grammar as somehow fascist, a view limited to literary theory and one that Fish himself was instrumental in creating. Because syntax and semantics are inseparable for Fish, he fails to distinguish Chomsky's claims for the syntactic and semantic apparatus of the grammar. Despite Chomsky's purely descriptive aims, the terms "apply," "acceptability," "ill-formedness," and the like thus assume the status of value judgments. Despite narrow definitions of grammaticality intended (in *Aspects*) to account for certain literary effects (see also *Logical* 149), possible/not possible syntactic orders are translated as proscriptions of poetic experiment. Despite the abstract nature of proposed linguistic universals (for instance, the structure dependency of rules in all languages [Chomsky, "On the Nature" 65]), syntactic universals become repressive limits on possible sentence meanings

---

[37] See Katz 115–16 for discussion.

("Consequences" 108–9; see also Norris, "Theory" 92; Stewart 46; MacCabe, "Opening Statement" 298). Claims for the biologically triggered acquisition of *syntactic* rules are read as arguments for distinguishing problems of meaning from matters of use and context (125). Arguments for the separation of grammar from pragmatics are interpreted as a refusal to admit that pragmatic constraints exist. And the limitation to competence alone of a theory now defined as primarily semantic comes to seem peculiar indeed.

The irony is that reader-focused criticism participates to a large degree in the limits of the linguistics-based analogies it continues to use. In his theory of interpretive communities, Fish's description of interpretive principles vacillates between a psychological explanation and a mechanistic one. On the one hand, readers construe, make their own meanings, with the consequence that the central task of the literary critic is to evaluate interpretive practices; in this sense the critic is no longer "merely a player in the game" but a "maker and unmaker of its rules" (*Text* 367). On the other hand, interpretation is inevitable and automatic both because, according to a strong reading of speech-act theory, "meanings come already calculated," embedded as they are in a prior network of cultural norms (*Text* 318), and because, following a structuralist account of the individual, readers themselves are "constituted by a set of conventional notions" that are triggered, "put into operation" (*Text* 332), by the texts they confront. By the time of the "Consequences" essay, this formulation changes slightly: readers never loosen the constraints under which they function (113), but they are nevertheless enjoined (having recognized the implications of a project such as Chomsky's) to reject the practice of (literary) theorizing altogether (127–28). The reader/critic is both an active meaning maker, someone able to make such choices, and a text processed by an all-encompassing cultural grammar. Thus Searle (or at least arguments influenced by Fish's reading of him) and Chomsky (now a symbol of conformity and determinate meaning) enter into the language of freedom versus repression.

Of course Fish bravely articulates paradoxes we may not solve. Who can claim to characterize interpretive actions precisely? And he understandably valorizes literary views of language, literary problems. Yet an alternative perspective highlights traces of the (revamped) generative model that ironically remain. While reader-oriented critics argue against the passive acquisition of syntactic rules, this notion limits and forms the literary account; just as the linguistic rules of a community are given in advance, so the norms of analogous interpretive communities are often unavailable for inspection or analysis. Just when critics impute to generative grammar a totalitarian political authority, they may fail to address such political matters as how critical practices come to gain legitimacy, how individuals are inscribed in particular interpretive communities, and to what extent individual interpretive choices are determined and absorbed by institutional norms.

I have just denied that generative grammar is a theory of meaning in Fish's sense, but we might nevertheless step back from this internal critical argument to ask briefly just what it means to characterize it as such. From a broader point of view, it would seem reasonable to wonder how it is that the writer of *Towards a New Cold War* or *Manufacturing Consent* (with Herman) could come to promote a language model that has acquired in critical discussion the reputation of a conservative or authoritarian interpretive theory. One could of course claim that Chomsky is simply blind to the political ramifications of his own generative model, despite his demonstrated willingness to accept, and contribute to, massive revisions of the theory on other grounds. Yet such an explanation hardly seems credible in the light of his relentless examination of political discourse—the rhetoric of postwar statements on Vietnam, for example (*Towards* 115–53), or the selective media coverage of political events (*Manufacturing* 37–86). A more plausible explanation is that there is no necessary conflict of interests here, simply because, as Chomsky has insisted, there is little relation between his formal concerns in syntactic study and his analysis of political matters (see *Language and Responsibility*). Critical models of any kind inevitably involve larger interpretive problems, as do literary grammars and competence theories, but to attach such issues to the apparatus of at least this syntactic model as those in the field now define it is to confuse the two projects. A possible—not so innocent—outcome of this mistake is a final dismissal not just of generative grammar but of the political work of someone who in the context of criticism has come to seem impossibly naive. Thus in an era of interdisciplinary, politically minded criticism, the discipline-internal sense of "conservative" somehow fails to mesh with an outside perspective on political commitments, and we end up participating in the well-documented marginalization of Chomsky's political work (see Hitchens).

This interdisciplinary backlash is not so much insidious as part of the unfortunate and uneasy dynamics that have long characterized the relation between literary criticism and linguistics. An earlier criticism imported the generative model with nearly unmitigated enthusiasm, and the prestige of the scientific account was enough to encourage critics to ignore its real limitations for the (literary) problems at hand.

Remade for these tasks, it was bound in this weakened form to disappoint, and this line of research thus only ensured the repudiation of the linguistic acccount. In later arguments the authority of the enemy (sometimes the generative model, sometimes Chomsky) is likewise part of the appeal. One can always, of course, claim that the controversies involve literary metaphors, not the details of the original imported accounts; and yet as the projects of linguistics-based criticism fail, it is not the literary analogy but the linguistic model that increasingly takes the blame.

Chapter 4

Speech-Act Theory Revisited

The hypothesis of this book is that speaking a language is a matter
of performing speech acts according to systems of constitutive
rules.

> —JOHN SEARLE, *Speech Acts: An Essay in the*
> *Philosophy of Language*

Can we trace the same fate for speech-act criticism as for projects
based on generative grammar? Certainly criticism would seem to have
first embraced, then rejected speech-act theory in much the same way,
and even at much the same time. But I think the answer is both "yes"
and "no"; the fortunes of speech-act theory are somewhat more complex. The cases are of course in some sense similar (and entangled): as
we have seen, both generative grammar and speech-act theory first
served a range of reader-focused critical concerns, then suggested an
account of criticism as a highly constrained, institution-bound social
practice. Just as generative grammar's critical role has faded, moreover,
so too newcomers to the field must find it difficult to imagine the
general enthusiasm with which critics once met linguistic philosophy.
Speech-act readings of literature proliferated, journals specialized in essays linking ordinary language philosophy and literary criticism, and a
variety of widely read critics—including Richard Ohmann, Jonathan
Culler, Stanley Fish, Mary Louise Pratt, Wolfgang Iser, and Steven
Mailloux—endorsed critical programs indebted to some extent to J. L.
Austin or John Searle.[1] And we might remark a similar critical paradox.

[1] Richard Ohmann's well-known articles on speech acts are "Speech Acts and the Definition of Literature" (1971), "Literature as Act" (1973), and "Speech, Literature, and the
Space Between" (1974). As I indicated in the last chapter, many books relying to some
extent (the degree naturally varies) on speech-act theory appeared in roughly the same

While such interest has indeed waned, it is again not so simple for literary criticism to disengage itself from its earlier preoccupations. Like the language of generative grammar, speech-act terms have quite clearly become fixtures in our lexicon; critical vocabulary has in good measure become the language of speech acts—"performative act," "speech institution," or "constitutive rule." So once more we could claim that criticism has not entirely left speech-act notions behind so much as it has somehow assimilated and absorbed them.

But the answer is "no" to an identity of critical history in the sense that critical discourse has returned more to worry over speech-act models than it has to generative grammar; it rather engages and reengages speech-act accounts for what it takes as central, shared problems of meaning and intentionality. To be more specific, a new, reevaluated Austin (thanks to Jacques Derrida and Shoshana Felman) haunts literary conversation; references to Austin, Searle, and H. P. Grice still abound in debates on intention and interpretation; and critics echo speech-act models in accounts of gender and social position as enacted and performed.[2] To cast the matter positively, this recurring interest reflects basic differences between models; although the literary and philosophical goals do not entirely match, I would agree that speech-act theory, unlike generative grammar, genuinely overlaps in certain of

period: Jonathan Culler, *Structuralist Poetics* (1975); Stanley Fish, *Is There a Text in This Class?* (1980); Wolfgang Iser, *The Act of Reading* (1978); Steven Mailloux, *Interpretive Conventions* (1982); Mary Louise Pratt, *Toward a Speech Act Theory of Literary Discourse* (1977); Susan Sniader Lanser, *The Narrative Act* (1981); Roger Fowler, *Linguistic Criticism* (1986); and Ellen Schauber and Ellen Spolsky, *The Bounds of Interpretation* (1986). Selections by Culler and Fish also appeared in Jane Tompkins's popular anthology *Reader-Response Criticism* (1980); Susan Suleiman's introduction to another—Susan R. Suleiman and Inge Crosman, eds., *The Reader in the Text* (1980)—discussed speech-act models briefly. Related discussions proliferated in the mainstream journals, including special issues on literary convention (1981 and 1983) by *New Literary History*, and a now-defunct journal (*Centrum*) specialized in ordinary language philosophy and criticism. A second wave of interest, especially in Austin, accompanied the rise of deconstruction.

[2] I refer here to Derrida's well-known account of Austin and his debate with Searle (1977–1983), topics discussed in the next chapter. Felman's engagement with Austin is *The Literary Speech Act* (1983). For ordinary language philosophy in accounts of literary meaning, see W. J. T. Mitchell, ed., *Against Theory* (1985), especially the essays by Steven Knapp and Walter Benn Michaels, William C. Dowling, and Richard Rorty; see also Knapp and Michaels, "Against Theory 2" (1987). This work obviously overlaps with the speech-act accounts I mention earlier (see note 1), but it constitutes a second wave of (deconstruction-influenced) interest. For an excellent overview of the interaction between literary criticism and speech-act theory, see Sandy Petrey, *Speech Acts and Literary Theory*; see also the substantial essay by Barrie Ruth Strauss, "Influencing Theory." A recent use of Austin's sense of the performative power of speech acts is the "Critically Queer" chapter in Judith Butler, *Bodies That Matter*, which draws on Eve Sedgwick, "Queer Performativity."

its initial concerns, and the model is apparently rich enough to prompt both literary elaboration and counterargument. Again such discussions understandably focus on discipline-internal questions, for which speech-act models are not always well equipped; yet in this case I would claim that critiques more authentically interact with their sources.

Of course other realities complicate discussion of a link between literary criticism and linguistic philosophy. Not the least of these is that literary critics often mistake the aims of theories such as Austin's and Searle's; again the apparent aptness of the model then frustrates the literary projects that necessarily remain at odds. Austin's project, which Searle elaborated, was a contribution to philosophic semantics, not a supplement to linguistic or syntactic theory. Intervening in a semantics based on an utterance's truth conditions, Austin proposed instead to determine the rules and conventions entailed in (nondefective, rather than true) everyday speech actions. For critics, what this means is that Austin and Searle focus on precisely defined linguistic intentions, not literary or textual ones; on the institutional expectations implied in linguistic conventions, not on literary grammars or interpretive heuristics; and on single utterance acts, not texts. Within the original tradition all this makes perfect sense; in another discipline it inevitably seems narrow.[3]

A second problem for any analysis is the already complex history of speech-act theory within literary discussions. If speech-act theory is now more rarely a topic, more often the assumed context of critical discussion, its specific influence is difficult to trace and discuss. When a writer uses the term "performative," for example, how are we to know whether its sense derives for this particular critic from Austin, from Emile Benveniste, who discusses Austin, or from Shoshana Felman, who, besides writing on Austin, writes on Benveniste writing on Austin? Or how are we to know how much of Stanley Fish's interest in the notions "rule" and "institution" derives from Searle, and how much generative grammar or his reading of Wittgenstein have shaped his theory of literary meaning? I raise these questions only to admit that I do not expect to answer them. Since speech-act notions entered literary criticism in that period of general interdisciplinary experiment, they have indeed become so loosely metaphorical in some cases and elsewhere so enmeshed with concepts drawn from a variety of sources as nearly to defy precise analysis.[4] But I do believe that speech-

---

[3] In this discussion of initial issues, I am indebted to Wallace Martin. See Donald Kalish, "Semantics" for background on Austin's philosophical contexts.

[4] This is understandably true of the term "performative" in drama and cultural criticism, but it is worth noting that earlier on many readers wanted not to expand but to

act accounts significantly influenced a crucial period of reader-oriented criticism in ways it is possible to outline and that in any case many of the goals and problems of speech-act models are revealingly parallel to those critics once faced and, I might add, face still.

Again I address such issues first through important early critical accounts, returning afterward to argue that this critical history is especially relevant to later concerns. In the next chapter I consider speech-act theory from a more general perspective; for the moment I concentrate on a narrower range of borrowed concepts. The specific critical analogy that is my initial and immediate focus—one that by now may sound all too worn and familiar—can be roughly paraphrased as follows: The act of reading literature involves rules or conventions similar to other (perhaps lower-level) linguistic rules. No matter how many vocabulary items one is taught, a new language remains unintelligible unless one also acquires knowledge of its syntactic rules. Similarly, one can master the vocabulary and syntax of a language without solving basic interpretive questions. Since sentence meaning is more than a matter of adding up word meanings or syntactic units—an ironic statement is an obvious example—one must appeal further to conventions of language use, to rules referring to the context of the utterance or to shared language practices (to assumptions about compliments, the institution of marriage, or what it means to promise or lie). In much the same way, a literary text requires more than a reader's knowledge of its language and even of everyday speech events and practices. That is, literature remains indecipherable unless one also has access to certain shared assumptions regarding readers and writers, to genre conventions, to a variety of literary-interpretive norms. And just as rules regulating language use constitute well-defined speech institutions that at the same time define social behavior (promising or marrying), so too, interpretive norms make up particular critical institutions or communities that sanction and legitimate interpretive practices (the business of criticism in general, university English programs, or, say, new historicism or deconstruction).

Now this broad connection between linguistic rules and institutions and critical norms and practices is of course not uniquely determined by reference to speech-act theory (and thus it will be impossible to avoid reference in this discussion to other language models, especially

---

resist Austin's major project in *How to Do Things with Words*, his dismantling of the performative-constative distinction. See, for example, Emile Benveniste, "Analytical Philosophy and Language"; and Paul de Man, "Semiology and Rhetoric" and "Excuses." Benveniste wishes Austin would not collapse these categories; de Man does not recognize this as Austin's goal.

to generative grammar). But it is clearly a speech-act-influenced account highly representative of familiar reader-focused criticism, and for this reason it would bear more detailed comparison with the original speech-act model, no matter how generally the analogy was once meant to be applied. For once again we might ask how the borrowed model functions in both its original and its literary contexts, how it adapts and permutes, and how it prompts and curtails literary questions. Since it is an especially influential speech-act source for literary criticism, I choose to press here the connection between John Searle's *Speech Acts* and well-known reader-oriented critical texts.[5] In this case I believe that as much as Searle's model has extended our understanding of literary matters in the criticism of the last several years, theories of literary convention and reading communities imitate problems in the original account, which, in turn, function still to limit the related criticism.

SPEECH-ACT RULES

To explain this state of affairs will require first a brief consideration of the notions "rule" and rule-based "institution" in Searle's analysis of speech acts, those concepts which literary critics found so compelling. I should say that this discussion begins as an overview, but I shortly analyze those connections I find most problematic. In Searle's account, the speech act (as opposed to the word or sentence) is the basic semantic unit, since propositions are always used to accomplish some intentional goal in the world—acts of stating, requesting, predicting, and the like. Searle explains how such (illocutionary) acts are formulated and interpreted by distinguishing between two rule types: regulative rules, which merely regulate preexisting behavior (traffic rules or rules of etiquette), and constitutive rules, which actually enable the activity they describe to take place, although they may also then regulate it (see *Speech Acts* 33–42). All linguistic rules, including rules for speech acts, are rules of this last type, as are rules for games such as football or chess. A game cannot exist independently of the rules that define it, without the participants' knowledge of its goals and a codified means of achieving them; likewise speech acts first require institutionalized conventions governing the practice (34). Regula-

[5] The discussion that follows concentrates mostly on pages 3–71 of *Speech Acts*, Searle's most influential work for literary studies; I do not claim to represent here his current thoughts on speech acts. I am indebted in this section to many discussions with John Wenstrom.

tive rules are usually imperative in form: "Do X" ("Stop your car when the light turns red"). Constitutive rules, on the other hand, since "they create or define new forms of behavior" (33), are somewhat "tautological in character" and take the form "X counts as Y in context C" (35). Thus, following Searle's analogy, in a constitutive rule such as "Scoring a touchdown counts as six points in the game of football," "touchdown" and "six points" do not explain each other so much as refer to the absolute givens of the game, and neither notion (unlike the movement of traffic) has meaning outside its context.

Searle's method of analysis is continually informed by the game analogy. Just as it is possible to outline the rules for football by listing the conditions that result in such specifications as "touchdown" or even "winning," so it is possible, he says, to derive from an inspection of a speaker's linguistic knowledge a set of "necessary and sufficient conditions for the performance of particular kinds of speech acts" (22). Here he echoes Noam Chomsky's (1965) remarks on the goals of a generative grammar; one asks what characteristics a sentence (here speech act) must exhibit in order for speakers to consider it nondeviant or well formed (here "felicitous") (see also *Speech Acts* 12–15).[6] In the case of promising, Searle's central example, one begins by asking what conditions would be necessary for an utterance of "I promise" really ("nondefectively") to count as the undertaking of an obligation (35).

In answer to this question Searle formulates both a list of conditions and a second list of rules derived from them. His analysis of promising involves conditions general to all speech acts but also such conditions as that the speaker believes the promised action is one the hearer desires; the speaker has the power and ability to perform the promised action; the speaker is not already expected to perform the action in the normal course of events; the speaker is at least apparently sincere and means to be so taken (57–61); and finally, an "essential condition," the speaker "intends that the utterance . . . will place him under an obligation [to perform the action]" (60). From these contextual conditions Searle later extracts the second, somewhat narrower set of rules he describes as representing a new viewpoint, "rules for the use of the illocutionary force indicating device" (62), that is, rules for the use of "I promise," the conditions stated in quasi-imperative form ("Pr ['I promise'] is to be uttered only if the hearer H would prefer S's [the speaker's] doing A [the action] to his not doing A, and S believes [this]" [compare

---

[6] Searle explicitly cites *Aspects of the Theory of Syntax*, 21–24. His language recalls Chomsky's discussion: game playing is on the basis of a set of "internalized" rules; speakers' intuitions are "notoriously fallible"; the goal of description is linguistic knowledge (*Speech Acts* 14).

58, 63]), and the essential condition in the form of "*X* counts as *Y*"
("The utterance of *Pr* counts as the undertaking of an obligation to do
A").[7] Violations of such rules produce defective or infelicitous promises—insincere promises, but also utterances of "I promise" that are
not promises at all (see 54, 63).

The problem, which I necessarily address in outline here, is that in
the course of this analysis at least three possibilities associated with
the various implications of the game analogies emerge for the interpretation of the "*X* counts as *Y* in context *C*" formula, and it is thus
sometimes unclear what the notion "constitutive rule" is meant to
explain.[8] These are subtly different inflections of the rule model which
will take some effort to sort out. The initial question is formulated as
analogous to a single move within a game: "How can scoring a touchdown create six points?" (35). Thus, when Searle lists the conditions
"for the performance" of a promise (the phrase implies the conditions
are prior to the act), making a promise is apparently equivalent to saying "I promise" in the context of certain preexisting contextual factors
(the specified list of conditions) (55), and the constitutive rule in question is simply one governing the conventional association between the
utterance and those institutional principles (see 39–40). A paraphrase
of the formula might then read: "Saying 'I promise' counts as the undertaking of an obligation in the context of an established procedure
for promise-making." In short, Searle's interest here is in how individual speech acts come to mean in reference to an established practice
(see 35) and in how speakers invoke institutionalized expectations in a
single intentional gesture.

Whereas this first account describes behavior already defined as institutional, however, a second version of the formula aims to describe
either the nature of institutional knowledge or how single actions become institutional actions (which is not certain). Here Searle remarks
that the entire list of conditions is itself constitutive of promising or a
promise. Constitutive rules, he says, "come in systems," and "it may
be the whole system which exemplifies this form [the '*X* counts as *Y*'
formula]" (63). While not every rule of basketball can be phrased in
constitutive form, Searle argues, "acting in accordance with all or a
sufficiently large subset of the rules does count as playing basketball"
(63). This somewhat different use of the game analogy reflects its natu-

---

[7] Searle stresses that despite the regulative form these rules take, they are still really
constitutive; constitutive rules can be reformulated into imperatives without changing
their essential nature (*Speech Acts* 36).

[8] For a more extended discussion of the game–speech-act analogies see Henkel, "Promises According to Searle," from which some of this material is derived.

ral ambiguity: Is promising like scoring a touchdown in football, or is it akin to playing football? Whereas earlier one constitutive rule (presumably the "essential rule") links an utterance to some "states of affairs" or the shared knowledge outlined by the conditions (40), now the conditions themselves (though Searle concedes they vary in character) are all constitutive of promising or a promise, the institution or a single act. A paraphrase of this new account might read: "The list of (necessary and sufficient) conditions defines the institution of promising or, when fulfilled, counts as an act of promising." The C variable in the formula has been lost, since there is no longer a distinction between a constitutive rule and its background conditions.

When Searle derives a final list of rules from his initial conditions (in quasi-imperative form, save for the "essential rule"), it is by way of a third reading of the game analogy. His goal, he says, is to outline rules for uttering "I promise" as one might ask "under what conditions a [chess] player could be said to move a knight correctly" (63). These rules, now stated from the point of view of what individuals must do to formulate promises, are said to define correct, felicitous promises. Making a promise once meant uttering "I promise" in a certain context; it now means adhering to a set of instructions. This paraphrase of Searle's formula would read: "Carrying out a list of rules counts as the formulation of a correct, recognizable promise," as a series of satisfied requirements counts as a proper move in chess. Like his first game analogy, this description focuses on behavior falling within the scope of an already established practice (once again a move within a game), but like the second game analogy, it implies that a series of constitutive rules (all the rules for chess) constitutes a promise (a correct move). Here, however, the rules admit deviation; one can violate some rules, Searle notes, and such violations are not always "sufficient to vitiate the act in its entirety," just as one can move a piece incorrectly in chess and still purport to play the game (54).

It seems to me that only in the first case can we preserve the concept of constitutive rule as Searle first defines it: "An utterance of 'I promise' counts as the undertaking of an obligation in the context of an established procedure for promise-making." A constitutive rule relates a single utterance (of "I promise") to a set of institutional norms; it simply by convention "counts as" a speaker's gesture toward the institution or practice.

A set of conditions, as in Searle's second version of the formula, is not sufficient to "count as" or define the institution, if that is the purpose of constitutive rules, as at least one writer interprets him here (see Cherry 301–8). That is, a list of existential conditions ("There are five men on a team"; "Balls are thrown through hoops") could not fully explain the nature of institutional behavior. We could easily concoct a case, after all, in which such a conjunction of conditions occurred accidentally. But to be fair to Searle, this is exactly his point in stressing the distinction between brute and institutional facts in a preliminary discussion (50–53; see also Anscombe). Institutional actions presume purpose. The "essential rule" is obviously his solution to this problem; it is the one rule on the list stated in constitutive form, it specifies what the whole system of conditions is to "count as" or mean, and it somehow activates the conditions by indicating their intentional context. As Christopher Cherry remarks, however, this solution presupposes rather than explains the practice of promising, since a conjunction of such conditions normally requires the institution in the first place; and he does not see the notion "constitutive rule" alone as strong enough to explain how brute facts become institutional facts (Cherry 302–8). In addition, it is only in a rather odd sense that we could talk about practices (rather than conventions for invoking them as in the first reading of the formula) as defined by constitutive rules. A legal system is literally constituted by rules: "Behavior X counts as illegal." Yet it seems more natural to say that what constitutes the institution of promising is speakers' shared knowledge of the practice, especially since this shared background information cannot be stated in constitutive form: "H is not expected to perform A in the normal course of events." Of course, Searle's list elaborates this knowledge, but it does not follow that what speakers know is how to follow rules. There is an important distinction to be made between the rulelike regularities that result from persons acting on the basis of similar inferences drawn from shared knowledge of a practice and behavior deriving from following rules.

Perhaps the second reading of this somewhat ambiguous "speech act as whole game" analogy applies instead: the set of conditions together "counts as" a promise rather than the institution itself. Then, however, the claim that the conditions are necessary and sufficient is not correct, since one can imagine promises that violate one of the conditions and still serve the crucial function of obligating the speaker. For instance, it seems plausible for a speaker to violate ordinary speech-act expectations (the non-obviousness condition) and still have promised ("I promise to take out the garbage" when one always does).[9] Such

---

[9] The exception is the sincerity condition. I do not think that a speaker can openly violate the sincerity condition and still promise. But I think that in some cases one can violate the condition that the hearer desires the promised action. One can imagine a case, for instance, in which one uses such a promise both to promise or pledge an action and to

examples cast doubt on Searle's claim that the essential condition entails the others (see 54); in any case it is still difficult to reconcile a claim that *all* the rules together are necessary and sufficient with the essential rule's distinctive function.

Finally, one could say that the rules for promising in Searle's last version of the formula (the rules as opposed to the conditions) do constitute correct, felicitous promises, if not promises in general. But since these rules are indeed stated from a significantly different viewpoint—they are in nearly imperative form; they are expressed not as definitional rules but as strategies for speakers' actions or hearers' judgments; and they again admit violation—one might simply term these rules "regulative." In fact, once one sees these rules for promises as regulative, perhaps as a narrower version of Grice's conversational maxims, one is in a better position to discuss deviant cases.[10] For example, one could state more specifically what actions besides promising the (garbage-toting) speaker accomplishes with this somewhat odd promise—say, an implied criticism of others not usually willing to help with this task. Searle's focus on the institution-defining function of constitutive rules sometimes treats defective promises as nonpromises.

It seems that Searle uses the notion "constitutive rule" to explain the answers to questions that are not quite of the same order. Practices and acts are conflated; in his account, "promising" (as an institution) and "promises" (single acts defined by institutions) require a single explanation.[11] He sets out to describe not only how saying "I promise"

---

imply that the hearer *should* desire the promised action (a man who says "I promise to enter a monastery" to his wife, who obviously does not wish it, could both commit himself to the action and imply she should share his religious goals). One could keep a single constitutive rule by adding the condition of sincerity: "*Pr*, uttered with apparent sincerity, counts as the undertaking of an obligation."

[10] Grice describes shared assumptions about conversation deriving from a "Cooperative Principle," simply interlocutors' expectation that others want to be clear, relevant, brief but informative, and give information for which they have evidence ("Logic" 45–50). Speakers routinely violate these subprinciples, but often they do so obviously, signaling to interlocutors that the Cooperative Principle is nevertheless in effect, that they mean hearers to notice the violation. Listeners then construe what is meant or implied, as opposed to what is said. Thus a letter of recommendation that violates a quantity maxim implies a lack of enthusiasm; an apparently irrelevant response to "How's Smith?" ("He hasn't been to prison yet") implies Smith is dishonest (versions of Grice's examples [43, 52]). My point here is that one could take Searle's rules for promising as more specific versions of Grice's conversational maxims. The example in note 8 is the kind of explanation one can give if one assumes that rules for promises are liable to "flouting" or overt violation; the apparent promise is an "implicature" or implied speech act in this case, not just a nonpromise. See also Grice, "Further Notes."

[11] The importance of the distinction between practices and acts defined by practices was suggested to me by John Rawls's essay on utilitarianism, "Two Concepts of Rule."

obligates a speaker but also, at various times, how speakers encode felicitous promises, how hearers recognize promises and distinguish defective promises from "happy" ones, and what shared knowledge makes promising possible. All these questions fall within the scope of promising, certainly, but not all of them can be answered by the same formulation of constitutive rules.

SPEECH-ACT METAPHORS

Now the analogy between literary norms and Searle's constitutive rules (or any sort of linguistic rule), and between interpretive practices and speech-act institutions, makes a great deal of immediate intuitive sense. The success reader-oriented critics themselves often achieve in codifying interpretive strategies suggests that literary analysis is highly constrained and therefore amenable to analysis by rules. Many reading habits seem, like linguistic rules, below the level of conscious control or awareness. Literary texts are for many critics less intelligible than other linguistic objects outside a given structure of interpretive assumptions. And the operation of this complicated set of literary norms demands as much shared agreement from a number of actual persons—reader, writer, even colleagues when interpretation involves published criticism—as does the speech-act practice of promising.

Indeed, just such analogies have generated much of the literature on reading norms and conventions (special issues of *New Literary History* are just one example), and the widespread reference to literary interpretation as an "institutional practice" is often in conscious reference to speech-act accounts (as in the essays of *Against Theory* [Mitchell]).[12] As I noted at the outset, the loose and suggestive way critics imported speech-act concepts precludes a precise history of their relation to literary criticism, but it will be useful to outline the general course of this discussion. Early on, some critics relied explicitly on Searle's rule distinctions as necessary to reader-oriented literary theory. In a 1977 essay, for example, Fish criticized Iser for diluting the constitutive-regulative opposition in his description of literary discourse (*Text* 222–23), and Michael Hancher, at the appearance of Pratt's *Toward a Speech Act Theory of Literary Discourse* (1977), faulted her work for outlining regulative, rather than more properly linguistic, constitutive rules ("Beyond" 1085–86). It seems, in fact, that much of the initial appeal of

[12] In the 1981 and 1983 special issues of *New Literary History*, see especially the essays by Hilary Putnam, Jonathan Culler ("Convention"), Lawrence Manley, John Reichert, and Steven Mailloux ("Convention").

the notion "constitutive" as applied to literature was its association with an essentially formalist claim. That is, the term suggested that literary discourse was distinct from ordinary discourse and that one could outline the rules that exclusively constitute literariness, though this time from the point of view of reader rather than text.[13]

As I mentioned in the last chapter, the simultaneous critical interest in generative grammar complicated speech-act issues and metaphors. Again the idea here was that literary rules could receive the same treatment as syntactic rules and grammars. A "literary grammar" aims at the "internalized" knowledge and shared assumptions of experienced readers of literature (their "literary competence"), and the rules of this grammar explain readers' sense of what interpretive operations "generate" acceptable ("grammatical") or legitimate readings of literary texts.[14] Despite the very different source, scope, and goal of Chomsky's grammar as opposed to Searle's account of speech acts, at the (understandably) general level critics imported the two models they seemed rather similar: both aimed at a rule-based description of linguistic knowledge, and both described the assumptions shared across a linguistic community. This reading of the theories was perhaps complicated by Searle's analogy between his own goals and the internal linguistic knowledge of Chomsky's grammar. We thus find in critical discussions felicitous speech acts loosely equated with well-formedness, acceptability conflated with grammaticality, institutional rules analogous to syntactic rules, and language practices (in Searle's sense) associated with (Chomskyan) speech communities.[15]

Somewhat later reader-oriented criticism is rather differently oriented toward these two language models (sometimes working antagonistically, sometimes asserting a perceived opposition between Chomsky and Searle), but at the same time it has indulged in the ever-broadening

[13] Mary Louise Pratt, *Toward* xi–xix, 3–37; and Roger Fowler, *Literature*, chaps. 7–10, *Linguistic Criticisim* 175–179, make a similar point about linguistic-literary models in general.

[14] This is, of course, a reference to the issues of the previous chapter. Again, on the notions "literary grammar" and "literary competence," see especially Culler, *Structuralist Poetics* 5–10, 20–31, 113–30 (reprinted in Tompkins), and *Pursuit* 48–53; and Fish, *Text* 5–10, 44–50; 366–67.

[15] Culler, for example, sees speech-act theory (language institutions and constitutive rules), Saussurean linguistics (Saussure's remarks about semiology), and generative grammar (the performance-competence distinction, syntactic rules) as similarly suggestive for literary theory (*Poetics* 5–10). Both Chomsky and Austin are structuralists in Culler's analysis (*Poetics* 26–28; *On Deconstruction* 110–11). Fish, as we have seen, retains metaphors drawn from both theories—"constitutive rule" from Searle, "interpretive community" analogous to Chomsky's speech communities, "acceptability" from generative grammar as equivalent to "felicity" from speech-act theory (see *Text* 303–7, 356–58).

use of the borrowed linguistic and speech-act terminology.[16] That is, while there is now less interest in issues such as the constitutive-regulative distinction per se, echoes of speech-act terminology survive. Norms of interpretation are said to "count as" the institution of criticism; such rules not only constitute genres and texts, even readers, but are "constitutive" of criticism as a political practice; the act of interpretation is a "game" like football or chess; and in accounts of literary meaning, literary texts are analogous to individual illocutionary acts. Because it is not always obvious that such connections have indeed been operating in critical discourse and because there are other possible sources for such literary metaphors as "game" or "rule," I wish to return very briefly to the example of the paradigm texts of the last chapter, Culler's *Structuralist Poetics* and Fish's *Is There a Text in This Class?* Given Culler's explicit orientation toward generative grammar in this work and to some extent in the later *Pursuit of Signs*, and given further the later animosity between Searle and Culler, it may seem odd to speak of the influence of *Speech Acts* on Culler's thinking.[17] But it does appear that at least in the earlier book, which predates his later interest in deconstruction, Searle is a direct source. Specifically, Culler refers to Searle in much of what he says about rules and, I believe, derives his use of the term "constitutive rule" from him. Thus Culler argues: "The cultural meaning of any particular act or object is determined by a whole system of constitutive rules: rules which do not regulate behaviour so much as create the possiblility of various forms of behaviour" (*Poetics* 9; compare Searle, *Speech Acts* 33). Linguistic (Chomskyan) competence is his central analogy, the model for literary interpretive conventions, but such conventions operate in the context of an institutionalized practice, and this Culler often defines in speech-act terms. When he describes the cultural context of critical acts, for example, Culler paraphrases first Searle's remarks on games, then his analysis of promising: "One can score a goal only within a certain institutionalized framework. . . . various social rules make it possible to marry, to score a goal, to write a poem" (5); and later: "Many promises are in fact broken, but there still exists a rule in the system of moral concepts that promises should be kept; though of course if one never kept promises doubts might arise as to whether one understood

---

[16] Pratt (*Toward* 83–86) and Fish (*Text* 106) contrast Chomsky and Searle, and in "Consequences" Fish assumes Chomsky has the same explanatory goals as does Searle. According to Fish, he just fails to realize them (107–15, 125).

[17] The animosity is expressed in Culler's remarks in *On Deconstruction* (110–12, 117–22), Searle's review of *On Deconstruction* ("The Word"), and Searle's reply to Louis Mackey's defense of Culler ("Exchange").

the institution of promising and had assimilated its rules" (9; compare Searle, *Speech Acts* 33–37).[18]

Fish's text is a more obvious source of speech-act analogies, especially in the earlier essays of the volume. Searle's discussion of brute and institutional facts supplies Fish with ammunition against stylisticians who mistakenly see textual units as context free; characterizations of the effects and meanings of linguistic elements, he maintains, require the same complex institutional and contextual knowledge as statements about games ("He scored a touchdown") (84–89; see also Searle, *Speech Acts* 50–53). Austin's (*How to*) and Searle's (*Speech Acts*) insistence that all speech acts (even apparently true-false utterances) are performative, felicitous relative to local goals and intentions, both shapes his argument against a hard-and-fast ordinary-language–literary-language distinction (106–11, 231–37) and suggests the notion of a "standard story," a set of conventional notions against which utterances are normally, though not inevitably, interpreted (197–200, 238–44). Austin and Searle appear less explicitly in the later essays of the volume, but the language of speech acts continues to inform them. Just as one cannot predict the perlocutionary effects ("success") of speech acts, Fish argues, one cannot ensure or determine the meaning of literary works (317). Critical understanding is "institutional" and constrained (306), and interpretive rules come in systems that both determine what will "count as" (echoing Searle's formula) a successful (felicitous) interpretive act (356–58) and "constitute" the consciousness of the interpreter (332, 338). Interpretive communities account for differing interpretations, differently constituted interpreters, since each is a subinstitution, sanctioning alternative rules of the literary game (366–67). Such formulations naturally recur in Fish's later work, informing especially his sense of interdisciplinary projects and legal practice, since these involve disjunctive sets of interpretive conventions (see especially "Being"; "Fish"; "Force").[19]

If the notions "rule" and "norm" have so permeated early reader-oriented criticism and if general interest in interpretive communities continues to focus on the legitimating function of the literary "institution," it would seem useful to test these metaphors further against a speech-act version: How much are literary norms like linguistic rules, and what does it mean to compare them? Are literary rules constitutive in Searle's sense, and do they fully comprise institutions and ac-

---

[18] Searle's *Speech Acts* is in the bibliography of *Structuralist Poetics*.

[19] These issues, along with Fish's revisions of Searle, resurface in *Doing What Comes Naturally*, which includes "Fish" and "Force."

tions? And how analogous is the practice of criticism to other linguistic institutions?

An alternative account of rule types will supply a new perspective. In *Models and Metaphors*, Max Black outlines a schema of rules somewhat different from Searle's. While he admits that kinds of rules overlap (114–15), Black identifies four basic types, usefully contrasted in terms of their violations and consequences. "Regulation rules," in his terms, really a restricted version of Searle's regulative rules, regulate existing behavior in some way, have a specific time of appearance and are enforced by an identifiable person or institution (109–10); penalities for violations of regulation rules include legal punishment or perhaps ostracism from some group. "Instruction rules," Black's second rule type, guide behavior in a similar way but with a view to effective means-ends results, as in (his example) "Do not plant tomatoes until after the last frost"; such rules differ from regulations in that no (externally imposed) penalties attach to them and they have "neither authors nor histories" (110). Black's third category, "precept rules," are maxims or rules of thumb that imply some moral judgment about rule followers and nonfollowers; they are related to instructions in that they suggest a good way to behave (for example, "Practice what you preach"), but their ends are vague and indefinable, not subject, like instructions, to the designation "effective" or "ineffective" (111–12). Finally, "principle rules," his fourth category, are lawlike mechanical rules that merely characterize some sort of uniformity in the world. So different does Black consider principle rules from other rules, since they "do not seem to identify a class of human acts," that he is almost unwilling to call them "rules" (113). He notes, however, that even these expressions of laws, uniformities, and universals can in some contexts acquire an instruction-sense when used as mnemonic devices, as in "If you want to remember and distinguish the two kinds of cases that arise in electrostatic phenomena, bear in mind the formula 'Like poles repel, unlike attract'" (113–14).

Now the general statement that literary rules are somehow like linguistic rules would imply that they are of the principle-rule sort, especially if the analogy is to (Chomskyan) syntactic rules, as in the familiar "literary competence" models. Such rules state lawlike mechanical regularities ("English objects follow verbs"), are morally neutral and descriptive rather than regulative and prescriptive, and despite frequent interpretation to the contrary, are not meant to function as instructions for behavior, for communication, or for the encoding or decoding of sentences (see Chomsky, *Aspects* 8–11).[20] Searle's rules for promises, inasmuch as they are practice-defining necessary and sufficient conditions for promises (or promising), similarly aim to be rules of this sort, although as we have seen, this goal is complicated by a number of his other interests. Note that Black accords a much different sense to the term "constitutive" than does Searle. Since rules constituting institutions always come in sets and inevitably describe purposive, intentional behavior, Black would categorize them with instructions rather than principle rules, as Searle sometimes seems to prefer (123–25); and this difference perhaps explains the contrasting role of rule violation in the two accounts.

It is more difficult to sort out rule notions precisely in critical discussions, but there are at least three (overlapping) contexts in which literary rules appear, if not distinct types. A first kind of literary rule is principally associated with generative grammar, though often with some reference to speech-act theory (as in Culler's and Fish's earliest literary-reading models). Here the rules of a literary grammar (derived, as we have seen, from construing generative grammars as text-processing mechanisms) are loose, cross-generic characterizations of literature or of basic interpretive norms. Since "literature" in reader-oriented criticism is defined as a way of reading, these accounts naturally concentrate on translating formalist characterizations of literariness ("Literary works cohere") into literature-defining reading operations ("Read so as to achieve coherence"). Roman Jakobson's "set toward the message" ("Closing" 356), originally a focus of language on itself, is now a disposition to read something as literature (see Pratt, *Toward* 31–37, 87; Culler, *Poetics* 66–67, 163–64), and this is in a sense its constitutive feature, so that the rule is at once active and statically definitional. Often, however, such a discussion gives way to more specifically formulated reading operations—the search for tension or binary oppositions, for example, or the recuperation of thematic unity—and these are more emphatically described as heuristics, whether analogous to rules of a generative grammar or rules for speech acts. They are stategies readers apply, chosen from a "repertoire" (Fish, *Text* 314), they are "recipes" or "instructions" (Fish, *Text* 326–27), they guide readers in "construing" meaning (Pratt, *Toward* 170) or in "making sense" (Fish, *Text* 313; Mailloux, *Conventions* 149), they involve solving

[20] As I mentioned in the last chapter, I refer to Chomsky's *Aspects of the Theory of Syntax* (1965) rather than a more recent account, because it is nearly the only linguistics text cited in literary criticism.

enigmas (Culler, *Poetics* 180). Rules referred to in this manner consequently demonstrate a clear purposive force, but their implied ends
may vary—from the recovery of a work on some basic level (more
analogous to lower-level linguistic rules) to the working out of better,
more acceptable interpretations (closer to the sense of Black's instruction rules).

In discussions of genre conventions, a second context for rule metaphors, literary rules are more often directly analogous to speech-act
rules. A genre consists of a set of shared conventions (analogous to a
speech-act practice) which texts invoke in single instances (see Pratt,
Toward 86–87, 201–10; Culler, *Poetics* 5; Mailloux, *Conventions* 132,
156–58; Schauber and Spolsky, *Bounds* 44–55, 57, 70). Not surprisingly, genre conventions, like speech-act rules, are amenable to two
kinds of analysis. Sometimes, for instance, the implication is that
genre rules are lists of existential conditions ("Lyric poems consist of
the following conventions"), a reasonable way to formulate rules that
critics stress are simultaneous with acts of interpretation (see especially Fish, *Text* 305–21); surely no literary object could be actualized
from outside some such framework of preexisting expectations. Thus
Fish can speak of texts as "preread" according to generic expectations
(*Text* 311), Culler can define genre rules as "constitutive of functional
categories" (*Poetics* 137), and Mailloux can characterize generic traditions as becoming constitutive of textual meaning, once they serve to
model expectations for readers approaching texts (*Conventions* 151).
The literary model in this scheme would consequently list rules corresponding to readers' understanding of what murder mysteries and historical biographies *are*. Elsewhere, however, a critic will emphasize not
such ideal definitions but the interpretive space between generic expectations and a particular work. An ideal set of (again, shared) conditions outlines the possibilities and limits for the genre, but these do
not so much constitute an immediate apprehension of the text as provide a background against which a particular reading experience is
consciously and actively measured. From this somewhat different
viewpoint, Fish describes sets of rules as "organizing rubrics" that
guide the *process* of interpretation by a "route" not "wholly determined" (*Text* 314); Pratt, who sees all language as essentially generic
(even conversation being governed by narrative expectations), explains
literary meaning as a function of violation of genre conventions (*Toward* 152–233); and Culler speaks of the generic expectations that
guide and limit readings (*Poetics* 127, 136), generating meaning as the
text resists or complies with known rules. There is a sense, then, in
which genre rules can be formulated as principle rules, as lawlike uni-

versals that exist independent of individual human agency; like Chomskyan syntactic rules or one sense of Searle's systems of constitutive rules, they define knowledge without immediate reference to behavior. Yet they also correspond to rules as instructions, to heuristic devices that guide means-end activity. And while generic expectations seem to be nonpurposive in nature, inasmuch as they precede and determine interpretation, they also seem liable to conscious choice both prior to interpretation and during the reading process. This point Culler and Fish illustrate, as we have seen, by reading normally nonliterary texts as poems (Culler, *Poetics* 161–62; Fish, *Text* 322–29).

A final kind of rule-based discussion is increasingly echoed in later criticism. In these accounts, interpretive principles intersect with the world beyond the institution of literature or derive from certain critical approaches (sometimes "interpretive communities"), as opposed to the institution of "literature" as a whole. Thus these rules of reading attach not to a specifically literary competence but to "cultural codes" (Culler, *Poetics* 123, 143) or New Criticism or deconstruction (Fish, *Text* 320–21, 336, 343–55). Such rules (often "norms") can receive neutral treatment, as in Mailloux's (*Conventions* 126–30) and Culler's (*Poetics* 141–45) earlier accounts: knowledge of critical and cultural conventions is simply necessary to an understanding of a work that is a product of a particular period or practice. Or moral judgment can be implied, as when Fish complains that readers lack awareness of specific historical and cultural sources for their reading strategies (*Text* 342, 358–61). Rules like these, then, not only expand beyond the practice of criticism to include cultural clichés and even critical loyalties but border on (Black's) precept rules or prescriptions. They can assume the form of apolitical strategy applicable to more than canonized literary texts (as in a rule: "Actualize so as to achieve overall coherence"), but one can often imagine for them a specific legitimating authority, a time and a place of origin, much more easily than one can even for speech-act institutions or genre conventions (essentially such a rule would read: "Texts should cohere; so read primarily for this effect").

This simple schema of rule types reveals further problems in the literary accounts. First, the confusion over whether "literature" in general or a genre is being defined (in terms of principle or constitutive rules), or a particular interpretive act (in terms of regulative or instruction rules) is akin to the practice-act conflation in Searle, the collapse of institutional knowledge, the invocation of shared practices in individual acts, and the formulation of felicitous speech acts into one rule description. In a literary theory it seems particularly difficult to describe an interpretive operation consistently according to the principle-rule model, as the general analogy with linguistic rules would suggest. In the instance of genre rules, for example, any definitional statement of an institutionalized convention cannot help but imply something about its application, so that a rule-statement such as "A mystery novel withholds the murderer's identity until the final pages" is more usefully conceived as a heuristic—"Read for clues as to the murderer's identity." In fact, for a number of reasons genre rules are best characterized in this fashion. A list of apparently necessary and sufficient conditions for genres would draw the arguments that apply to such institutions as promising (no enumeration of existential conditions is enough to explain institutional behavior, and in any case, since texts are reader actualized, there are no such brute facts to contend with). And given that generic norms apply to texts rather than single speech acts, given the resulting complications—mixed genres, the possibility of reading a text as invoking other than its apparent genre conventions—a list of conditions that necessarily and strictly constitute (in Searle's sense) any one genre would be impossible to formulate. Further, the lawlike nature of principle rules would not allow for the central role of deviance and distance from generic expectations. Just as Gricean rules tell us more about deviant promises, it is rather the resistance to than the compliance with a generic ideal that is meaning producing here.[21] Most important, characterization of reading operations in terms of principle rules involves a fundamental contradiction: since the task defined at the outset is the description of interpretive *behavior*, production of a mental object, it is impossible in the analysis to separate rule knowledge from rule accord, from interpretive activity. In this case, knowing rules must entail knowing how to use them in any one instance. Principle rules, which characterize regularities as nonpurposive in nature, do not illuminate purposive behavior.

A possible rule-based solution would be to distinguish between institutional expectations and specific gestures toward them, but to explain

---

[21] Pratt explicitly applies Grice's Cooperative Principle and maxims ("Logic") to literary texts (deviation from a general norm is thus the basis of interpretation). She believes that the same interpretive operations hold for literature that hold for conversation and conversational narrative, and so she differs from many critics in her (refreshingly) nonmetaphorical use of speech-act and linguistic models (see *Toward*, chaps. 4–6). My minor reservation is just that in her discussion of William Labov's analysis of natural narrative Pratt turns his narrative units into a somewhat more rigid schema than I think he intended (compare *Toward*, chap. 2; and Labov, *Language*, chap. 9); the result is that she searches for orientation passages in narratives that gain interpretive significance precisely by *not* containing expected orientation material (see 52). At times she also applies speech-act terms to narratives (narratives are assertives), and this treatment means that the terms lose their original significance ("appropriateness conditions" become loose expectations; Searle is indistinguishable from Grice) (132–39).

the application of rules as another rule, a position Fish sometimes implies ("With the Compliments" 711). But this kind of analysis, as others have complained (Putnam 1–14; Tyler 125–26), develops into an infinite regress of rules, with the consequence that the crucial behavior involved is never sufficiently elaborated. At any rate, such a rule would correspond to Searle's essential rule, serving to activate a series of more static conditions, to signal their institutional context. An analogous rule would, possibly, characterize the one constitutive feature of literature, the intentional stance of a reader toward the text (what defines a literary work is the reader's disposition toward the literary institution, a decision to read it as literature). But once again it is doubtful whether such intentional acts can be meaningfully described as conventions. To draw once more from the discussion of Searle, what readers know about literature is, of course, embodied in the institution, but what they know is less how to follow rules than how to make inferences based on institutional knowledge. It is not so much that some "essential" intentional decision transforms the conventions embodied in the text as that it signals the reader's sense of the interpretive space between text and context.

A further problem is that the general notion "rule" designates an even wider range of behavior than the practice-act conflation alone would suggest. The rule-associated interpretive behavior is sometimes highly purposive (extending even to the elaboration of a critical viewpoint in a professional article), sometimes unconscious (as in the oft-cited focus on the message or in an assumed critical habit). Of course, if one wished to tighten the analogy with lower-level linguistic rules, one would want to claim interpretive operations are generally below the level of conscious awareness or control. Indeed, this view has a certain automatic validity. Why else would interpretation have seemed to depend all this time on texts rather than on readers? But at the same time, interpretive rules, corresponding as they most often do to Black's instruction rules, imply some amount of volition, if not full awareness, and some extended event or process. Again the suggestion is that some immediate perception of the text is "constitutive" of the literary experience or is analogous to a recognition of the speech act invoked; and yet it would be impossible to contend that all literary experience is of this sort. Perhaps an alternative metaphor—a schema, for example— better models the duality of literary interpretation.

The question of the source of language institutions is similar in each account. Obviously both speech-act and literary-interpretive rules differ in kind from other linguistic rules in that they involve generalization, repeated experience with speech events and texts, as opposed to the passive, biologically triggered acquisition of syntactic rules. By implication, the linguistic knowledge involved is of a different order. But the speech-act analogy suggests that it is necessary to distinguish kinds of institutionalized linguistic knowledge even further. In Austin's scheme and in Searle's, performative acts such as marrying (saying "I will" in a certain context) are similar to promises in that they both require analogous appropriateness conditions—the correct persons (able to carry out the promise, not already married), an accepted procedure for carrying out the speech act (conventional actions and locutions), apparent sincerity, and so forth (Austin, *How to* 1–24). But the speech acts "I will" and "I promise" contrast in the sense that marriage involves more complicated nonlinguistic conventions, as Searle acknowledges (*Expression* 16–20). In addition, conditions for promising exhibit more extra-institutional logic: persons cannot, for instance, promise to carry out an action that basic life experience tells everyone is impossible ("I promise to flap my hands and fly"). Marriage, on the other hand, rests more on its own internal logic; it is not from any general experience of the world that we know one cannot marry a penguin but from an understanding of the institution of marriage itself. The consequences of rule breaking again illustrate these differences: violations of syntactic rules result in nonsentences, unintelligibility; violations of rules for promising sometimes imply meanings beyond the apparent illocution (as in the earlier example of the odd promise); and violations of conditions for marriage result in an empty procedure, but with complex social and legal consequences.[22] Similarly, literary norms specifying interpretive operations that apply everywhere in the world, in extra-literary contexts (the basic search for coherence, for example) differ from historically specific, literary-institution–internal genre rules. (This last distinction is, in fact, one of the insights of Mailloux's taxonomy of literary rules [see *Conventions* 126–58].)[23] This is

---

[22] This is to claim not that insincere promises do not generate social or legal complications but that the conventional apparatus of marrying or christening make implication difficult. Speech acts can, of course, be void in the way that "I will" uttered in the wrong context can (when a speaker asserts a nonexistent car needs repair), but such an utterance can draw from hearers extra interpretive effort and make sense on another level (the speaker wishes she owned a car). One cannot imagine an analogy for the speech acts of a marriage ceremony.

[23] Mailloux, *Interpretive Conventions*, is to my mind the best account of literary rule types. He insightfully distinguishes between exclusively literary conventions and general interpretive operations (126–58). My quibbles are merely that he, too, conflates practices and single acts (constitutive rules for him are both institution defining and rules of

not to say that such rules are entirely distinct but simply that literary accounts often conflate different senses of "institutionalized."

A possible rule-based solution for some of these problems would be to define several kinds of (specifically textual) interpretive operations and characterize them by means of different rule types. This is exactly what Ellen Schauber and Ellen Spolsky propose: an integration of a Chomskyan "autonomous linguistic system" ("Stalking" 404) with pragmatic and literary-interpretive components ("Stalking" 397–413; *Bounds* 17–23). In a first version of their model "well-formedness rules" (principle rules that govern phonology, syntax, and sentence-level interpretation) characterize (most of) the formal linguistic component, whereas "preference rules" generally explain higher-level pragmatic and literary-interpretive behavior ("Stalking" 401). Such a model could usefully distinguish between a narrowly conceived sentence-level semantics (involving anaphora, negative scope, and the like as in familiar linguistic models) and textual concerns. Unfortunately, in order to justify the two levels of their particular system, Schauber and Spolsky are forced to revive a meaning-significance distinction of the sort E. D. Hirsch advances (1–13). This distinction naturally involves an argument about a "basic," immediate, context-independent meaning of a broader sort (than I have just suggested), as opposed to interpretive meaning ("Stalking" 402–3), and to adhere to such a distinction is to oppose a central tenet of speech-act and most reader-based literary theories—namely, that context-independent sentence interpretation is not possible. In any case, that the model is a temporal, text-processing one represents a problem for the Chomskyan part of the literary grammar, which is not equipped to explain linear interaction between text and reader. In a later version the model is more detailed—well-formedness rules also describe basic conceptual processes (*Bounds* 24–25), and preference rules apply at lower levels (28); but there is some confusion about the diversity of facts and behaviors accounted for by two rule types. It also is not entirely clear how the model's subsystems interact (35).[24]

---

thumb, part of a broad communicative competence, and really include rules Searle would call regulative [127–29, 150–51]). By the end of the account some of the initial distinctions erode (all rules are in some sense "constitutive"; "illocutionary act" defines a mode of behavior ["disrespect"] or a general process of interpretation) (150–58).

[24] Schauber and Spolsky offer an account of contrasting rule types, a detailed examination of genre conventions (*Bounds* 56–77), and an interesting elaboration of Grice (114–19). My reservation is just that it does not always grapple with the problems raised by attempting to integrate linguistics with speech-act theory and by applying speech-act theory to discourse concerns ("illocutionary point" becomes the rhetorical purpose of an entire text [44–55]).

As another possibility, one could dissolve the problem of volition altogether by relying on a (strong) structuralist version of the individual, by describing readers as sets of rules rather than as sources of intentional gestures or interpretive decisions: readers too are "constituted by a set of conventional notions" that texts "put into operation" (Fish, *Text* 332; "Consequences" 113). By this analysis, even interpretive operations that imply some process, a development or outcome, would be as inevitable as any initial stance toward a text. According to this view, both readers and the world with which readers interact are artifacts of language (all knowledge is thus in some sense linguistic). But as much as both these claims may be true to some extent, the result of holding them absolutely and simultaneously is particularly unrevealing for literary theory. Readers process texts the way they do because they process texts as they must. World and reader, text and reader intersect, but since this action is inevitable, there is nothing to investigate or explain. This is not to deny that critics might reconsider the individual implied in reader-oriented theory; as Pratt has suggested ("Ideology"), speech-act literary models in particular have assumed a culturally specific ideal reader. It does seem best to conclude that claims about the minimal awareness or consciousness of interpretive behavior, however expressed, are not useful criteria for arguments about the specific nature of rules in a literary theory; for most critics would want to argue for the role of both unconscious constraint and active meaning-making.

In examining the implicit claim of many literary theories importing rule-based models—namely, that literary-interpretive activity closely parallels the structure of linguistic knowledge and behavior at lower levels—I have in all likelihood pushed the analogy between literary rule and speech-act institution farther than most reader-oriented critics should like to go. Yet the exercise is instructive, I think, since it leads one to suspect that constraints on literary interpretation more nearly parallel everyday constraints on interpretive behavior in the world at large than they do the recognition or production of principle-type rules (see Manley 47). And this is where the speech-act account is revealing, once we see institutional behavior as improperly characterized by principle or Searle's (rather than Black's sense of) constitutive rules. Rules in a literary theory, as we have seen, sometimes correspond to principle rules (as literature- or genre-defining conditions), sometimes to instruction rules (as purposive or projecting a specific end or descriptive of some process), sometimes to precept rules (as attaching to some code), or sometimes to regulations (as legislated by an identifiable group). But interpretive activity in general is not well explicated by a mere nod toward linguistic rules and institutions. Behavioral regularities at the discourse level might be better characterized by a different metaphorical complex (specialized literary knowledge that intersects with more general cultural knowledge, maxims and instructions, deviance as meaningful) than that associated with linguistic rules (specifically literary knowledge, principle rules, deviance as unintelligible). In fact, this analysis in some ways merely describes how the literary object is always implicitly explicated according to one set of concepts in its systematic resistance to another; the rule formulations of literary theories, like Searle's constitutive rules, inevitably assume the characteristics of instructions and heuristics the more they are applied to single acts of interpretation.

SPEECH ACTS REVISITED

I hardly need explain that Searle's attack on Derrida soon affected the status of his model, although literary critics have remained to some degree ambivalently invested in its terms. They have partly because of Searle's connection to Austin, with whom deconstructionists engaged more positively, but also, as I remarked earlier, because speech-act accounts genuinely border on literary interests. Searle's debate with Derrida is a subject in its own right and a topic in the next chapter. Here let me just briefly note why thinking about the earlier work on speech acts in the way I have suggested—as simultaneous accounts of conventions and invocations of conventions, of institutions and specific acts instantiating institutions—might bear on recurring critical issues.

Problems of literary intentionality and meaning are most obviously connected to speech-act concerns. While intentionalist accounts in the New Critical sense are no longer much at issue, "intention" of a sort remains important to certain arguments about literary communities; that is, one may invoke "illocutionary intent" to free meanings from texts and situate them instead in specific contexts and in shared literary conventions and norms. Consider, as a brief example, Steven Knapp and Walter Benn Michaels's contributions to the debate collected in *Against Theory*, the debate to which Fish adds an essay on Chomsky (see Mitchell). Here Knapp and Michaels outline a speech-act-based theory of literary meaning, one meant to underscore Fish's point that readings are immediately interpretive and interested. This argument itself he elaborates along the lines of Searle's distinction between brute and institutional facts.[25]

Knapp and Michaels initially describe two groups of critics, those who follow putatively objective procedures in order to ensure valid readings and those who deny that correct, text-determined interpretations exist ("Against Theory" 13–24). Both camps, say Knapp and Michaels, commit a single error: they "imagin[e] the possibility of language prior to and independent of intention" (19). The first kind of critic attempts to recover authorial intention (12); the second sort subtracts intention from language, claims that intention cannot be reliably reconstructed (12, 22). Knapp and Michaels follow Searle in arguing that "all meanings are intentional" (15). To recognize language as language involves assuming agency, and to interpret involves recognizing some context or other; language cannot mean, cannot be language, in an intentionless, contextless void (16–18). If meaning acts are by definition intentional, Knapp and Michaels conclude, then "the meaning of a text is simply identical to the author's intended meaning," and one can neither search for authorial intention ("illocutionary intention" [17]) after reading a text nor deny its interpretive necessity (12). Both critical projects thus become "incoherent" and further theorizing altogether useless (12, 18).

I should emphasize again, if it is not obvious, that Knapp and Michaels do not intend to fix or valorize authorial intention; rather, by way of Searle, they hope to resist the pitfalls of centering textual meaning in the (abstracted) linguistic code. Thus Knapp and Michaels recall Searle's arguments that locutions in themselves do not mean. They remain mere sentences, since identical locutions uttered as speech acts in different contexts mean differently. If we cast their project in this way, then code-based theories are again of two types. One finds in the linguistic code transhistorical meaning; the other imagines a code that permutes and interacts with itself, a solution that multiplies meanings at the same time as it detaches them from specific (historical) moments and human agency. On the one hand, Knapp and Michaels would seem to have simply argued for context-dependent interpretation and for historically situated speech acts, an agency that if not real is construed and would confer on literary language the political force of the nonliterary. On the other hand, they conclude, as we have seen, that utterances just then mean, and their injunction to stop theorizing bespeaks an apolitical impulse.[26]

Pressing the speech-act model clarifies how such a position develops. The analogy that underlies the argument is between speech act and literary text, as opposed to literary and nonliterary speech act, and this allows Knapp and Michaels to conflate several senses of "intention" that both Austin and Searle are at pains to distinguish. The "intention" that preoccupies speech-act accounts is illocutionary intent, the intention to mean and to get hearers to recognize this intention to mean by uttering a conventional token (an illocutionary verb ["I promise"]) (Searle, *Speech Acts* 44–50). The "meaning" in question is thus simply the recognition of the type of speech act invoked (that a proposition has been promised or asserted). The illocutionary intent is distinguished from other intentions (a speaker's desire to please or intimidate an interlocutor); and the meaning-effect, or recognition of the speech act (sometimes called "securing uptake"), is distinguished from other (perlocutionary) effects (a hearer's reaction of pleasure or of disbelief or belief in the speaker's assertion) (Austin, *How to* 117; Searle, *Speech Acts* 42–50). While Searle asserts clearly, as Knapp and Michaels do, that locutions and illocutionary intentions are inseparable (*Speech Acts* 24, 42; see also Austin, *How to* 114), such intentions are a great distance from both the problems of authorial intention and the questions of textual meaning that preoccupy literary critics. "Speech act" in Searle's sense is an utterance with a single illocutionary verb, not extended discourse, and "illocutionary intent" does not extend to the broader significance of texts.[27] The meaning-effects that Knapp and Michaels describe fall under the scope of perlocutionary effect, typically described as beyond convention and speaker control (see Austin, *How to* 94–120); literary meaning would seem open, therefore, to exactly the kind of theoretical questioning they resist.[28] In this case the

[26] In further responses Knapp and Michaels change their position somewhat: they associate illocutionary intent more fixedly with a generalized authorial intention ("Critics" 103; "Rorty" 142). This is particularly true of their follow-up essay, "Against Theory 2," in which Knapp and Michaels again maintain that linguistic convention is not a stable source of meaning but then also say that it provides "clues" to authorial intention (57). What they need here is some account of the relation between intention and convention, and thinking along these lines would once more necessitate a distinction between kinds of intention, between broadly construed authorial intention and illocutionary intent.

[27] This distinction does not rely on a supposed difference between meaning and significance, but it depends on a contrast between recognizing the speech act as a speech act with a particular propositional content and any other meaning—in a general sense—it might convey.

[28] For discussions of different senses of the terms "meaning" and "intention," see Grice, "Utterer's Meaning, Sentence-Meaning, and Word-Meaning"; and Hancher, "Three Kinds

terms of the original model preserve contextually positioned meaning without closing off interpretive speculation, as does the distinction between an intentional gesture toward conventions (the illocutionary intent) and the institutionalized conventions themselves (which open questions about which conventions are at play in particular contexts).

But I should also say that the notion "intention" is vexed in ways the speech-act model does not as easily solve. That is, critical discussion has also focused on the intentionalism of speech-act theory for the kinds of speakers and social structures the notion entails. Pratt was perhaps the first to articulate this now-familiar position: locating intentional force in individual speakers as speech-act theorists do assumes speakers are ideally or usually straightforward, that Anglo-American speech conventions are universally shared, and that interlocutors effectively control all possible and potential communicative intentions ("Ideology" 62–71). I think it is clear that Austin, Searle, and Grice are vulnerable to such charges. Searle's paradigmatic promises tellingly focus the discussion on social contracts, and Grice, as Pratt notes, assumes a universal norm of efficient and informational conversation (65–70).[29] Austin's account, too, fits Pratt's sense that speech-act theory's interlocutors are good old guys who are reliable and sincere, although Austin's self-mocking speaker, who treads on snails and gambles with his employer's money, suggests a more complex persona (see "Plea" and "Three").

But we might also recognize competing impulses in speech-act accounts in order to consider more seriously what we can salvage from this discussion. We could at least note that the theory rather naturally invites such arguments, for when Austin asks for what acts adults in this culture can apologize, whether one speaker can apologize for another, it seems appropriate to ask whether or not such assumptions always hold. Indeed, work on speech acts has suggested cross-cultural

---

of Intention." Although I was not explicitly recalling Hancher's essay at the time I first wrote this chapter, I am certain that reading his clear account of the difference between literary and illocutionary intention has helped form my thinking on this matter.

[29] Butler remarks the centrality of the heterosexual marriage ceremony in Austin's account of speech acts in order to raise questions about the structure of authority behind them (223–30). Although I have said I agree with Pratt that Grice's norm of efficient and informational conversation is culturally specific, it is perhaps more accurate to say that this is not even an Anglo norm (Deborah Tannen provides abundant examples in *Talking Voices*). I believe, however, that Grice's framework remains useful. If we replace his generalized Cooperative Principle with the culturally specific norms of conversational behavior interlocutors expect for particular speech genres, then the principles of flouting (or rule-violation) and implicature (or unstated speech act) work quite well.

studies of politeness and alternative "logics" of indirection.[30] Questions about the individual speaker who invokes such conventions are more difficult, however. Again Austin and Searle clearly do not cast individual speakers as coerced, speaking as they must, or as reaffirming broader social institutions as they speak; neither do they imagine in detail, as Pratt does, corporate speakers or speakers who speak for groups rather than themselves (see "Ideology" 61–62), although theirs is of course a speaker shaped by conventions and other speakers.

On the other hand, as I have said, "illocutionary intent" defines only a conscious intention to invoke a type of speech act (with specific propositional content) that interlocutors will recognize as such. Again, this formulation, far from excluding the unconscious intentions—linguistic and otherwise—of inconsistent speakers, implicitly casts these as largely unavailable; and in fact "perlocutionary effect" invites interpretive speculation on such matters. Note that Searle assumes interpretive questions bear on which conventions are in force: he revises the sincerity condition to describe speakers who are *apparently* sincere, obviously because his account has no inner access; it must address sincerity simply as conventionally coded (*Speech Acts* 62). As Austin remarks, the habits of ordinary English speech, its language institutions, inadequately characterize well-known unconscious behavior—displacement, compulsivity, and the like ("Plea" 203–4). Whereas this observation leads him to underplay how much ordinary speakers think about such matters, it means Austin stresses the way in which the language itself models, distorts, and simplifies social action: "We take *some very simple action* . . . and use *this* . . . as our model in terms of which to talk about other actions and events . . . even when these other actions are pretty remote and perhaps much more interesting to us . . . and even when the model is really distorting the facts rather than helping us to observe them" ("Plea" 202). Searle and Austin thus strongly assume that unconscious intentions and actions exist alongside conscious linguistic intentions, but they tend to assume unconscious intentions and actions will not submit to the kind of analysis they apply to conscious linguistic intentions.[31] Such assumptions understandably

---

[30] Interesting early examples are Penelope Brown and Stephen Levinson, "Universals in Language Use" (a cross-cultural analysis of politeness); and Tannen, "Ethnic Style in Male-Female Conversation." See also John Gumperz's collection *Discourse Strategies*; these essays draw principally on discourse analysis and sociolinguistics, but often they also borrow accounts of indirection and implicature. For a brief but insightful assessment of the limitations of speech-act theory for political projects, see Norman Fairclough, *Language and Power* 9–10. For an overview of issues, see Ronald Wardhaugh, *An Introduction to Sociolinguistics* 282–311.

[31] Pratt says that it is not enough to point out that speech-act theory intends to identify

limit speech-act theory, but they also suggest how one might elaborate and productively reverse it: what is important is not whether utterances issue from individuals in some pure sense but that the speech institutions of our culture assume that they do, and such assumptions speech-act accounts might begin to describe. Again the terms I have just elaborated distinguish between an intentional gesture—codified in a historical moment—and its context of open-ended conventions, other prior and possible speech acts. Following this outline, we might consider more fully the ways in which specific speech acts enact and reify speech institutions.

The purpose of this chapter has not at all been to suggest that constraints on interpretive behavior do not exist, that we can dispense with rule-based models and return to some notion of a free, individual mind encountering texts in direct, unencumbered fashion. Rather, the point is precisely that the nature of those literary constraints requires further investigation. To reiterate from a somewhat different angle, it is not that interpretation does not lend itself in any way to analysis by rules but rather that one begs central questions by responding to the natural affinity of literary matters to rule-based analysis by characterizing interpretive norms and literary criticism as simply like other linguistic rules and practices. After all, many questions remain about the status of such entities in the original disciplines. Neither will it do

---

not real intentions but just those that the speaker takes public responsibility for, since "complex and contradictory subjective states obviously have an impact on what gets said," particularly in the case of indirect speech acts ("Ideology" 64). I agree with her basic point that construed and conflicting motives, attitudes, feelings, and the like obviously bear on interpretation—in a broad sense—of speech events, but I have some honestly conflicting responses to both her statement here and the underlying agenda. On the one hand, I do think that accounts of implicature and indirect speech acts begin to get at the matter of calculating the distance between announced and unannounced linguistic intentions. On the other hand, I would have to agree that Austin's account of presumed psychological states (sincerity especially) and Searle's (gratefulness for thanks, and so on) badly need elaboration; neither writer is clear about how much the feelings and beliefs accompanying speech acts are real or signaled, how interlocutors locate or construe them, and how speech acts serve generalized rhetorical aims in longer stretches of discourse. At the same time, however, I question whether one can ask the theory to address all such issues. Speech-act theory, once again, does not much address unconscious intentions, but I feel it is a bit much to ask a theory to explain how speakers communicate conscious linguistic intentions, directly and indirectly, and also implicitly ask it to be a psychoanalytic theory, however important such a project may be and however more important it may be for literary criticism. No one, after all, asks psychoanalytic theory to explain how hearers can process grammatical assertions as requests for information. One might, of course, ask how such issues interact, as Labov and David Fanshel did some time ago in *Therapeutic Discourse*. But such projects can explore only how one model might shed light on another's issues. In our discipline we often hope for an ideal and all-encompassing metatheory; all we can do, I think, is piece together models of limited scope.

to abandon such projects altogether, for as I have just suggested, critical theory has in common with other fields questions about "rule" as a central notion, particularly the matter of where convention ends and intentional behavior begins.

Chapter 5

Linguistics and Speech-Act Theory since Deconstruction

Since there is no nonmetaphoric language to oppose to metaphors here, one must . . . multiply antagonistic metaphors.
—JACQUES DERRIDA, *Of Grammatology*

Early linguistic criticism had both optimism and energy. Should a linguistic model fail, the solution was to update the model, to replace data-focused structuralism with linguistic mentalism or to enhance generative accounts with discourse theories. To a question I implied in an earlier chapter—What happened to this investment in linguistics, to all this enthusiasm?—it is tempting to respond, simply, "Deconstruction happened."

Now as I have already said, matters were more complicated than that. Certain discipline-internal needs ensured that such projects could not survive, at least not without a radical revision of the underlying premises. Uneasy at the start in its interdisciplinary projects, a discipline that had begun to exhaust the borrowed paradigms soon resumed a much earlier position: critics must more fully define their own goals, relinquishing the dream of scientific criticism. This time, however, deconstruction clearly formed much of the disciplinary rhetoric, and it set many of the specific terms of the new orientation toward both linguistics and speech-act theory.[1]

This is not to say, I must emphasize, that deconstruction was wholly responsible for the change in critical climate. On the contrary, linguistic models in particular independently disappointed former enthusi-

[1] An excellent introduction to the general issues is Vincent Leitch, *Deconstructive Criticism*.

asts. Besides, it is possible to draw from Jacques Derrida the sense that linguistics and deconstruction are thoroughly and inevitably opposed and also the sense that linguistics is a positively necessary project. The fact remains that many critics so exclusively read deconstruction as oppositional that for some time it was difficult to approach linguistics or linguistic philosophy—without risking the label "conservative," that is—in less than hostile terms. From this trend I must exclude some later criticism, but this newer discussion is perhaps possible only as deconstruction itself declines in prestige.

In this new context, then, we must also ask whether deconstruction's engagements with linguistics and ordinary language philosophy are any longer of moment now that its critical heyday is past. I would argue that in both abuses and productive uses of linguistics and linguistic philosophy those early deconstructive readings very much persist. One has only to recall that critical positions on specifically linguistic topics have not changed much since then. More positively, the most inventive of these accounts—Derrida's reading of Saussure, Shoshana Felman's reading of Austin—inform ongoing projects: historical readings of "mimologism," in the first case; accounts of gender as constructed and performed, in the second.[2] Such a history suggests it will be profitable to revisit the original scene and contest, this time with a view to points of (admittedly ambivalent) interaction between deconstruction and these language theories. The important moments here are, first, Derrida's analysis of Saussurean linguistics in *Of Grammatology* and, second, his engagement with ordinary language philosophy, his essay on J. L. Austin and the ensuing debate with John Searle.

DERRIDA ON SAUSSURE

It is not, I think, an exaggeration to say that, more than any text of deconstruction, Derrida's analysis of Saussure is the most generally familiar, its movement serving as a master pattern for other deconstructive projects. In fact, I have already mentioned critiques of Roman Jakobson's preoccupation with the aesthetic value of sound, which were clearly inspired by Derrida's critique of Saussure's phonocentrism. This (second) chapter of *Of Grammatology* is well known, in part because it handily outlines Derrida's basic premises. More important for this discussion, the text simply remains a compelling critique of Saussure's *Course in General Linguistics*, both in its appreciation for its radical potential and in its pointed treatment of Saussure's attitude

[2] The last allusion is to Judith Butler's and Eve Sedgwick's elaborations of Felman.

toward speech and writing.

But in an unfortunate contrast, Derrida's remarks for some time encouraged a general sense among deconstructive critics that little of merit could be read in Saussure's account; and many essays echoed Derrida's arguments without as much a sense either of Saussure's project or of Derrida's own engagement with linguistic theory as one might, in retrospect, wish. One reason to return to Derrida's text is thus the sheer perspective of changing critical positions and passions. A second reason to reconsider Derrida on Saussure is Saussure's rehabilitation. That is, both critics and linguists have since returned to reexamine the *Course in General Linguistics*, particularly, in the case of literary discussion, Saussure's views on language history, which in the era of *Of Grammatology* soon also drew critical fire. In an especially elegant analysis, for instance, Derek Attridge credits Saussure with dismissing only simplistic models of language evolution but, in the process, locates (contra Derrida and yet very much in the pattern of *Of Grammatology*) Saussure's romantic impulse in his treatment of etymology, conceived as a type of narrative. A second example is Gregory Jay, who politicizes Derrida on Saussure by reviving the ideological premises of the Saussurean notion "value."[3] In any case, my remarks here are in this spirit, save that I wish to concentrate the focus principally on the question of Derrida's own investment in linguistics. Thus in what follows I consider whether or not Saussure's sign theory and phonologism are consistently of the sort Derrida describes, but I do so as a point of entry into Derrida's position on linguistic theory in general, not solely his position on Saussure. Ultimately I ask if the deconstructive project works as it claims on linguistic theory from within its own premises.

DERRIDA ON SAUSSURE ON WRITING

Derrida's comments on Saussure frame his more general remarks on linguistics, which may be understood only from the perspective of that analysis. Briefly put, Derrida's immediate (and well-known) objection to the *Course in General Linguistics* is that it privileges (in the most loaded senses of the term) speech at the expense of writing. Saus-

---

[3] Jay eloquently defends Derrida against the charge that he is ahistoricist or apolitical by emphasizing the political underpinnings of Derrida's argument with Saussure (158–70). In so doing, Jay points to both the ideological critique the *Course* itself poses and its limitations. That is, Jay finds in the *Course* a "demystification of a social contract theory of language" and conscious reference to the larger political meaning of value (163), but like Derrida, he sees Saussure revert to an idealist or materialist metaphysics (169).

sure's commitment to empirical investigation, Derrida says, generates this position. His phonologism, his exclusive regard for the sound-sense dimension of language, results from a practical empirical need, the need to delineate a strict scope of analysis (*Grammatology* 28, 34); and in this rigorous exclusion of the extraneous (here writing and all that writing famously entails for Derrida) it is a model of scientific description (29). In short, Derrida's analysis of Saussure is simultaneously an unhappy pronouncement on science, for science inevitably excludes that which would correct and undermine it.[4] In Saussure's account, Derrida notes, writing consistently assumes "a *narrow* and *derivative* function" (30); it exists merely to represent speech, as a sign of a sign (33–35).

Saussure is actually contradictory on this point, at one moment citing historical evidence (*Course* 24) and Chinese ideographic writing (26) to claim that spoken and written language make up two self-contained and independent sign systems, at another declaring that writing exists "for the sole purpose of representing [speech]" (23). And Saussure goes farther, characterizing writing as "fictitious" and "superficial," in danger of usurping and disguising the sound-image, which, in contrast to writing, naturally constitutes language (24–25, 30). Now Saussure's opposition, between sound as natural and writing as artificial, Derrida points out, contradicts the doctrine of arbitrariness, his emphatic claim elsewhere that all sign systems are thoroughly conventional (*Grammatology* 44). More interesting, Derrida argues that Saussure in fact changes his mind about what is "natural," excluding writing from linguistics according to two competing justifications. When he describes writing as a sign of a sign, a secondary sign system, Saussure casts writing in a dependent and reflective, therefore natural, relationship to speech; when he emphasizes the prior and natural bond of language and sound, Saussure characterizes writing as artificial and derivative (44–46). Writing is paradoxically neither independently conventional enough nor natural enough to constitute an object of inquiry.

Now commentators have since suggested some reasons—offered from Saussure's perspective—why in his brief remarks on writing Saussure should strive against the substance of his own general theory. David Holdcroft, for example, convincingly argues that Saussure falters in his choice of "acoustic image" as a key term (38). And James Porter faults both the editors of the *Course in General Linguistics* and Der-

---

[4] For a reading that emphasizes this aspect of Derrida on Saussure, see Sam Weber, "Saussure." See also Weber, "Stroke."

rida's substitutional quotation for contributing to the apparent textual emphasis on the naturalness of sound (872–76).[5] One clear contributing factor, however, is the purely pedagogical perspective of the *Course*, the explicit position Saussure assumes in these pages. Anyone who teaches phonology to new students must warn them not to confuse speech with writing; students are otherwise unable to grasp the historical sound changes under discussion, since speech sounds do not correspond to orthography. Derrida accuses Saussure of ethnocentrism here, for were he to consider in detail a variety of writing systems, pictographic systems in particular, and were he not to associate ideograms with words, he would hesitate to find writing dependent and derivative (*Grammatology* 32–33). But again, from the point of view of a teacher of linguistics, the aim would be to confront the assumptions of a text-focused culture and to include in analysis unrecorded languages and dialects.[6]

Such explanations admittedly fall short of the mark, however, for Derrida convincingly maintains that Saussure's stridency here signals an unusual investment in defining writing as derivative (*Grammatology* 38–41). Saussure, after all, calls a pronunciation influenced by writing a "pathological" mistake or a "monstrosity" (*Course* 31, 32), apparently because the dependency relation between speech and writing is here reversed. As Derrida asks, "Does not the radical dissimilarity of the two elements—graphic and phonic—exclude derivation?" (54); if all signs are arbitrary, how can one enforce distinctions between graphic and phonic systems? (44). Roy Harris (seconded by Holdcroft) suggests a more compelling (than pedagogical) motive for Saussure's obvious stake in this position—his wish, as a historical linguist, to preserve the text-based practice of historical phonology. This is only apparently contradictory; if Saussure says that writing is secondary, it is because he sees writing as a reflection of *langue*, not just of speech.

[5] Holdcroft comments that a term that did not refer to sound as the basic element of *langue* would be more "fully in the spirit of the idea that language is a form" and avoid the implication that writing is parasitic on speech (38). I have not explored here the question of which texts of the *Course* Derrida consults or his quotation of Saussure, since this is the focus of other discussions. See Porter, for example, who points to editorial changes contributing to the emphasis in standard editions of the *Course* on the naturalness of sound (especially 894), and who objects to certain of Derrida's paraphrases of Saussure; his ultimate aim is to dispute the philosophical affiliation Derrida assigns Saussure.

[6] Saussure's pedagogical aims are often assumed; I am not the first to notice them. But for some reason many commentators do not sympathize with linguists' curiosity about what a language sounded like in an earlier period, the direction of phonological change, and similar concerns.

And if it is, then linguistic studies of historical documents, which now accurately reflect the otherwise unrecoverable *langue* of the lost language, remain valid (Harris 41–45; Holdcroft 41–42).[7]

In fact, I think Saussure's status as a historical linguist is significant here in other respects. We might shift the emphasis a bit to consider not just the characterization of writing as corrupting but also what it is said to corrupt. That is, sounds shaped by writing become as unnatural as writing itself. Saussure wants to preserve ongoing historical phonetic changes (the Great Vowel Shift is an example), sound evolution set in motion by general processes, from the influence of a print pronunciation that could partly alter its course. This wish, of course, suggests a narrow conception of naturalness; alternatively, one might define (as a sociolinguist now would) socially accepted reverses of an overall historical phonological trend "natural" as well. As Harris remarks, Saussure often absorbs individual concerns into social ones, and this problem prevents his successfully addressing the details of face-to-face communication (202). He similarly limits himself in this case; his emphasis on the shared and the social obscures the potentially systematic role of idiosyncratic sound changes in the larger phonological system. And of course this position is hardly consistent with his account of the interaction between *langue* and *parole* (see *Course* 19, 98).

Whatever its sources, as Derrida points out, Saussure's attitude toward writing is also not a legitimate consequence of his statement that language is a system of differences without positive terms (*Grammatology* 52–53). Since language is, by Saussure's own account, form, not substance, its units a mere function of "the differences that separate [one] sound-image from all others," language resides no more in verbal than in written matter (Derrida quoting Saussure 53). (Often Saussure maintains that the materiality of sound is not the relevant object of study [66, 119].) Difference, as Derrida says elsewhere, "remains inaudible" ("Differance" 133). The phonological system is also a kind of writing, as Saussure himself says, which is to say that both systems are constituted by difference. Intrinsic qualities distinguish graphemes no more than phonemes; graphemes, too, exist by virtue of their differences from other graphemes in the written system (*Grammatology* 52, 326–27n.17). By such arguments Derrida inaugurates a "science" of "grammatology," which would take as its object "arche-writing," a (metaphorical) writing that subsumes both graphic and verbal "writing" and announces the essential and thorough artificiality of

---

[7] As Harris also notes, Saussure's position on the dependency of writing significantly complicates the project of a general semiology (see 16–18).

all language (56–57, 74–81). As Thomas Pavel comments, Derrida's text suppresses the distinction between writing and arche-writing (*Feud* 69), by which I take him to mean that Derrida conflates (these) on-the-ground empirical arguments about the general nature of sign systems with (developing) philosophical comments on the absence or resistance of analytical objects. This is a movement from within and without Saussure's terms, a movement Derrida will repeat later, though perhaps less consciously than here.

In any case, this discussion also bears importantly on Saussure's sign theory, for "difference" applies not just to signifiers but also to signifieds. If thought in the *Course*, like sound, exists on an amorphous plane before the onset of language, then the principle of difference defines conceptual space as well (*Course* 112). Derrida's arguments on this head are apparently contradictory; the first, detailed elsewhere, attacks Saussure's too rigid distinction *between* signifier and signified (see *Positions* 18–20); the second faults the *unity* of the Saussurean sign. Both tacks are consistent, however. The first objections focus on Saussure's distinctive treatment of signifiers and signifieds. If signifieds are differentially and negatively defined, as Saussure says, if their "value" is a product of oppositions, what each signified is not, then, says Derrida, signifieds are essentially other signifiers, referring as they do to absent terms. Meaning is thus system-derived, the presence of the signified continually absent and deferred. In critiquing Saussure's opposition between signifier and signified, Derrida thus questions—in Saussurean terms but more pressingly—the existence of any a priori signified (*Grammatology* 46–51; see also *Positions* 19–20).

Derrida's complaint about the fixed components of the Saussurean sign works similarly. Saussure, Derrida notes, posits an indivisible bond among graph (since it is entirely dependent on the phonetic system), phoneme, and a concept or signified. Here Saussure's interchangeable treatment of "phoneme" and "word" produces the mistake. Once more Saussure envisions no slippage; he assumes instead absolute correspondence among word divisions, phonic units, and concepts. The monolithic unity of the "word" is thus paradoxically similar to the problem of the hard-and-fast distinction between signifier and signified (*Grammatology* 21–22, 31–32). Both are attempts to stop the play of difference—that is, to fix reference and meaning—and to preserve objects in the world outside the system. One hardly need elaborate the famous terms in which Derrida casts his solution—the neologism "différance," which captures two senses of the French verb *différer* ("to differ" and "to defer"), and "trace," the differential principle that resists both abstraction and substance ("Differance" 136–37; *Positions*

24–30; *Grammatology* 46–47, 53–55). Derrida thus effectively rewrites Saussure's key concepts.

Now critics have occasionally complained that Derrida is too quick to link Saussure to what he terms "classical" sign theory, which in any case, they claim, he characterizes as too consistently naive.[8] But again Derrida addresses an important problem, and this time a more textually obvious and more generally discussed one. Specifically, notice that the *Course* conflicts between its negative definition of language—a system of elements defined by difference—and its account of value. The notion "value" is in fact meant to follow from the principle of difference. French *mouton* and English *sheep* have the same signification, Saussure remarks, but not the same value, since in English *sheep* contrasts to *mutton*, whereas French contains no such second term (*Course* 115–16). Value, then, is a systemwide notion; *sheep* and *mouton* have different values arising from their relation to other elements, from their exchange and identification functions in the system (115).[9] Saussure gives other examples—the value of the French plural as opposed to the plural of Sanskrit, which distinguishes singular, dual, and plural (116). Although Derrida focuses on Saussure's account of signs, the passages on value in effect elaborate the problem. For reading from a Derridean perspective, such examples sometimes revert to nomenclaturism; and they distinguish between (something like) meaning and reference in such a way as to assume a world before language.[10] Saussure clearly anchors "sheep" and *mouton*, that is, in a nonlinguistic reality, even though he mitigates this impulse in the succeeding grammatical example. Thus the demonstration of how value works backfires against the motivating notion of difference.

One issue here is that Saussure attempts two things at once. His "difference" theme is a pronouncement on the nature of language, read

---

[8] For example, Newton Garver, 670–71, and Umberto Eco, *Semiotics* 23–26, argue that Derrida misplaces critical energy here. For comments on Derrida's conception of philosophical history, see Garver; and Richard Rorty, "Derrida."

[9] Saussure also relates "difference" to "identity"; perceiving a distinction between one linguistic element and another involves construing an identity between different realizations of that element. The classic example is phonetically distinct realizations of a single phoneme. See *Course* 107–11, 114–15.

[10] "Nomenclaturism" is Holdcroft's handy characterization; see 51, 140–43, for discussion. Harris insightfully elaborates the same problem from a slightly different perspective. He analyzes Saussure's account of value as involving a conflict between two metaphors illustrative of irreconcilable tensions in the *Course*. One metaphor imagines the two amorphous planes of thought and sound, mutually (and somewhat mysteriously) defining one another in a moment of contact; the other (economic) metaphor compares linguistic to monetary systems, implying a correlation between two independently existing systems (see 118–23).

as a radical statement on the reality-constituting function of *langue*; yet this discussion Saussure also applies as a concrete theory of word meaning. So while Derrida rightly objects that the second project does not follow through on the implications of the first, we might also remark that, unlike Saussure, Derrida has no interest in the practical problem of a developing semantic theory. This is an interesting contrast to Saussure's linguistic critics, who bypass the general philosophical project and ask instead whether Saussure's principle of negatively defined difference indeed applies to word-level semantics. As Holdcroft in particular notes, Saussure never demonstrates that word meaning is so created; semantic oppositions presuppose some measure of similarity ("man" versus "woman"), he notes, and word meanings additionally require positive characterizations that do not ("in any natural sense") involve oppositions (129; see also Pavel, *Feud* 72). Once again it pays to recall that Saussure works on historical phonology, for the negativity principle works largely from that perspective; phonemes one indeed defines oppositionally, and Saussure has simply developed a semantics through that fact.[11] Statements that hold for language at one level, however, do not necessarily work at another: we have already witnessed the syntactic limitations of Saussure's approach. In this case, general positions on the nature of language and meaning fail to translate readily into specific and relevant analytical tools. But I might also note that here Derrida echoes Saussure. While he locates Saussure's problematic confusion of phoneme and word, Derrida's analogous account is metaphorically phonological, and it shares the assumption that one locates both semantic arguments and metaphysical questions at the level of "sign."

Derrida finally associates Saussure's logocentrism, his conception of signs or words as unambiguously linked to objects in the world, with Saussure's phonocentrism, his wish to cast spoken language as the natural and transparent expression of inner consciousness. Saussure's position on writing and on signification, then, is not simply mistaken; it betrays a suppressed but real nostalgia that undercuts his initial project, a desire for a fully and simply perceived object, either empirical or ideal (see *Grammatology* 40). According to Derrida, Saussure must believe there is some natural connection "between phonic signifiers and their signifieds *in general*," and it is only within this larger context that the arbitrary relationship between *particular* sound images and

[11] There are issues here I naturally bypass: the *Course* preceded the distinctive feature conception of the phoneme, and there are, of course, nonbinary phonetic facts of interest. But the point is that sound yields to the negative principle ([p] as perceivable because it is not [b]) in ways that word meaning does not.

concepts obtains (44). Thus Saussure, in Derrida's account, ultimately stands within the philosophical tradition of a metaphysics that equates "voice" with "presence," a position that motivates Saussure's metaphors of exclusion—sound as internal and natural to language, writing as debased and fallen (35). Speech, however, consciousness metaphorized, escapes analysis and control; in Derrida's (recast) Saussurean terms, language is prior to individuals and acts, and writers and speakers fail to "dominate" it (158). Subjects, too, are then in some sense linguistic functions.[12]

But we might briefly reconsider the matter of Saussure's alleged metaphysics of presence. Now Derrida unquestionably locates in the *Course in General Linguistics* Saussure's suppressed resistance to his own general program, especially as it involves the confused dimensions of "natural" and "conventional"; since Derrida's analysis of the passages on writing, the problem seems no longer subtle. Clearly, too, as Derrida and others notice, Saussure's sign theory falls short of its aims. And there is the additional evidence of certain of Saussure's less-recognized intellectual preoccupations; as Jonathan Culler (on Saussure's study of anagrams) and Tzvetan Todorov (on Saussure's account of glossolalia) show, Saussure, like Jakobson, in some sense longed for transparently meaningful signification (see Culler, *Saussure*; Todorov, "Saussure's").[13] Even so, and as fascinating and important as such demonstrations are, I am not sure that the text of the *Course* is guilty in the same way, or that every instance of "sound" or "sound-image," so often rendered "voice" in Derrida's account, represents the same kind of problem; and so perhaps the accusation "phonocentric" does not

---

[12] Nancy Holland reminds Derrida's readers of his affinity to Sartre; the flux of ongoing mental states can never be present to the individual as an object of inspection, since the act of objectifying experience alters its nature (17–18). (For useful general remarks on this topic see Alan Bass xvi–xx; and Gayatri Spivak 30–36.) Deconstruction-influenced discussion often focuses on the social constructedness of individual identity, but this is not precisely the character of the argument here. For discussion of Derrida's "psychological nominalism" (Rorty's term), see Rorty, "Philosophy/Writing" 150–54; and Walter Benn Michaels.

[13] As Todorov's study illustrates, Saussure's wish for unmediated signification is idiosyncratic; he resists in his study of glossolalia the possibility of unconscious symbolism ("Saussure's" 259–70). Culler examines several motivations for Saussure's study of anagrams, but he decides that Saussure did not find the practice self-expressive, nor did it form a critique of the sign or suggest interpretive freedom from linguistic constraint (*Saussure* 124). As Julia Kristeva notes, the limitation of any sociological and psychological interaction with linguistics is characteristically the matter of unconscious symbolism, which essentially remains outside the limits of linguistic study (see "Speaking"). Saussure's problems here are not surprising.

precisely characterize either the vexed issue of what Saussure calls "natural" or his complex position on the significance of conventionally shaped sound.

Some of the issues here are essentially those that pertain to Jakobson's linguistics, developed in an earlier chapter as a distinction between "phonocentrism" and "phonologism." That is, from the perspective of literary discussion, all reference to sound has come to seem problematic since Derrida (see Norris, *Derrida* 69). But once again an interest in phonological issues is not inevitably premised on the association of sound and individual consciousness. In Saussure's case as opposed to Jakobson's, however, the biological foundations of the conception of sound as natural are less in evidence. Certainly biological concerns are implicit in the notion *faculté de langage*, the general sign-making ability that generates the acquisition of a particular *langue* (see *Course* 10). While Saussure obviously did not have access to much of what is now known about biological constraints on perception and language acquisition, some facts about language learning would have been obvious, simply that sound is the usual form *langue* embodies, shaped and constrained, as Saussure notes, by physiology (8, 38–41). This is not to say that even this general picture is entirely clear in the *Course*. As Holdcroft notes, though Saussure announces *faculté de langage* as a primary notion, he fails to elaborate it (42–43). And Harris points out that Saussure's phonetic theory contains the surprisingly un-Saussurean notion of a fixed and universal phonetic repertoire from which languages arbitrarily select. Apparently such a scheme follows for Saussure from the physical facts of human articulation and acoustic perception, but it effectively collapses purely acoustic and cultural factors, since the account does not distinguish phonetic constraints from culturally conditioned choices (see 46–51).[14] Yet despite such confu-

---

[14] Harris discusses in detail Saussure's prephonemic theory (in the current sense of the term "phoneme"), in which universal and natural sound units emerge from the undifferentiated dimension of sound as a result of "the conjoint discriminations provided by the articulatory and auditory processes of speech" (Harris 47). Of course once again I do not claim that an interest in the biological aspects of sound production and perception necessarily precludes another agenda; I only begin to sort out Saussurean senses of "natural."

Saussure differs from Jakobson here in a number of respects, principally in a conception of (biological) naturalness based on auditory and articulatory apparatus as opposed to a more limited innate language-learning ability that affects perception. Saussure's approach to phonology (*Course* 38–64) thus sometimes does not seem to allow for the interaction of biology and culture which Jakobson's does (see Harris 46–51 for discussion), but note that some passages contradict by depicting alternative analyses for the same stream of sound (*Course* 104–5).

sions, these passages in the *Course* focus on the universality of both acoustic units and physiological equipment, not on a sonorously awakened perception of self.

Indeed, unlike Jakobson, who ultimately fuses the universal-biological and personally experienced aesthetic dimensions of sound, Saussure is difficult to credit with any interest in individual speakers. The *Course* outlines a particular speech exchange, of course, but the attempt founders on a phonologized conception of meaning; meanings for (passive) hearers are automatic, reflexively processed versions of meanings for speakers. Such a scheme fails precisely because it does *not* imagine conscious—or meaningfully unconscious—varied, individual interpretive effort.[15] The central concept *langue*, in contrast to the "competence" of generative grammar, is a thoroughly generalized notion, as Saussure says, complete only in the collective, not within individual speakers (*Course* 19).[16] And Saussure's account of historical change does not give much to individual linguistic effort; as he says, conscious arguments for linguistic change are futile in view of linguistic arbitrariness, since no form is superior to another (73–74; see also 98). Of course one might maintain even so that Saussure sets up a general equation between sound and consciousness, a possible sense of the amorphous plane of thought before language (see 112); but such a reading for the *Course* simply works best when one already assumes it. For Saussure's phonologism foregrounds automatic, unconscious linguistic behavior, but persistently it is the processing either of semantically detached phonological units or of system-established word meanings; this is not Jakobson's unconscious linguistic experience, an encounter with self or world.[17]

[15] That Saussure has no developed conception of collective knowledge or collective action is not a counterargument, for without such a theory he feels no pressure to negotiate between individual and collective linguistic experience.

[16] Contrast Saussure's *langue*, "the sum of word-images stored in the minds of all individuals" (*Course* 13), and Chomsky's (early) "competence," knowledge more or less complete within the individual (*Aspects* 3–5). Although Saussure sometimes invents formulations close to Chomsky's (contrast *Course* 13 with *Course* 19), in several passages Saussure's is a more collective notion, complete only in the linguistic community. Norman Holland develops other contrasts between Saussure and Chomsky, though some of these perhaps underestimate Saussure's psychologism (see chap. 20).

[17] It is perhaps even stretching things to say that Saussure much discusses linguistic behavior in the usual sense, except in the section on diachronic linguistics, for his obvious focus is the collective fund of linguistic knowledge, as opposed to linguistic actions and experiences. Once again, however, this does not mean that Saussure's conception of world-word relations is consistent. As we will see, I am not the first to question the putative link between sound and consciousness in the *Course*. Holdcroft finds the thesis difficult to credit since Saussure did not believe the importance of sound would be obvious in a manuscript culture (40). See also Porter, who doubts the possibility of a subject prior to

I would rather locate Saussure's defensive position on the natural-ness of sound in a certain romance of the collective linguistic experi-ence, a position that involves both his suspicion of institutionalized authority (as represented by print culture) and his unwillingness to as-cribe agency to linguistic change. While Saussure describes a variety of forces for linguistic change he terms normal and (in some cases) natu-ral—political upheaval, language contact, and the like—he particularly focuses on the phonological processes he characterizes as internal and more clearly natural, acoustically conditioned change (*Course* 144–45, 150–51).[18] (An example is a sound that changes when it falls between vowels; the sound is thus "conditioned" by its [sound] environment.)[19] These processes Saussure casts in natural metaphors; they direct an evolution either "calm" or "torrential" (140), and they develop sporad-ically even in situations of political and social stablity (150–51). The standard written language, says Saussure, retards this natural and inev-itable evolution, introducing an artificial linguistic stasis; and it ob-scures for the linguist the nature and direction of change (140, 150).[20]

Acoustic processes are regular, but their sources for Saussure remain uncertain (*Course* 147).[21] Saussure rejects uninformed theories of lan-guage difference—which attribute phonological variety to climate or ethnicity. But he seriously considers that phonological change may de-rive from a principle of least effort (in pronunciation) or from the diffu-sion of errors in child language development, though such explana-tions—given the available contradictory evidence—are necessarily partial (147–51).[22] Saussure thus centers naturalness on "free," sponta-

---

the Saussurean sytem (893). Although he faults the rigid binarism of the Saussurean sign, Peter Steiner similarly does not associate it with an individual consciousness ("Defense" 422).

[18] The (apparent) confusion here is just that Saussure terms institutional, geographic, and political forces external to the inner workings of language early in the *Course*; these impinge on language and form it but are not part of language itself (20–23). In his discus-sion of diachronic linguistics, however, Saussure casts such forces as part of normal, in some sense natural, diachronic development (150–51), although this hypothesis in itself does not serve to make history part of *langue*.

[19] A familiar synchronic example of acoustically conditioned change is the alternation between "write" and "writer," "shut" and "shutter" in American English; the [t] sound becomes [D] (called a "flap") between two vowels, providing the second vowel is in an unstressed syllable.

[20] Saussure's remarks here echo his earlier suspicion of grammarians' categories; his fear again is that these may not reflect realities for speakers (*Course* 167).

[21] Obviously Saussure was working in the context of rudimentary information on acous-tic processes.

[22] A law of least effort cannot explain all linguistic change, Saussure notes, simply be-cause phonological changes develop sometimes in one direction, sometimes in another (148).

neously developing collective pronunciation; the direction of change is largely unpredictable, the linguistic choices unmonitored and unconscious (147–53). This organic conception of linguistic change explains both Saussure's exclusion of "wrongly" permuted sound (in addition to writing) and his doubts about all planned and legislated linguistic change. Although Saussure pictures idiosyncratic (individual) and institutional forces as inevitable, they clearly remain outside the realm of *langue* (*Course* 19); in contrast, the phonological laws of historical phonology are more ambiguously both inside and outside the system. The chart relating *langue* to *parole* and synchrony to diachrony, for example, suggests that diachronic change is part of the study of *langue*, despite contradictory pronouncements elsewhere (*Course* 98; cf. 20–23).[23] It seems the lawlike regularities of diachrony would remain at the heart of the shared linguistic system, could Saussure but separate natural from "unnatural" historical forces.

In his analysis of the *Course in General Linguistics*, Attridge also claims that Derrida mistakes Saussure's position, which is only partly a response to the question of writing. Attridge points especially to Saussure's discussion of folk etymology, for which Saussure assumes the same tone; ersatz word history, like print-shaped pronunciation, awakens Saussure's ire, superficially because it is naive and just plain wrong. Now Attridge's focus is Saussure's opposition between the synchronic and diachronic dimensions of language, and he has aready defended Saussure against the accusation that he lacks interest in history, when both the *Course* and Saussure's career suggest quite otherwise ("Language" 90–98). But Saussure's take on folk etymology, Attridge claims, betrays a subtler problem. Whereas Saussure wishes only to exclude simplistic approaches to linguistic history—the usual appeal to etymology that fails to explain the present and relational meaning of a term—he finally dismisses popularly shared and invented (or even academic) history—that is, narrative—which is also a part of synchronic linguistic reality (116–18). Thus Saussure's failing is a broader sense that it is unnatural for history—a history invented—to leak into and shape the present (117). Seen in this perspective, print pronunciation is problematic because it represents a kind of etymological folk narrative, a misapprehended record of pronunciation (116).

Such a reading of the *Course in General Linguistics* is not at all incompatible with the argument here; in fact it, too, moves the focus of interest from the problem of sound per se to Saussure's investment

[23] The chart in question (*Course* 98) pictures "language" and "speaking" as the two aspects of human speech and, surprisingly, "synchrony" and "diachrony" as the two branches of "language" (*langue*).

in peculiar forms of "naturalness." The account raises a problem, however, since it highlights Saussure's rejection of folk etymology, essentially of group-based, noninstitutionalized accounts of linguistic change, when I have cast Saussure as romanticizing unconscious collective speech behavior at the expense of print-backed authority. Saussure is not without contradiction here, but I think that for him folk etymology is imitatively intellectual; so his emphasis is not so much on its "folk" origins as on etymological practice, on bad linguistics. Thus Saussure gets caught between his interest in synchronic linguistic reality—whatever its source—and his obvious investment in academic scholarship.

But I prefer to center Saussure's discomfort on the general issue of agency as opposed to history per se, hence narrative. This is admittedly a minor quibble, especially since notions of history and agency so closely relate, but I wish at least to suggest complications. To begin with, I am not sure one can easily treat print pronunciation as a species of narrative; no obvious story presents itself here, only a printed, authoritative alternative pronunciation. There is also the evidence of Saussure's approving remarks on analogy, the diffusion of one paradigmatic sound alternation by (a kind of false or contrued) analogy to other sets in the system. (Latin *honos: honosem* becoming the phonetically created *honos: honorem*, then becoming *honor: honorem* on grammatical analogy with *orator: oratorem*.)[24] As Attridge remarks, analogy and folk etymology are essentially similar processes, depending as they do on invented linguistic connections. Since the obvious distinction is that analogy is synchronic, folk etymology apparently diachronic, Saussure must reject folk etymology because he remains uneasy with the synchronic effects of history ("Language" 116).[25] But Saussure also contends that analogy is systematic, affecting whole classes of words, whereas folk etymology remains idiosyncratic (174, 178). Changes introduced by analogy, says Saussure, start from an awareness of grammatical patterning but soon operate as uncon-

[24] The creation of Latin *honor* is Saussure's main example. The "diversifying action" of a phonetic change (rhotacization of [s] between vowels) first changed the contrast *honos: honosem* to *honos: honorem*. But this alternation seemed at odds with the existing pattern *orator: oratorem*; so an analogy on this set created the new form *honor*, which eventually replaced *honos*, a change that must now be characterized as grammatically motivated, since phonetic conditions do not predict it. See *Course* 161–64. Saussure follows neogrammarian wisdom on historical change: phonological processes introduce changes, which are spread and adjusted by grammatical factors.

[25] Actually, as Harris points out, analogy also confounds the distinction between synchrony and diachrony; that is, it suggests an evolutionary process at the heart of the system (150).

sciously meaningful units (165). Analogy belongs to collective experience rather than to the suspect decisions of grammarians (165, 167). And the grammatical forms analogy creates are triggered by an ongoing phonological change that the analogy spreads rather than inhibits (169). Analogy, Saussure concludes, is a lively and creative source of language evolution (170–71), but etymology is ahistorical, inasmuch as it works on forms that never did exist (175). Once again we must confront Saussure's sense that only unconscious linguistic behavior is natural, that language (especially in its phonological laws) has its own life, independent of human choice and direction.

Yet even should such speculations redeem Saussure from a presumed association of sound and consciousness, they fail to save him from Derrida's point about ideal objects; for Saussure, Derrida says, ultimately locates "source" and "presence" in the apparatus of the abstract linguistic system itself. Thus Derrida's critique ends as it began—on the general problem of empirical projects. It complains of the persistent failure of linguistics, a discipline that would explore language and yet remains a "telling example" of a "logocentric metaphysics," a science that does not pause to question the assumed transparency of the language in which it fashions its own arguments (*Grammatology* 46). Linguistics is, after all, a semantics, Derrida says, which modern linguists found on a "signified thinkable and possible outside of all signifiers," with the "full presence of an intuitive consciousness" (73).

DERRIDA ON LINGUISTICS

As such remarks illustrate, Derrida intends his analysis of Saussure, whose work he descibes as "the base of all the modern theories" ("Linguistic" 148), to apply to linguistic study in general; and in *Of Grammatology* he extends and elaborates the original critique with surprising care and energy. I say "surprising" because this task involves him in something of a paradox. That is, Derrida's final pronouncement on Saussure requires that he reject all empirical projects; yet his expanded confrontation with linguistics involves him in linguistic controversies that his own anti-empiricism would seem to deny him. The Derrida everyone cites and remembers is the Derrida who locates in Saussure a problem paradigmatic for linguistic study: Saussure's phonocentrism is a species of empirical idealism. But the other Derrida is considerably enmeshed in linguistic debate and struggles with its specific terms in passages that have none of the flavor of the nonengagement to which I alluded earlier. It is this second Derrida, temporarily and ambivalently engaged with general problems of linguistic theory, whom I wish briefly to consider here.

But I might pause at the outset to ask, given the mismatch of projects, how possible a conversation between linguistics and deconstruction may be. In this case, I believe there is no lack of willingness to connect, but the barriers are considerable. Saussure's *Course in General Linguistics* does not entirely support Derrida's concerns, in the simple sense that its own focus is largely elsewhere; neither can Derrida's phenomenological reading of the linguistic project fully connect with its terms. Specifically, Saussurean linguistics does not represent, as Derrida would have it, anything like a full-fledged semantic theory; and its rudimentary semantics is certainly not the source of its influence on succeeding linguistic theory. I am particularly impressed with Jay's attempts to politicize Saussure's discussion of value, hence Derrida's critique, but we learn here—more than is usual—from Jay through Saussure rather than from Saussure. As Paul de Man remarks, the confusion of natural and linguistic signs is an ideological issue, which linguistic study since Saussure clarifies ("Resistance" 11); but we cannot closely explicate Saussure much more in this direction, simply because his account of semantic issues is largely about matters phonological. That it is, in turn complicates Derrida's equation of phonologism and logocentrism. For it is not so much that phonologism masks a faulty metaphysics as that phonological arguments inadequately model a semantics capable of sustaining metaphysical speculation. To cite an example, the problem of Saussure's fixed relation between signifier and signified is somewhat moot, given the theory's phonologism in my sense, given its exclusion of syntax, not to mention the facts of *parole*. Such problems, of course, interact with Derrida's own limitations on linguistic projects (in the narrow sense of "linguistics"). Derrida, that is, reads Saussure through Husserl, with the result that he sometimes locates metaphysical issues in language meant to address purely linguistic concerns.[26]

Given these initial problems, the movement of Derrida's arguments on linguistic theory in *Of Grammatology* will be of particular interest in this account, not just because, as always, his juxtaposition of terms is as important as any conclusions he states about them. Here, to draw on Pavel's comments, Derrida alternates between philosophically speculative and empirical modes of argument (54); yet this process is not simply stylistic but reflects these particular difficulties of his response

---

[26] This complaint is, of course, not new. For discussion see Garver; Nancy Holland; Rorty, "Derrida"; Pavel, *Feud* 54.

to linguistics. One set of objections to linguistic phonologism is an extension of Saussure's own theory lodged from inside the discipline; the other is an ambivalent dismissal of empirical projects. And it is not so entirely clear as one might suppose which arguments prevail.

I begin here with what Derrida has to say about the materiality of linguistic signs, since it is quite clear that this topic continues to focus his general response to linguistics. As Derrida's coauthor remarks, the central mistake linguistic study makes is to privilege the substance of expression, for this theoretical decision undermines the founding principle of "difference" (Bennington and Derrida 33). Such, of course, is already the argument in *Of Grammatology*. Here Derrida reiterates Saussure's own arguments for the "reduction of phonic matter" (53). "The linguistic signifier," in Saussure's words, "is not [in essence] phonic. . . . The idea or phonic substance that a sign contains is of less importance than the other signs that surround it" (Derrida quoting Saussure 53; Derrida's interpolation). In fact Derrida recognizes that were Saussure not to exclude from the language system the phonic substance he describes elsewhere as necessary and natural, his distinction between *langue* and *parole* would find no basis (53). That is, the study of *langue* observes only the differences and oppositions functional for that language, whereas the province of *parole* includes accidental and random (including acoustic) elements. Thus the study of actualized sound, "phonology," as Saussure terms it, as part of *parole*, becomes an "auxiliary discipline" (Derrida quoting Saussure 53).[27]

It is from this perspective that Derrida launches his more specific critique of linguistic study, first by focusing on Roman Jakobson and Morris Halle's distinctive-feature phonology. Jakobson and Halle are natural targets inasmuch as *Fundamentals of Language* is a landmark text in the history of phonological study, but they are idiosyncratic objects in the sense that they attempt in this book only an analysis of the English sound system, of the features that make up English-language phonemes. Since phonemic distinctions (/b/ versus /p/) do not directly signify but only contribute to higher-level meaning, Jakobson and Halle set aside (in Jakobson's case for other projects) problems of signification in Derrida's sense. Perhaps from Derrida's perspective this

---

[27] There is some confusion here over the terms "phonetics" and "phonology." In their current senses, the first term refers to the study of acoustics or actual sound, the study of sound produced. The second denotes phonemic analysis, in some sense sound perceived, the study of sound units operational in a language (productions of /p/ may vary, but nondistinct acoustic variations—aspirated [pʰ] or unaspirated [p]—do not affect interpretation as a relevant linguistic unit). Now Saussure reverses these terms, so that Jakobson and Halle's "phonology" is not at all what Saussure means by that term. It is unclear how much this difference in terminology affects Derrida's analysis.

itself constitutes a problem, but Jakobson and Halle simply and plainly have other interests—specifically curiosity about the makeup of sound units in a language, ultimately about how native speakers can process and decode them. Since Derrida reads Jakobson and Halle's phonological theory as a semiotic one, he in effect asks an account of the English-language sound system to reject reference to acoustic phenomena. In any case, Derrida cites Saussure in order to take the linguists to task for not going "beyond" the usual "phonologism" of linguistic science (53); in so doing he invests distinctive phonological features with the same semantic import Saussure attaches to signs. Jakobson and Halle, Derrida notes, declare the "inseparability of matter and form" (55); for them the "sonorous substance" must be taken into account "at every step of the analysis" and so cannot be practically excluded from the study of phonology (Derrida quoting Jakobson and Halle 54). Further, they repeat Saussure's objections to writing as an independent sign system; they thus fail to outline the substance-free abstract systems underlying both writing and speech (54).

Continuing to engage local linguistic disputes, Derrida declares his preference on these points for the glossematics of Louis Hjelmslev.[28] Hjelmslev, as Pavel notes, is an unrepresentative selection for linguistic study (*Feud* 54), and I might add that "glossematics" was not a historically productive approach to phonological issues. To be fair, however, Hjelmslev does share Derrida's interest in a broader semiotic account, and he is thus a more likely object of analysis. Hjelmslev's "glossemes," Derrida notes, exclude both "the substance of expression" (phone or graph) and "the substance of content" (meaning); such units of pure "linguistic function," of "formal difference" as opposed to "phonic difference," accord more faithfully to the differential principle of language (57). Hjelmslev's approach permits study of graphic as well as verbal systems (58); and its emphasis on the "play of form" allows the theory to extend also into the domain of literature (59). Such advantages, Derrida concludes, are of more than "theoretical" interest (56).

But questions about the origin of such theoretical systems soon arise, and Derrida reevaluates these projects from that perspective. Since linear or temporal models for Derrida would imply a suspect foundation, a stable source of meaning, he in some sense approves the distinctive-feature approach. That is, like Jakobson, he dismisses the temporal, "physically continuous" aspect of oral speech as central to phonological study (69). Since linguistic analysis reduces the sound stream to phonemes and phonemes to distinctive features, Jakobson

---

[28] See Hjelmslev, *Prolegomena to a Theory of Language.*

finds in language a "manifestly granular structure" not much different from the discrete bundles of structures found in the written word (Derrida quoting Jakobson 69). Thus Derrida retains some hope for a linguistics in this context; as he explains, phonology must "renounce not itself, phonology, but rather phonologism" (69). Here Jakobson and Halle, I might remark, benefit rather too easily, for the language of distinctive-feature phonology—a "granular" structure of "concatenations" (Jakobson's term) and cross-oppositions—would seem to avoid the strict one-to-one graph-phoneme-concept association Derrida also resists. It does so, but by default: Jakobson and Halle have (necessarily, at the level of sound) deferred questions about the overall shape of meaningful speech events. On the other hand, such miscommunications highlight a competing (linguistic) perspective on the relation of oral and written speech, which Derrida echoes in his remarks on authorial death—a contrast between the monumentality of writing and the elusiveness of the spoken word (see "Signature" 7–8; Bennington and Derrida 45).

Because the moments Derrida cites in Hjelmslev's work are semiotic rather than phonological in focus, Hjelmslev cannot as easily as Jakobson and Halle defer questions about ideal form. So it is through this account that Derrida once again repeats the movement from "writing" to "arche-writing" which informs his analysis of Saussure. Whatever theoretical "progress" Hjelmslev may represent (61), his abstract objects are objects nevertheless. Derrida cites two objections, one specific and internal, one general and external. First, though Hjelmslev identifies "original and irreducible" "form[s] of expression," these forms refer to graphic (or, presumably, phonic) substance in a "very determined" manner (60); in effect, the underlying substance-free form is an object itself. Second, one must finally ask of any such theory "the question of the transcendental origin of the system" (61). No closed (that is to say, scientific) theory may model "difference," meaning deferred, since meaning ultimately derives from the system as a whole (61, 68). Once again only "trace" and "différance" successfully resist such closure. As Derrida earlier comments, the goal is not, as in Hjelmslev's model, to describe "play in the world"; rather one must think through "the game of the world" (50). Of course, this theoretical game the linguist cannot win, whether the specific project is phonological or semantic, for accounts of interpretive regularity necessarily involve abstract identities.

Derrida is not indifferent to this problem, but in many moments it only demonstrates to him the general condition of science: it cannot locate its objects from a point outside language; yet it requires descriptive objects. Such arguments naturally apply to Jakobson and Halle's distinctive feature analysis, since binary oppositions imply the presence of opposing substances. Here the analysis might end, but Derrida, more sympathetic to the empirical program than one might guess, begins to press the Saussurean opposition of form and substance. In an important but unnoticed deconstructive movement he finally dismantles the source of the original critique.

Science, Derrida notes, "can only describe the *work* and the *fact* of differance" (63). Any expression or perception of "difference," that is, requires some material or substance. And "to keep sonority on the side of the sensible and contingent signifier," to keep it distinct from the difference between substances or becoming-substances, is "strictly speaking impossible, since formal identities, isolated within a sensible mass are already idealities that are not purely sensible" (29). Form and substance are inseparable, in other words; since form in language locates within that otherwise undifferentiated mass of sensible material (the sound stream), that substance is no longer mere substance but form. Likewise form cannot be substance free, since material expression is prerequisite to the perception of form. Thus develops a central paradox. Phonology's conflation of matter and form, its focus on sonorous substance at the expense of "difference," is first a point of evaluation between one account and another, then the discipline's final failure. Yet it follows from "difference" itself that the confusion of matter and form is a necessary mistake, if indeed it is one. After all, the form-substance opposition is also subject to deconstruction. If the condition of science is the fusion of form and substance, then one might want to reject scientific programs in general, but one cannot at the same time fault phonology for a local and particular analysis of phonic material.

The argument thus comes momentarily to rest on the general problem of scientific abstraction. Although he sometimes campaigns against a particular view of phonology from within its own framework, the (empirical) search for a transcendental signified remains Derrida's firm objection to linguistics. Approval may temporarily focus on a linguistic account's oppositional scheme, read as a semantics, but the system of analysis is itself finally a concrete object of study. As Derrida says, there is never a science of "nonorigin" (63); and as his coauthor reiterates, only "difference" preserves an ideality that is not material—"sensible" (Bennington and Derrida 32–33). This position does not entirely explain Derrida's lengthy discussions of phonocentrism in modern linguistics, however, since its entanglement of substance and form seems inevitable from his arguments elsewhere.

Thus to anchor the charge of ideality, inasmuch as its key terms to some extent dissolve, Derrida turns to press a second objection, here to linguistic psychologism. To disengage form from substance, Derrida contends, one must pose the question of the origin of form, and this move implies a presence, a place of perception from which to delineate forms within the sensible mass. The linguistic model that resists objectively defined elements nevertheless locates and stabilizes signs in a further kind of ideal object, the mind of the perceiver (see 40). The analysis that follows extends his earlier account of "voice" in Saussure. Once more, however, Derrida is considerably ambivalent about the scope of the original critique.

Returning to the distinction Saussure institutes between sound in an objective, purely acoustic sense (its phonetic realization) and the "sound-image," "psychic image," or "psychic imprint of the sound" (its status as a phoneme), Derrida considers under what conditions such mentalist terms could be preserved (Derrida quoting Saussure 63). First, the linguistics must distinguish between the psychic image (Derrida is not happy with this term) and ordinary sound, essentially as Saussure suggests: the sound-image is abstract, immaterial, "not the *sound* heard but the being-heard of the sound" (Derrida's remarks 63). Second, the theory must specify that psychic images designate neither external nor "natural," "internal" realities (64). Further, sound-images must not derive from unified, individual subjects, in short, from a naive Western metaphysics: The "essence of the *phonè* cannot be read directly and primarily in the text of a mundane science, of a psycho-physio-phonetics" (64–65). Rather, one must think through sound-image as "trace," the "condition of all other differences," "the absolute origin of sense in general" (65).

Now linguistics can accommodate Derrida's first requirement; indeed, it is its source. The sound-image–sound (or phonology-phonetics) distinction should actually remove some of Derrida's objections to phonology's reference to phonic matter. The material in question is not sound but the "sound heard" in some potential, not actual sense, and its objects of description are at least not objects in the world. Since this definition of phonology places Jakobson and Halle's scheme—their phonologism—roughly in the same position for Derrida as Hjelmslev's glossematics, it is once more difficult to see on what internal basis Derrida rejects it. (The distinction also helps to explain why a different position on the status of writing would not affect Jakobson-Halle phonology.) The second of Derrida's criteria, too, represents an argument from within linguistic study; he in fact cites Jakobson's objections to mentalism of the sort that treats phonemes as psychic reflections of external sound (64). Derrida's final requirement is, of course, entirely problematic, given that it appears to exclude all reference to perceiving subjects, and amounts to rejection of even the narrow sort of reference to perception that he had seemed about to accept. To speak of the "absolute origin of sense" is to speak of "non-origin" (65), Derrida notes, since the source of sense, "difference," has no location; it exists beyond individuals and individual perception. That is, because phonemes for Derrida are on a par with meaning-bearing signs, representation of shared phonemic distinctions seems to derive from (theoretically) conscious subjects in full possession of linguistic intent. Once again the deconstructive aim is to transform the sound-image from within and to remove all suggestion of a psychology or of actual perception. But the result is a proscription of any analysis at the level of sound.

If Derrida acknowledges that Jakobson anticipates his wish to block a linguistic psychologism unnecessary for an investigation of phonic difference, one might ask why the discussion arrives here. The analysis, for which Saussure serves as the master pattern, opens up the interesting matter of Saussure's psychologism without considering in any detail whether it is of the sort described, whether it assumes speakers' immediate intuitive consciousness. Certainly Saussure's chapters on writing and linguistic change founder on competing conceptions of "naturalness." Nevertheless, his accounts of the speech exchange and of analytical procedure actually suffer from a curtailed, rather than overwrought, psychologism. And if Saussurean psychology is undeveloped and inconsistent, it is not clear that it so "infects" the balance of the *Course in General Linguistics*. My point is that this is an open matter. In fact, I think that Saussure's extreme distrust of abstract categories—which Derrida shares—in itself constitutes a kind of suspect psychologism. The focus in *Of Grammatology* on a consistent tradition, a metaphysics of presence, blunts its statements on the *Course*. "Sound-image" is invariable, verifiable, and therefore a false notion (64); "trace," in contrast, is neither an "ideal" nor a "real" object (65). In short, the engagement with Saussure never develops, for Derrida rejects empirical projects in advance.

We may variously explain the missed interaction, for the ground of linguistic argument is in some sense both too distant and too close to Derrida's concerns to work as it might. Derrida is initially removed from linguistic theory to the extent that his general critique of empiricism prevents his engaging its specific terms. As commentators have sometimes complained, the demands of philosophy are perhaps too distinct from the concerns of science. Now this is not to say that Derrida's pronouncements on science are unmixed. On the one hand, he has undeniably contributed, if indirectly, to a general vilification of science guaranteed to appeal to readers in the humanities.[29] On the other hand, Derrida himself regularly declares that empirical abstraction is necessary, inasmuch as it exposes the limits of formalisms, that a metaphysics of presence in this sense is "good." Clearly he expects empirical projects to go forward. I may also add to these remarks the further complication of the term "science," which for Derrida sometimes means empiricism in general, sometimes linguistics, and sometimes systematic philosophizing as well.[30]

Derrida is also contrastingly enmeshed in Saussurean arguments in terms of his general debt to European structuralism. That is, his treatment of "self" derives from as much as it contrasts with Saussure. Further, as Rorty complains, Derrida shares Saussure's penchant for abstract objects, and it is not always clear that terms such as "différance" and "trace" satisfactorily resist Derrida's own objections to ideal form ("Two Meanings" 208).[31] Since Derrida explicitly rewrites Saussure, many of his own metaphors are naturally in some sense Saussurean; that is, the revised metaphors are likewise paradigmatic and phonological. Syntagmatic tropes suggest to Derrida stable origins, a suspect model of communication; thus his terms are not much invested in the temporality of speech. Most important from the perspective of this account, Derrida's linguistics is largely Saussure's. Specifically, he fails to distinguish phonological from semiotic projects precisely because he works in the Saussurean tradition that conflates them.[32] A Derridean account of meaning therefore consistently involves a single-level system, with signs analogous to phonemes.[33]

While he apparently engages linguistic phonologism, then, Derrida

[29] Jonathan Culler notes this problem early on in remarks that emphasize the role of deconstruction in baring the aims of science. See "Structuralism." For more elaborated remarks on structuralist and deconstructionist attitudes toward science, see Pavel, *Feud* 6–7, 54, 71.

[30] On the necessity of science, formalisms, a "metaphysics of presence," see Derrida's interview, "Some Questions" 252–53, 257, 260–61. The position is elaborated in Bennington and Derrida 61–62. On the notion "science," see, for example, Derrida on Husserl, *Speech* 10, 15, 54–55.

[31] Rorty's argument is that one cannot offer transcendental solutions when one is claiming that the possibilities of recontextualization are limitless.

[32] As Nigel Fabb remarks, nonlinguists have historically been attracted to the speculative moments in Saussure, but linguists have attended to the more concrete suggestions for synchronic analysis ("Saussure" 60). Here Derrida reads Saussure's phonology through his sign theory.

[33] Derrida's comments on the critic Jean Rousset highlight his greater resistance to literary, as opposed to linguistic, structuralism ("Force"). Spatial metaphors inadequately capture linguistic dynamism and instead impose a static textual unity (11). The unity the structuralist critic finds is rather the structure of his own model (17).

launches his main attack from without. Linguistics participates in a metaphysics of presence, assumes independently existing objects (even if abstractions) and subjects (even if cast collectively). Derrida's elegant account of "conventional" and "natural" in Saussure's chapter on writing, along with his critique of Sausssurean sign theory, are his most effective lines. He is less convincing when he saves phonology from "phonologism," for the analysis here pertains more to the inevitabilities of empirical projects than to the association of voice with nature and self-presence which Derrida finds in Rousseau. And this problem complicates any claim that deconstruction and linguistics actively address each other. In this sense the matter of phonologism is something of a false lead and not entirely equivalent to the latter issue: only at the more general level of a critique of Western metaphysics do the two coincide. It is here that deconstruction speaks past linguistics and linguistics past deconstruction.

DECONSTRUCTING AUSTIN

I turn now to that second moment of interdisciplinary interaction, this time with ordinary language philosophy, Derrida's reading of Austin and subsequent arguments with Searle. I should perhaps more accurately characterize these essays as documents of nonengagement, for as both Derrida and Searle remark, it is not altogether clear that the expected conversation between two philosophical traditions actually took place (Searle, "Reiterating" 37; Derrida, "Limited" 198).[34] Derrida's writing on Saussure, as I have just argued, also does not entirely engage Saussure's linguistic interests and arguments, but the gaps and mismatches between the texts of *Of Grammatology* and *Course in General Linguistics* seem to me of a more innocuous kind. That is, Saussure's linguistic program and Derrida's philosophical interests collide, occasionally intersect, with the result that Derrida reads some parts of the *Course* as participating in work more relevant to his project than it actually is. The discussion thus develops the independent interests of deconstruction, yet echoes and permutes Saussurean terms. Derrida's text is a classic of interdisciplinarity, effecting insightful critique in some moments, misreading by way of its own project in others.

[34] Derrida's general remarks on the exchange also include a critique of Searle's sense of his role as the legitimate heir of Austin's work ("Limited" 35–43); a momentary charge that Searle *did* understand the deconstruction of Austin, just evasively chose not to; and the claim that the assumptions he attacks in Austin and Searle are actually those they share with *continental* philosophers ("Limited" 35–43; "Afterword" 130–31).

Whereas Derrida's account of Austin begins in the same spirit, the ensuing exchange with Searle is a contrasting study in frustration. Of course, one anticipates that Derrida's and Searle's philosophical interests will not here converge, but one might have expected more agreement on the terms of debate, more open exploration of shared concerns.[35] Initially instead, the more the supporters of each side in the exchange talked, the more they diverged. Reed Way Dasenbrock has described the (immediate) after-discussion as Searle-bashing alternating with the occasional Derrida-bashing (8). The reasons for such events naturally depend on one's perspective: as various commentators put it, either Searle was territorial and obtuse in his "correction" of Derrida's remarks on Austin, or Derrida was irrelevant and abstruse in his response to the concrete issues Searle raised. Or perhaps the hostile tenor of the conflict was inevitable, given the contrasting histories and interests of analytic and continental philosophy (Maclean 21–22; Dasenbrock 7–8), given the ordinary language philosopher's emphasis on how communication works, up against the deconstructionist's focus on failed communication, on misunderstanding as intrinsic to language (Dasenbrock 7).

I can briefly sketch the general conditions responsible for this state of affairs. As I noted in the last chapter, literary critics have sometimes misread the projects of ordinary language philosophy, construed either as elaborations of linguistics or as comments on a broader conception of textuality. But Austin very specifically addressed semantic issues as they were then cast in the analytic tradition. This discussion, following Alfred Tarski, limited meaning to an equation with truth-value—a move that essentially restricted discussion of meaning to propositional sentences. Entering discussions that tried to address problematic utterances from this perspective ("Shut the door" or "The present king of France is bald"), Austin found these "felicitous" or "infelicitous," rather than true or false, and outlined the contextual conditions that make them so. Within this tradition, Austin was thus revolutionary. And as Stanley Cavell reminds us, Austin's more general aim was to complicate our notion of "ordinary" language, to challenge our sense of what goes without saying, and to call into question our vision of

[35] The texts of the Searle-Derrida debate are Derrida's analysis of Austin, "Signature Event Context"; Searle's response to this essay, "Reiterating the Differences"; Derrida's response to Searle, "Limited Inc a b c . . ."; Searle's review of Jonathan Culler's *On Deconstruction* (in which Culler summarizes Derrida's position), "The Word Turned Upside Down"; Searle's response to Louis Mackey's comments on this review, "An Exchange on Deconstruction"; and Derrida's remarks on the debate in the *Limited Inc* collection, "Afterword." A bibliography of commentary on the debate is in Dasenbrock, *Redrawing the Lines*.

philosophy as a privileged form of discourse (184). Outside his original context, however, many of Austin's insights seem commonplace, and especially when Searle is called upon to defend as more generally applicable concepts not meant to solve literary problems or address the issues of deconstruction. Derrida, as I am not the first to note, reads Austin outside the analytic tradition; that he does should not insulate Austin from analysis, but it does finally affect the flavor of the succeeding exchange with Searle.[36]

With this unpromising start, one would hardly expect to improve the situation with still more talk. And yet somehow the Searle-Derrida exchange has remained surprisingly productive even as a nonconversation, its controversies continuing to attract both philosophers and critics. Later commentary, represented by such collections as Dasenbrock's *Redrawing the Lines*, attempted to map out in less partisan manner the connections between kinds of philosophy and between philosophy and criticism. Dasenbrock outlines a number of positive effects of the Searle-Derrida debate for philosophers, among them a developing sense that the exchange represents something more complex than a "stark confrontation" between two traditions (8); an interest in widening the discussion to Anglo-American philosophers beyond Austin and Searle (8); and a focus on the shared concerns highlighted by recent attempts to "rewrite" philosophical history (9). Thus for Dasenbrock and others the exchange is not yet over; issues rather are "still emerging" (see Alfino 143; Dasenbrock 8–17).[37]

Now Dasenbrock wrote before the exchange between Searle and Richard Rorty began, a somewhat disheartening reenactment of many of the arguments of the original debate. In any case, I have always been less sanguine about the first debate's consequences for literary theory, as opposed to applied criticism. Dasenbrock had reason to be encouraged, for he took the discussion surrounding the Searle-Derrida debate to signal to philosophers that literary critics had replaced their former

[36] I am grateful to Wallace Martin for outlining these points as clarifying, even necessary, context. Again, see Donald Kalish for discussion of Austin's philosophical context. See also Richard Rorty's frustrated comment that while Derrida often appears to be discussing the same kinds of problems as linguists and ordinary language philosophers, his issues are decidedly different. Rorty wishes that Derrida would more explicitly acknowledge that they are. See "Derrida" 674–75.

[37] I am generally indebted in this introductory section to Dasenbrock's excellent overview of the scene, "Redrawing the Lines." Christopher Norris, "Deconstruction and 'Ordinary Language,'" for example, elaborates interesting connections between the two philosophical traditions. Dasenbrock does mitigate the optimism of this picture with some realities: analytic philosophers, he admits, take a guarded view of continental philosophy, and continental philosophers remain rather unfamiliar with work in the analytic tradition (10–11).

insularity with a sense that philosophical debate could contribute to literary concerns (8–9).[38] And certainly Derrida's analysis of Austin has prompted a good deal of inventive criticism, particularly that which develops the so-called "new" Austin for literary analysis, an Austin invested in language as game and play. But it seems rather that (the several) especially balanced discussions of the Searle-Derrida debate itself have circulated relatively little among critics, that the field has not entirely sorted out its hero-villain perspective on the issues.[39] As tempting as this approach may be, given the original tone of the debate's participants and especially their mutually intractable positions, it is clear that a more generally productive interdisciplinary exchange is yet to be had. What follows, then, is a modest contribution to this conversation. My purpose here is to explore a few of the reasons why Searle and Derrida essentially fail to argue, without pretending they may in any way reconcile; and in this respect the discussion at least aims to distribute its sympathies.

DERRIDA ON AUSTIN

"Signature, Event, Context," Derrida's essay on Austin, is an appreciative account of *How to Do Things with Words* that nevertheless takes Austin to task for certain of his failings. What Derrida finds appealing in Austin's project is its provisionality—he calls it "patient, open, aporetical" (14)—its interrogation of descriptive truth, and its treatment of meaning as haunted by misfire and failure. He finds what Christopher Norris calls a "commonsense" model of the speech exchange more problematic ("Home" 6–7), and in famous remarks Derrida challenges especially its consequences for fictional language.

In *How to Do Things* Austin himself dismantles certain commonsense notions about language. The argument relies on the observation that utterance form does not transparently encode meaning. One formulation may represent many different speech acts, depending on the context ("Bull!" may be a warning or description), and one kind of speech act (a promise or commitment, say) may take different forms

---

[38] Dasenbrock again has his reservations; he notes in particular that literary critics are much less familiar with analytic than with continental philosophy (11–12).

[39] Charles Altieri, Stanley Cavell, Christopher Norris, Richard Rorty, and Henry Staten are the names that come to mind when one thinks of sustained attempts to outline disputes and convergences between philosophical traditions (see Dasenbrock for discussion and bibliography). But as central as these writers are, and as much as others admire their work, it seems to me that their audiences give less credit to their positive than to their negative assessments of analytic philosophy.

(59, 99). If meaning does not inhere in form, speech acts are not predictable from word meanings but depend crucially on other factors of the speech situation, including the linguistic intention speakers signal and the shared knowledge participants in the speech exchange assume. Hearers interpret utterances according to what they construe about (deliberate) speaker intention (whether or not the utterance is delivered ironically, for example), and according to what they know about the speech situation (whether or not a promised action is possible) (see 12–24).

This discussion develops in the context of an initial contrast between constative utterances (ordinarily descriptions one can characterize as true or false) and performatives, utterances for which to say is to do: an umpire who says "You're out" does not merely describe but changes the status of a player in the game (1–11). Performatives are "infelicitous" rather than false; one notes whether or not they succeed, or one thinks of them as faulty or incomplete. Many (entertaining) pages in *How to Do Things* are devoted to analysis of the "appropriateness conditions" or contextual factors pertinent to such speech acts, principally those that frame highly institutionalized performatives. In Austin's well-known example, for the speech act "I do" to result in marriage, to be felicitous, the speakers must be appropriate (not already married), and another participant must wield a specific social authority (be licensed to perform marriages). Faulty participants, botched ceremonies, and the like are "misfires" in which the speech act does not succeed; instances of insincerity are "abuses," acts purported but hollow (see 12–38).

The dramatic action of *How to Do Things* develops as Austin's exploration of contextual conditions on performatives gradually undermines the original contrast between performatives and constatives. First Austin discards grammatical criteria for performatives; performatives one may cast in first person with a performative verb ("I hereby promise *X*"), but they also assume unpredictable forms and in any case the formula does not exclude constatives ("I hereby state that *X*") (see 53–82). Both performatives and constatives rely on linguistic conventions that promote uptake, recognition of the speech act as such, and on hearers' assumptions about intentional states (sincerity or belief). Both kinds of utterances also affect hearers in unconventional, ungovernable ways (in effects of surprise, disbelief, or belief). And appropriateness conditions apply to both performatives and constatives; speakers must have (institutionally defined) knowledge of events in order to constate appropriately about them, just as speakers must be capable of proposed actions in order to promise felicitously (see 133–47).

Finally, judgments about performatives and constatives are both contextually relative; the description "France is hexagonal" is true relative to immediate conversational purposes and to the status of speaker and hearer (143). The dimension true-false on constatives is thus a species of felicity, and finally all speech actions are in some sense performative (see 142–45).

Derrida credits Austin with foregrounding failure and deconstructing truth value and reference (13, 15), but he questions an account of meaning essentially modeled on analogy with physical action. The word applied in such discussions, "communication," itself suggests transmission or displacement of a unified meaning, in Austin accomplished by the notion "illocutionary force" (1–2, 13). Such a scheme assumes a message communicable in a self-identical and self-contained way (1, 3). That is, it originates in a simple linguistic intention; ideas and thoughts precede communication, are then encoded and represented, and unproblematically decoded (4, 13–14). Nothing in the model suggests this chain is not continuous; the account does not acknowledge a gap between sensation, representation, and perception (3–6).

Austin himself does not much discuss writing, but Derrida imagines that the concept of writing consistent with a model of speech acts would be the sort familiar elsewhere: writing functions in the absence of a receiver, serving as a modified presence of the writer or sender (7). But the case of writing particularly underscores what goes amiss in Austin's account, that he assumes a speaker's conscious intentional control over the meaning of the speech act (14). Writing, which ruptures the message from its sender, implies that speech acts escape the authority and control of consciousness (8); speech acts do not represent solely conscious intentions, nor do they fully express and represent them (12). The iterability of the linguistic code or mark renders the initial act of enunciation no longer decisive; the speech act survives to function in new contexts, weaned from referent and origin in the radical absence of the sender (10). Set adrift in this way, the message is no longer predictable and transparent but "illimitable" (12).

Once Austin frees the performative from the authority of external reference, says Derrida, he seeks to stabilize interpretation not only in intentional states of speakers but also in other features of the speech context (13). The uniqueness of the speech act Austin associates with both a transparency of intention and a full saturation or availability of the speech context to interlocutors (15, 18). But the speech context is unstable and never fully determinable (2–3). Austin's account of fictional language is instructive here. Austin terms the fictional utterance "parasitic" on normal discourse because it lacks specific intentionality or the usual illocutionary force. Thus in Austin's work writers of fictional language do not seriously invoke commands, and hearers or readers of fictional utterances do not hold actors or writers to fictional promises (*How to* 21–22, 104). Derrida responds that Austin (uncharacteristically) treats fictional citation as anomaly, when in some sense it is the condition of all language. That is, no performative could succeed without its recognition as citation, without receivers' knowledge of the (iterable) locution (14, 16–18). If all utterance acts are acts of citation, if they graft onto new contexts in the absence of an original sender and receiver, then the entire speech context is no longer recoverable (12). Austin's emphasis on risk and failure, essential to the very idea "performative," suggests an endless alteration of context which he does not later acknowledge (16–17).

Given the context of the succeeding polemics, this brief account of the two initial pieces, set side by side, will be essential to the following discussion. Critics who had invested themselves in ordinary language philosophy first stressed Derrida's affinities with Austin (Stanley Fish, "Compliments"), and similarly minded critics (Shoshana Felman) developed engaging versions of Austin's arguments, highlighting the qualities Derrida found most attractive; this Austin is suggestive, amusing, and ironic, though one may well remark that this "new" Austin was already much in evidence.[40] Other critics, in contrast, took Derrida to have decisively repudiated Austin, just as he had, in this view, forever settled matters with Saussure. This version of events gained momentum from Paul de Man's essay on Austin, which deconstructs an opposition between "grammar" and "rhetoric" already under attack in *How to Do Things with Words*, but which was largely read as elaborating Derrida (see "Semiology").[41] I merely suggest, then, that what was said and what was meant were not obvious even at the start and will not now easily sort out.

[40] Since Cavell mounts an impressive defense of Austin in "Politics as Opposed to What?" I will not belabor his points here, but Cavell reminds us that visions of Austin as a conservative thinker bent on protecting the sensible and ordinary misapprehend his ironic public "mask" (182). See Norris, "Home" 18, for comments on contrasting views of Austin.

[41] As Cavell notes, de Man remains unaware that the disjunction of meaning and grammar is the founding insight of ordinary language philosophy, and he never recognizes that Austin aims to dismantle a distinction between constatives and performatives (192–93). De Man's analysis thus repeats many of Austin's insights; and in reading Austin as attached to a notion of descriptive truth that Austin in fact interrogates, de Man misses what is for Derrida his major appeal. Michael Hancher remarks (in informal lecture) that the French translation of *How to Do Things with Words* may have contributed to de Man's reading of Austin.

DERRIDA AND SEARLE ON INTENTION

Searle's response to Derrida ("Reiterating the Differences"), particularly as it addressed the status of writing as opposed to speech, was especially positioned to fail with literary critics. The reason is not news: Derrida's initial focus on the written word was obviously more appealing. The issue is so much foregrounded in deconstructive criticism that philosophers—including Derrida himself—sometimes characterize literary deconstruction as a kind of vulgarized philosophy; specifically they charge that critics privilege Derrida's textual experiments over his serious philosophical arguments.[42] In any case, we are at least familiar with critical projects that begin with putative deconstructive aims yet end with valorized literary language. Consider Searle in this context, then: Derrida's comments on writing are precisely what Searle is most liable to misconstrue, and he has thus lost a literary audience at the outset, even those critics who have already missed Derrida.

And why should Searle mistake so many of Derrida's remarks on writing? I will resist psychologizing on this point (since Derrida already speculates) and simply note that Searle's unfamiliarity with the conversation of deconstruction means that references to an arche-writing—since *Of Grammatology* simply "writing"—figure in arguments that seem to promote a special status for the written word (see "Reiterating" 199). His contributions to the debate then elaborate what naturally follows: it is the written, not the spoken, word that has enjoyed historical privilege, and writing is thus not in need of redemption ("Word" 76–77) (a legitimate perspective, considering the status of texts in literary studies and philosophy); speech and writing both originate in speakers' intentions and in formative local contexts ("Reiterating" 200–201); written and spoken utterances similarly rely on linguistic codes and conventions (206). But since he had determined in his essay on Austin to dismantle the contrast between written and oral speech, such arguments irritate Derrida, who then reads Searle as repeating his insights ("Limited" 46–47).

Of course, Searle also argues for the distinctiveness of writing in

---

[42] See, for example, Christopher Norris's response to Richard Rorty's essay "Philosophy/ Writing." Norris accuses literary critics of turning deconstruction into a rhetorical theory and of misreading the significance of such notions as the "freeplay" of signifiers ("Philosophy" 192–98). See also Derrida's comments on this point ("Afterword" 115–16). Rorty replies in "Two Meanings," but he also does not like the literary version of deconstruction: critics, he says, keep rediscovering that language cannot be read like the phenomenal world (209–10).

ways that betray his own disciplinary focus on single utterances as opposed to texts. The resulting position on text-based interpretive problems again does not find a literary audience. Texts are permanent records of past intentional acts, Searle maintains, and their separability from their origins distinguishes them from oral utterances ("Reiterating" 200). Such comments remind us that Derrida focuses a good deal on what the case of writing has to tell us about problems of intentionality in speech-act theory, which I take to be the heart of the debate. Let me say at the start that failing to theorize intentionality in a fully satisfactory way is for me speech-act theory's major vulnerability. Yet inasmuch as Searle's remarks share some of Derrida's premises, we might question whether a contrast of positions is altogether clear. And it will be productive to ask whether the players in the debate are consistent on such matters and even whether Searle represents his position in this context as he does elsewhere.

It is not easy to characterize the conflict succinctly. Searle takes Derrida as attacking communicability in general and the communicablity of the written word in particular, at least as rooted in a specific historical intentional act. Searle finds this project incoherent since, following Austin, interpretation without intention then rests entirely on the linguistic code. But the linguistic code cannot mean in a vacuum, in abstraction ("Reiterating" 202); as Austin demonstrated, a single locution means differently in different contexts. If interpretation cannot rely on linguistic form, it must depend on shared extralinguistic conventions, including some calculation of past or present speech intention. In the context of Searle's other work, as I noted in the last chapter, such intentions are not global; they are intentions to get hearers to recognize a kind of speech act as such—a promise as a promise. For Derrida, the appeal to intentionalism is an attempt to limit and control meaning. In the debate he asserts repeatedly that Searle is wrong to see him as positing through the case of writing a complete break with speaker intention ("Limited" 55–60, 64, 105). He also, however, reiterates his earlier argument. Signs are by definition repeatable; every repetition implies a difference of context and an absence of a present and controlling intention ("Limited" 56–58). A fully realized speech act is thus not possible ("Limited" 58).

Now I have already expressed sympathy for Derrida's general position on speech-act intentions. Intentionalism of a specialized sort substitutes both in Austin and in Searle for faith in linguistic form, and yet not much is said about such linguistic intentions—including how they differ from intentions of other kinds. As Norris complains, speech-act accounts fail to sort out conscious and unconscious motives affecting linguistic behavior ("Home" 19); and Ian Maclean notes that the theory depends on an inexplicit conception of the relation of speech to thought (4). However one might characterize the problem, speech-act accounts of linguistic intention—typified by Searle's claim that whatever can be meant can be said (*Speech Acts* 19–21)—directly conflict with the Derridean doctrine of inexpressibility, cast sometimes as an infinite regress of interpretation, sometimes as communicative failure and loss.[43]

No discussion will reconcile such positions, of course, but we may at least reconsider the specific points of Derrida's critique. A central question is simply whether the intentionalism of speech-act theory, as far as Austin and Searle explicate the notion, is entirely as Derrida characterizes it. In an interview with Derrida, Gerald Graff presses this issue. Does Derrida make speech-act theory seem "vulnerable," he asks, by associating its intentionalism, meant merely as a "pragmatic concept," with "metaphysical claims [it] need not entail"—specifically, desire for "metaphysical plentitude" ("Afterword" 115)? I think one may defend Austin on this ground. In passages Derrida himself cites ("Limited" 73, 109 n. 3), Austin remarks problems of agency; intentional actions play out in a context of local circumstances and actions of other agents. One's own sense of what one is doing—what one intends—is always limited and incomplete, says Austin, a "miner's lamp on our forehead" illuminating only what is just ahead ("Three" 284–85). Austin's analysis of performative "abuse" similarly focuses on intentional uncertainty. Are broken promises infelicitous at the start or not? The point is moot, since one judges such intentions only in retrospect; at the crucial moment one cannot fully know them (*How to* 44).

Searle's account of intentionality is more difficult. Derrida's response to Graff focuses tellingly on Searle's language: Searle consistently calls speech acts achievements and realizations of intentions ("Afterword" 121–22). Yet of course this point does not address the presumed scope of such intentions, and my sense of Searle is that this language is unproblematic principally because for him the linguistic intentions at issue are exceedingly narrow. This limited intentionality is clearer in *Speech Acts*, less certain in Searle's response to Derrida, where he apparently seeks a more general interpretive stability—through recovery of original intentional acts ("Reiterating" 200–202). Even in this argument, however, he variously defines historically transmitted "understanding" as uptake, recognition of illocutionary intent, knowledge of

---

[43] I am indebted here to discussion with Larin Adams.

what "linguistic act" an utterance represents (202). In other words, Searle imagines hearers and readers distinguishing intended promises from assertions, reconstructing reference, and the like, but he does not seem to have in mind some larger issue of textual meaning and stability, of authorial intention in the literary sense. Certainly such a position would be at odds with his earlier accounts of indirect (and ambiguous) speech acts, which model multiple readings (see "Indirect"). In fact the problem is rather that Searle does not concern himself with textual meaning and interpretation at all; he focuses instead on single speech acts, on recognition of utterance type, on sentence-level proposition. The interpretive uncertainties so important to Derrida are not so pressing here, and are not obviously incompatible with arguments about illocutionary uptake. As Derrida remarks, the entire debate is perhaps a quibble over different senses of the term "meaning" ("Limited" 64).

Even so, I want to explore the specific quality of illocutionary intent, particularly through the revealing emphasis on conversational and transactional sincerity. The speech-act position is more complex than one would think from the usual characterizations, for both Austin and Searle are of two minds here. According to one impulse, speech acts crucially depend on some genuine intent. Simply put, in order for acts to be felicitous, speakers must mean what they say, or at least not obviously signal otherwise. And the flavor of the discussion is at least as significant: in Austin's account "our word is our bond" (*How to* 10). That is, his examples are of consciously made or flagrantly violated public commitments that enmesh the speaker in a complex of duties and obligations—promises to be delivered, christenings, marriages, and other verbal rituals to be executed correctly. While this contractual model of speech acts is appealing, one may object that it depends too much on honest dealing and on private certainty about public acts; who is to know whether or not speakers are sincere and hence whether or not a speech act is felicitous, whether it is direct or indirect?

But consider now competing and no less obvious passages in Austin and Searle, moments where both writers specifically undermine sincerity as a founding notion. Austin, that is, inflects "our word is our bond" in other ways. It makes sense, he says, to focus on verbal expressions as given, rather than as outward reflections of inward acts; after all, a promise is a promise even when given in bad faith (10). Words thus bind us regardless of particular inner states, and as we all know, many social exchanges—congratulations and apologies—depend on publicly expressed rather than "real" attitudes (78–81). As I noted in the last chapter, Searle similarly revises his sincerity condition on promises to describe *apparent* sincerity, so that what matters once again is what speakers openly signal (*Speech Acts* 62). It is not so much that particular speech acts require particular psychological states— gratitude for thanking, sincerity for promising—but that performative acts socially "count as" expressions of (conventionalized) psychological states (65). Thus if a speaker actively signals "unhappiness" in saying "congratulations," the speech act will nevertheless not be read as congratulations; if a speaker does not so signal, the congratulations count as sympathetic pleasure, though the speech act itself naturally does not forestall social speculation on such matters ("Was she *really* happy for me?"). As Steven Winspur remarks, Austin generally discards mental descriptions in favor of social acts (169), and we may add that Searle follows suit.

These conflicting positions frustrate an easy reading of "sincere" intention in speech-act theory, but we may appreciate the difficulties. The emphasis on outward and public acts severely constrains analysis of internal matters, except as one may simply cast such states as inaccessible to both speaker and hearer. Yet this position must account then for what *is* available and under conscious and public control. The answer is to focus on shared contexts and norms; yet this solution depends on a linguistically aware speaker who consciously invokes institutional conventions. The account somewhat paradoxically arrives at the controlling "I" of the performative formula, when the theory actually imagines an absence of control at the moment of its invocation. And this problem helps explain why some commentators find authoritative, self-present speakers in *How to Do Things with Words*, whereas others find only a pragmatically constructed subject (see Norris, "That the Truest"; Scholes, "Deconstruction").[44]

These last comments may seem surprising, given Derrida's central objection to speech-act intentionality, which focuses not so much as I have here on problems of mutual internal knowledge and scrutiny as on speakers' intentional certainty.[45] The notions "seriousness" and "sincerity," Derrida says, imply that intentions precede speech acts, that speaking and writing are entirely conscious activities ("Limited" 68–69, 74). Thus speech-act theory depends on a psychology, yet acknowledges no role for the unconscious (74). I would state the problem differently: Austin and Searle do not so much ignore the role of uncon-

---

[44] Winspur insightfully points to Austin's conflation of the grammatical subject "I" and the speaking subject (170).

[45] I say this though Derrida notes briefly that speakers in speech-act theory must be omniscient ("Limited" 75).

scious intention as assume a problematic position on it. That is, they both claim that conscious and unconscious intentions are impossible to distinguish, and Searle in particular argues against fully conscious and prior linguistic intentions ("Reiterating" 202). So we have here an understandable throwing up of hands at the the task of separating conscious linguistic intentions from embedding and motivating linguistic (and nonlinguistic) acts. As much as we might sympathize, and as much as Searle briefly sounds like Derrida at this moment, the theory invests too much in "intention" to rest here.[46]

In fact, one may argue that Austin and Searle implicitly sort out kinds of intention elsewhere in the theory, through such distinctions as illocutionary intent, illocutionary uptake, and perlocutionary intent, which they tend to associate respectively with speakers' narrow but conscious linguistic intentions, with hearers' recognition of (just invoked) linguistic and social norms, and with broad and various unconscious motives and unconventional effects impinging on hearers. I would not quarrel with these categories, but I want to note a few resulting difficulties. First, how will one begin to address the problem Searle himself raises of distinguishing unconscious motives from conscious linguistic acts? If such a project is confounded at the start, will one still characterize illocutions as entirely intentional? Are speech acts to be defined from the perspective of what the speaker intends or according to a hearer's reading of intention? That is, surely we imagine a contrast between purposely indirect speech acts and unconsciously ambivalent and ambiguous ones, a contrast that complicates notions of illocutionary uptake.

Since claims about intention in these accounts closely parallel claims about meaning, such questions extend to larger interpretive issues. Especially commentators have said speech-act accounts theorize only fixed and determinate meaning. Derrida in particular maintains that Austin's and Searle's imagined speakers, inasmuch as they consciously control their linguistic intentions, must then determine all meaning effects. Thus he reads no polysemy in speech-act accounts as others find no indeterminacy (Derrida, "Signature" 14; see also Norris, "Philosophy" 195; Rorty, "Two Meanings" 211).[47] Certainly readers of speech-act theory there find faith in speakers' presence or linguistic authority, which Derrida counters with the case of absent speakers and with the problem of writing to oneself ("Limited" 47–50; see also

[46] Yet recall my remark in Chapter 4 that it is rather unfair to ask a speech-act account to become a full-fledged psychoanalytic theory.

[47] Rorty sees in speech-act theory the attempt to stop a "regress of interpretation" by means of a "self-validating" intuition ("Two Meanings" 211).

Winspur 170). But the charges are perhaps too general, given that speech-act schemes depend on the basic problem of the multiple illocutionary aims possible for any one utterance; the arguments clearly begin with the observation that utterance forms are polysemic. Further, by Searle's account, actual utterance acts, not just speech acts in abstraction, may semantically double; that is, indirect speech acts essentially remain two speech acts at once ("Indirect" 30–31).

It is of course another matter to find speech-act discussions of a "freeplay" of signifiers—a term Derrida himself resists, preferring to speak about multiple or undecidable meanings ("Afterword" 115–16). Austin and Searle simply do not worry about interpretive uncertainty, perhaps because they relegate the problem, like so many meaning effects of interest to literary theorists, to the realm of perlocutionary actions. Austin (echoed by Searle) defines perlocutions, perhaps better understood as "perlocutionary effect," as "effects upon the feelings, thoughts, or actions of the audience, or of the speaker, or of other persons" (*How to* 101; *Speech Acts* 25). Yet he principally (Searle exclusively) depicts perlocutions as bearing on hearers—effects of belief, displeasure, or surprise, consequences such as further speech actions (*How to* 109–32). Speakers may intentionally or unintentionally trigger such effects (in hearers) in issuing an illocutionary act; but perlocutions—in contrast to illocutions—are in any case not governed by convention (*How to* 107; *Speech Acts* 46–47). Thus the speaker who intentionally utters a speech act controls linguistic intentions—themselves prompted by a variety of nonlinguistic intentions—but loses control over the speech act's extraconventional effects, over hearers' beliefs, over the resulting social consequences, over subsequent linguistic and nonlinguistic responses. Austin outlines a regress of effects beyond the intentional range of the speaker, everything from belief to humiliation, effects no longer specifically linguistic (118–19).

It thus makes sense to view speech-act positions on intention as more troubled than intractable. The kind of meaning within the theory's self-defined purview is public and social, and it specifically addresses questions related to linguistic form, even as it remarks the gulf between form and meaning. Some commentators have found the familiar resulting topics—interpretation of assertions grammatically cast as questions, for example—frustratingly narrow in scope, especially when Austin and Searle rarely discuss the theory's limits, what it can and cannot explain. And of course resistance to the general topic of unconscious aims further forestalls speculative conversation. (One can imagine postulating unconscious intentions associated with particular conscious linguistic actions.) On the other hand, something must be said about the explanatory power of restricted goals: the theory outlines quite well the shared linguistic conventions remaining in force despite varieties of local belief and motive. The controlling and omniscient speaker of speech-act theory is really the omniscient theorizer. That is, the theorist decides, for the sake of argument, what speakers know and intend. (Why else model unconscious effects as bearing principally on hearers?) The result is a focused but sometimes inconsistent explanatory perspective.

DERRIDA AND SEARLE ON FICTION

Since in Derrida's account fiction represents a decisive break with intention, the debate over fictionality and (Austin's) "parasitism" is an extension of the preceding quarrels. One would expect an especially lively interaction here, given the obvious vested interests—valorized fictionality for the literary critic up against the philosopher's defense of Austin's basic aims. To some extent the expected happens. Cavell, for example, says that critics focus on a "careless" mistake in the theory, one that Austin might well have acknowledged (190). Like Searle, he complains that critics too often mistake Austin's sense of "ordinary language"; the term means "nonphilosophical," not "non-literary," and it includes rather than derogates literary discourse (186–91). But for Derrida the problem cannot be cast as minor, for it neatly demonstrates what is wrong in speech-act theory with "context" as a founding notion. In arguments that echo his critique of the conscious speaker, he finds the "context" of speech-act accounts saturable, determined, exhaustive ("Limited" 64–65, 97; "Signature" 10, 14, 18).

To most readers of the Searle-Derrida debate in this field, Searle came across as recalcitrant on what seemed obvious points. He continued to argue for an original intentional moment encoded in literary speech acts and for the general concept "fiction" as logically dependent on a prior account of nonfiction ("Reiterating" 207; contrast Derrida, "Limited" 91–93). Derrida's argument focused on an initially straightforward point about the the problem of a simple, author-controlled origin (for reasons I have already discussed), arriving at the conclusion that all discourse partakes of fictionality. Now the interesting problem is how the debate stalled here more than at any other moment, with these positions stubbornly reiterated. For Searle essentially argued as characterized—from a position assuming interpretively stable speech acts and maintaining the distinctive status of fictional language. But it is by no means obvious to me that he should have done so, given Austin's description of fiction as something all speech acts are heir to, given, that is, the general theory's position on truth (see *How to* 22).

Indeed, it is especially instructive to set Searle's account of fictional discourse alongside the Searle-Derrida debate. In an earlier essay Searle begins with the proposition that literature is a set of attitudes brought to texts, since no unique set of properties serves to distinguish literary utterances from nonliterary ones ("Logical" 58). Whereas he takes too seriously the claim to "nonfiction" of newspaper accounts and the like (61–67), he observes that the characterization "fiction" is not coextensive with (traditional) literary texts; texts read as literature may be nonfictional in nature, fictional accounts partly nonfictional (74). Searle notes that what most strikingly characterizes fictional discourse is that the speaker is not held accountable for all its propositions (58), although these propositions have real-world force on some other, higher interpretive level, presumably in the form of some more general proposition the text as a whole can be said to represent (74–75). The solution is not altogether felicitous. Searle (following Austin) characterizes fictional language as consisting of pretend illocutions or pseudo-illocutions, illocutionary acts not false but with the usual illocutionary force suspended, since speakers can refer to nonexistent persons, signal noncommitment, and the like without the usual interpretive or social consequences (65). Yet what is appealing about the account is its assessment of the mixed properties of literary discourse, which significantly mitigates the treatment of fiction as pretense by emphasizing its nondistinctive functions. That is, some utterances in literary texts operate according to extraliterary norms: authors routinely refer to real-world persons and events; they often speak to readers in an essentially nonfictional mode; and fictional utterance acts ultimately result in very real commitments (67, 72). Here Searle's focus on single utterance acts works to advantage, for he is reluctant to develop some global principle defining all literary language.

In the debate itself, Searle's least attractive position for literary critics is his conception of a historically preserved speaker intention for fictional utterances. I am once again not certain that this makes him an "intentionalist" of the sort we recognize in literary discussions—someone who believes in a single and stable textual interpretation consonant with conscious authorial aims—simply because Searle speaks about intentions to assert and refer, rather than about interpretations of texts or literary works. And though he does not sort the matter out, his essay on fiction alludes to various levels on which the notion "intention" could be said to operate, including in covert authorial motives ("Logical" 66). In fact, the issues here become quite muddled. Neither Searle nor Derrida differentiates arguments about texts or discourse from arguments about speech acts or about signs, when such distinctions matter much to the direction of the conversation.[48] As an example, note that when Derrida discusses the written word (read "text") grafted onto new contexts that redefine its meaning, Searle, judging by his earlier interests, could well decide that the issue of new contexts pertains to how reference works for, say, the word "Paris" in an eighteenth-century novel, where the initial, historically determined referring act is relevant. Still, such matters are far from clear in the debate, and what goes wrong is partly that fictional speech acts are frozen past acts for Searle; he does not share the familiar literary assumption that fictional utterances are always new, reenacted and reinterpreted as read and reread. What Searle thinks about most in the discussion is the viewpoint of speakers, whereas Derrida credits the powers of readers and hearers.

A more positive way to characterize the missed contact here is to say that Searle's commitment to fictional utterances as illocutions with historically felt effects makes him resist arguments about iterability and citationality. The misunderstandings on this head are are worth tracing. For Derrida, the principle of iteration itself functions as a critique of the exhaustive context he finds outlined in speech-act theory. That is, fiction implies new contexts for future readings unconditioned by the author; if new contexts are always possible for utterance acts, the horizon of meaning retreats and multiplies ("Limited" 62–63). All utterances are in some sense citations—hearers must recognize features of the iterated code—but the notion "citation" also functions to question Austin's and Searle's focus on originating speech events, and it resonates for critics with familiar discussions about intertextuality, new texts fashioned from and dependent on prior texts. "Fiction" in Derrida's account is finally a special instance of citation, more obviously detached than other language from its origins, perhaps more contextually dependent and unstable (99, 105). For Searle, the conception of language as action means that locutions—utterance forms—are iterable, but illocutions—utterance acts—are not. Thus he takes the term "iterability" as pertaining to the possibilities of limitless syntactic production from finite means, as about linguistic form in abstraction, detached from context ("Reiterating" 199), and he naturally then wonders why Derrida so foregrounds the issue. Although elsewhere Searle him-

[48] I am not the first to note problems of this kind. Maclean observes that the exchange confuses terms or signs with propositions (see 15–18). Garver notes that Derrida does not imagine elements articulated into syntactic units at higher levels (671). Thus notions such as "iteration" interact with "sign" and do not refer to utterances at the level of speech act.

self illustrates ironic literary citationality as it bears on a single speech act, he misses Derrida's metaphorical and textual sense of "citation" and argues instead about "use" versus "mention" (see "Logical" 73–74; "Reiterating" 206).[49] Fiction Searle finally understands as a momentary and particular event—thus distinct from citation—for similarity of form does not imply identity of event.

While Derrida and Searle keep agreeing that interpretive processes depend both on (more or less) stable linguistic codes and on the particulars of the speech context, they are unable to make contact. Derrida focuses on the question of any context's descriptive availability, and Searle is distracted because the point seems to be about the iterability of linguistic form. (Derrida shares with Saussure a one-level model of language, which interferes with communication here.) Again Searle in other moments is illuminating, for elsewhere he treats "context" as a limitless notion. In "The Background of Meaning," in particular, Searle contends that the same word used in a variety of utterances does not have in each case the same truth conditions ("cut" as we understand it in sentences about hair cutting, cake cutting, or grass cutting are his examples) (223). What is more, these differences are not accounted for by such traditional notions as ambiguity or by positing that word meanings are vague or general and simply defined more precisely by further sentence elements (224–25). The explanation is extralinguistic; truth conditions are defined against a background of cultural practices and assumptions (227). Further, it will be impossible with any formal mechanism to render all such assumptions explicit, for one cannot predict what in the speech context will next be relevant, nor can one spell out this background in assumption-free language (228). I might well observe that Searle and Derrida here remain farther apart than necessary.

This is not to minimize actual and potential points of contention. The truth conditions Searle describes for utterances are nevertheless shared and available in a sense Derrida will want to reject (can interlocutors rely on each other's sense of which contextual factors apply?). Derrida already says that Searle must decide between two theories of context, one from within (in which the code itself creates its own context) or one from without (in which case the principle of grafting or citationality applies) ("Limited" 78–79). In this he echoes earlier arguments from within Searle's philosophical tradition—over how much meaning to credit to intention, how much to derive from convention.[50]

---

[49] Searle treats textual reference to past utterances as part of a present speech context. As Peggy Kamuf comments, one problem here is that Searle takes Derrida's discussion of authorial absence as argument for intentionless meaning (9).

[50] See, for example, the readings by P. F. Strawson and H. Paul Grice in Searle's collection *Philosophy of Language*, along with Searle's comments on Grice in *Speech Acts* 42–50.

Searle in some moments takes intention over convention; an invocation of convention is the formative act (see "Reiterating" 208). Elsewhere he defines intention as another convention.[51] To this conversation Derrida's emphasis on textuality adds the innovative element.

But it is not clear that Derrida has himself solved all such problems. The principle of iteration depends on a stable linguistic code, which then makes possible the absence of the speaking subject, but to account for new meanings in new contexts, the mark or code must at the same time permute. Derrida often remarks the paradox that the language code is at once repeatable and unique ("Limited" 83); repetition produces alteration, a remainder, which ultimately threatens the authority of the code ("Limited" 53; "Signature" 8). This effect is partly the effect of the code on itself. A "structural unconsciousness," really a textual function, replaces the determining subject; the mark is set adrift as a productive "machine" ("Signature" 18, 8). The argument explains Derrida's ambivalence about "illocutionary force"; he approves the notion in Austin, but prefers to understand it as emanating from the linguistic code rather than persons.

Yet, however much Derrida responds to Searle that these claims for iteration do not depend on contextless meaning for linguistic form, they obviously rely on a strong sense of a code in abstraction, as Rorty complains ("Two Meanings" 208).[52] Searle's claim that Derrida conflates the separation of utterances from origins with the separation of linguistic devices from their representational functions misses Derrida's point about self-interacting codes (see "Reiterating" 200–201). But it suggests that in dismissing intention Derrida valorizes and idealizes surface form—a position reflected in Derrida's (nearly Jakobsonian) celebration of repeated words and letters in Mallarmé (see "Mallarmé"). We are finally faced with a choice between the pitfalls of a transparent sense of source and the problems of a Romantic sense of word, issues a more engaged discussion might have pressed productively.

It is thus difficult to escape the conclusion that the Searle-Derrida exchange is a paradigm of failed interdisciplinary interaction, even

[51] Maclean remarks on the problem of describing as conventions both features of the speech context and psychological factors (4). Other critics prefer to describe performative force as a convention (see Winspur 172), but this strategy results in the regress of explanation I described in the last chapter. See Sandy Petrey for a contrasting analysis of Austin and Searle on matters of intention versus convention (131–46).

[52] Hancher points out an interesting related contrast between French and English law. French laws pertaining to signatures stress convention (only reasonably uniform, convention-based signatures count as legitimate); English law recognizes highly variable signatures, providing one can demonstrate the appropriate authorizing intention ("Law" 229–39).

though the conversation is really between subspecialties, between kinds of philosophy. The apparent connections—a shared familiarity with canonical philosophical texts, an interest in linguistic philosophy, a mutual admiration of Austin—ultimately complicate communication. When both writers discuss what seem to be the same topics, their vocabularies do not coincide: "mark" and "code" mean something far different to one who theorizes language through a semiotic model ("sign" and discourse then work the same way), than to one who distinguishes between syntactic form and speech act but does not address texts.[53] The Searle-Derrida debate is finally a dramatic contrast to the case of Derrida on Saussure. That is, Derrida works far enough from linguistics to impact discussion of Saussure rather than phonological study itself, and in any case reception of Saussure is such that no one will defend his phonology or his semantics in the way that Searle defends Austin. In the later exchange, Derrida elaborates his own position without fully addressing Searle, and Searle repeats his arguments without effectively advancing their cause. For all the difficulties surrounding intentionality, that is, a program that positions speech acts within a general theory of action is not without political appeal, as Richard Ohmann said long ago. As Cavell comments, one might alternatively cast Austin as recovering philosophy and the (suppressed, not valorized) "human voice" from oppressive philosophical systematizing. Thus he wonders whether a demonstration of textuality requires a complete deconstruction of presence (197).[54] Such reflections, surfacing since the exchange, are the major casualties of the debate.

[53] Rorty often remarks that Derrida (frustratingly) seems to be doing ordinary language philosophy when he is not. He comments that Derrida is easier to understand once one recognizes his interests are entirely different ("Derrida" 674–75; "Philosophy/Writing" 155).

[54] Derrida sets the terms, characterizing speech-act theory as politically oppressive, and since the debate is unsuccessful, Searle poses no counterargument (see "Afterword" 131–42). See Petrey for comments on reconciling these positions (145–46).

Chapter 6

The Language of Criticism Reconsidered

His best modern interpreter had to go out of his way *not* to understand him.

—PAUL DE MAN, "The Rhetoric of Blindness"

Literary criticism relates paradoxically to outside fields. Its textualism, its attention to a variety of discursive practices—the legacy of structuralism—renders it eminently flexible. And so we have reached a moment when the status of literary studies seems most secure, when in fact we export its methods to other disciplines, whose students read philosophical and historical texts as literary ones. Yet while we congratulate ourselves on this development, we might want to admit that literary criticism remains in some sense scavenger work; we actively mine other disciplines for our own projects. Our raw materials, if indeed we have any, suggest no single, no obvious analytical method, and ours is also a history of importation, a succession of borrowed, then rejected models—psychoanalytic, linguistic, sociological, historical.[1] Among these extradisciplinary models linguistics quite naturally assumes for literary critics the status of paradigm science, whether or not one approves of scientific projects. Since linguistic study addresses the nature of language, one can come, in an importing mode, to view it as a model discipline, to see its goals as related and complementary to critical methods. In a rejecting mode, by contrast, linguistic theory comes to illustrate the limits of science, to define this field negatively: the purpose of criticism is to say about texts what linguistics cannot.

[1] See Terry Eagleton for some interesting complaints about the eclecticism of literary studies (197–99).

The optimistic projects of the early chapters—stylistics, narratology, reader-oriented criticism—represent work in the first vein. Discussion of the second kind, represented in the last chapters, coincides with the rise of deconstruction; thus linguistic concepts come to illustrate reductive empiricism, its simplifying impulse.[2] We might then ask: Have three disciplines—linguistics, speech-act theory, literary criticism—productively engaged one another in the time frame represented by these projects? The answer is emphatically "yes" with respect to local applications of linguistics I have not discussed (studies of meter and rhythm, figurative language, narrative conventions) and also with respect to the more global linguistic-literary theories I have considered here. These last projects, I have argued, motivated new definitions of the literary canon, rethought what it means to read literature, problematized the literary-language–ordinary-language distinction, and began to examine the social scene of reading and writing. From the later direction of critical discourse, however, we can also see how difficult and precarious authentic contact with outside fields may be.

SCIENTIFIC CRITICISM

Thus I wish to conclude by emphasizing that the interdisciplinary projects examined here were positive and productive for literary criticism. But I also wish to address briefly the subtext of later (interdisciplinary) discussion, to think about what it means not just to import but to repudiate a borrowed model. Consider, for example, the sense of literary remarks on the topic "science." I offer no brief for either science or scientific criticism, whatever that may be (especially since linguistic study itself is only problematically "scientific"), but I do wish to note the function of "linguistics" and "science" as self-evident tropes in literary discussions.

Of course literary criticism has not always defined itself against linguistics in particular and science in general. Roman Jakobson was fond of remarking that Einstein's theory of relativity influenced his career more than any other single notion (*Verbal* 75). It apparently suggested to him resistance to censorship, a descriptive rather than evaluative literary criticism, and a focus on global explanation—on methods and foundations—as opposed to single texts. Indeed, the term "scientific" was in itself liberating for Russian Formalists and Prague School critics. Literary studies so-called would exchange the anecdotal, impressionis-

---

[2] See, for example, Ronald Schleifer, "Deconstruction" 393–94; "Responds"; and Christopher Norris, "Theory" 90–91, 95–97.

tic, and derivative criticism of the past for a rigorous methodology that would distinguish criticism from neighboring fields.[3] In one concrete sense the Prague School Circle represents an ideal of interdisciplinary activity. Many of its members simply *were* both literary critics and linguists (see Vachek 122–36), and work in each area applied to the single, unifying problem of explaining language in its literary *and* its nonliterary expressions.

In the United States, however, opposition between science and literature is firm and long standing. Scientific methods did not mesh with New Critical perspectives; linguistic analysis was at odds with texts conceived as organic and literary language cast as emotive.[4] The contrast of positions is particularly on display at the 1958 conference at which Jakobson delivered his famous paper ("Closing Statement"). Even within the context of a conference on style, speakers consistently acknowledge and anticipate the same objections: linguistics robs literary works of mystery, its categories are inflexible, it fails to locate the essential literariness of great works.[5] The early enthusiasm for new linguistic theory, as I noted in the first chapter, operated in this unfavorable climate. I. A. Richards's explictly territorial comments of the same period memorably illustrate. Linguistics, he remarks, though effective when "operating within its proper field," must not encroach on "any territory of the Humanities or of Literary Criticism or of the pedagogy for which they are responsible" (*Speculative Instruments* 8–9), both because aesthetic language resists linguistic description and because students of the humanities know of matters "deeper . . . than any science" (10).[6]

Viewed from this perspective, the period in which mainstream American critics willingly explored linguistic theory was really quite brief, sandwiched between the antiempiricism of New Criticism and that of deconstruction. Linguistic and speech-act models suddenly assumed status both because talented critics developed them in more

---

[3] See Boris Éjxenbaum for discussion.

[4] See I. A. Richards, *Speculative Instruments* 9.

[5] Edward Stankiewicz 81; Sol Saporta 83, 86; see also John Hollander 396, 407; and René Wellek, "Closing" 410, 417.

[6] This is not to deny that Richards was developing his own "scientific" approach, but it aimed at defining literary language as emotive and therefore not amenable to linguistic analysis. See Wellek, "Main Trends" 351–53, for discussion. Geoffrey Leech, however, comments that the implicit functionalism of Richards's analysis has something in common with Jakobson's communication triangle (78–80), and he reminds us that Richards later came to approve linguistic criticism (87n.1). Contrast Richards's attitude here to his later positive comments on Jakobson and Lawrence Jones's analysis of a Shakespearean sonnet ("Linguistics into Poetics").

attractive ways and because such theories were a particularly effective means of opposition to New Critical dogma, given the initial antagonism toward linguistic theory. It is also true, I have said, that linguistic models cannot take entire credit for these developments, for at the same time they served existing critical aims. But precisely the flexibility of such borrowed notions implies that many unexamined issues accompanied them from one field to another, since no special technical problem in the new discipline forced issues a critic either did not see or did not wish to face. That linguistic models proved so tractable in this process suggests that discipline-internal concerns, as much as pressures between fields, finally motivated critics to reject them.

The criticism of the 1970s and 1980s thus leaves us with a new orientation toward linguistics that in itself requires comment. Although frustration with the critical limits of linguistic concepts is inevitable, criticism echoes the earlier discipline-defining rhetoric: literature evades the descriptive capacities of normative grammars; if literary language is language at its most complex, it "can reassert its claim to be the central example, the creative paradigm, of all language-use" (Norris, "Theory" 91–93). Thus, inevitably, "the literary critic may feel that *his* kind of knowledge—his dealing with language at its highest, most organized power of expression—becomes the endpoint and justification of linguistic study" (91). If it fails to address literary problems, then, a linguistics should no longer set tasks for itself.

After a momentary enthusiasm we have thus returned to the rhetoric with which New Criticism once distanced itself from linguistics: literary theory does what science, the mere study of language structure, can never do. The underside of the rhetoric in each case is some measure of insecurity about the status of the discipline. Indeed, it is the interdisciplinary impulse itself that intensifies efforts at self-definition; if we should need the tools and methods of outside fields, we would nevertheless like to say what it is we accomplish that other disciplines do not. In fact, I think the same political impulse underlies both the initial connection and later disaffection with linguistics. For the Prague School, the association with linguistics served to define it against the encroachment of history and psychology; now, as critical theory embraces these same fields, current pronouncements work toward the same end. It is therefore not a surprise that later antagonistic rhetoric accompanies uncertainty about the future of criticism. But such a rhetorical position prevents the active investigation of literary issues by locating the difficulties in linguistics, that is, outside criticism, and it unfortunately suggests an insular and territorial perspective just at the moment criticism appears most open.

"LINGUISTICS": SEMANTICS

At the 1958 Indiana conference on stylistics, widely taken as inaugurating much of the American interest in linguistic criticism, Jakobson anticipated a broader, newer "linguistics," in his terms a study of language that would subsume linguistics in the narrow sense and a related study of literary language ("Closing" 350). Many critics were understandably offended, for not only did Jakobson seem to imply that literary critics would require training in linguistics, he also clearly saw much of the evaluative and interpretive work critics do as outside the realm of the linguistic criticism he was imagining (351–52). Many critics would now reverse both that argument and its imperialistic aims. Since an evaluation of an utterance's context is essential to its interpretation and analysis, an ideological criticism can provide a disciplinary model for linguistics; indeed, critics argue, such a literary theory poses an ultimate challenge to the central premises of linguistic study.[7]

What I want to suggest is that this general attitude, a product of disenchantment with earlier linguistic criticism, is essentially as mistaken as Jakobson's, although it, too, arises from eminently admirable critical aims. I wish to examine its principle premises, first to demonstrate some persisting misconceptions between disciplines, ultimately to question whether either field can or should set the terms for the other. That is, the rhetorical, perhaps not altogether serious, argument that literary studies should model linguistics regularly invokes two associated (very serious) claims: that linguistic study advances a failed account of meaning and that the discipline lacks social relevance.

As the first charge is so often asserted, linguistics is "unwilling to countenance" "indeterminate understandings" (Fabb and Durant, "Introduction" 2).[8] As I noted earlier, as a response to generative grammar, at least, this charge depends either on an inflated sense of the linguistic model's semantic claims or on the assumption that there are no syntactic—as opposed to semantic—matters of possible theoretical interest. In the first case, it is perfectly true that the generative model critics still address (Chomsky's extended standard theory) inadequately solved semantic problems. But this is not, as critics often suppose, because it failed to incorporate information about speech contexts;

---

[7] See, for example, Norris, "Theory" 91, 95–96; Mary Louise Pratt, "Linguistic Utopias" 60; Culler, "Towards" 176–77; Nigel Fabb and Alan Durant, "Introduction" 2; Schleifer, "Deconstruction" 394.

[8] See also Norris, "Theory" 96; Schleifer, "Responds" 333; Stanley Fish, "Consequences" 109.

rather it proved problematic to give even such phenomena as sentence-level ambiguity syntactic treatment. In the second case, it became difficult to motivate all syntactic operations semantically. In short, the relation of syntax to semantics remains an area of (interdisciplinary) confusion. If syntactic issues are separated in linguistic study from semantics and pragmatics, the critical argument goes, then this separation must constitute a claim that sentence interpretation is fixed and unproblematic, unrelated to larger contextual matters.[9]

But from a (brief and general) perspective on developments in linguistics, the central problem of the relation of syntax to semantics has been how to distinguish between points of connection and points of divergence. Leonard Bloomfield is famous for remarking that in order to discuss meaning a linguist would need "knowledge of everything in the speaker's world" (139). American structuralists might nevertheless discuss some semantic issues informally, as Bloomfield himself did, but it seemed best to focus on strictly syntactic and phonological problems, since the prevailing assumption was that a full semantic theory would require linguists to formalize knowledge of every sort, and such a project clearly did not make sense.[10] Yet Chomsky implied that this approach left many interesting connections between syntactic facts and semantic phenomena uninvestigated (*Syntactic Structures* 102). The initial solution was to exclude from the scope of linguistic models nonlinguistic factors that contribute to sentence interpretation—contextual conditions and social knowledge limitless or unavailable, impossible to formalize—but to include semantic knowledge closely related to syntax, knowledge of paraphrase relations between sentences, of semantic anomalies within sentences, and of multiple readings for ambiguous sentences (see Newmeyer, *Linguistic Theory*, 1st, 74).[11]

Debates about the legitimate scope of a linguistic semantics naturally ensued. Generative semantics represented the most expanded form of the impulse to integrate syntactic and semantic issues; and this approach later encouraged linguistic interest in broader pragmatic issues for the first time.[12] Central to this project was the notion that

[9] See, for example, Fabb and Durant, "Ten Years" 58; Stephen Muecke 159; Colin MacCabe, "Opening Statement" 300.

[10] Bloomfield's discussion of meaning is in *Language* 139–57, but it is severely limited by his extreme form of behaviorist psychology, which also affects his discussion of language learning and use. See 21–41.

[11] I am very much indebted in this overview to Frederick Newmeyer's clear discussion of the Katz-Fodor model and of generative semantics (*Linguistic Theory*, 1st, 73–81, 93–120, 209–19).

[12] Critics have sometimes echoed statements from this period, for such a project has seemed to them to represent a move toward a theory of discourse and away from the critical limitations of extended standard theory (see Fabb and Durant, "Ten Years" 56;

pragmatic factors accounted for previously undescribed but predictable syntactic phenomena. A (deep structure) representation of illocutionary force—an underlying subject and performative verb—could explain, for example, the distribution of mitigators and hedges (see Fraser). Or one could predict the interpretive consequences of syntactic operations; that is, syntactic deletions, it seemed, regularly constrained speech acts.[13] But as Frederick Newmeyer explains, this line of research eventually foundered on the attempt to find grammatical treatments for increasingly diverse and extragrammatical facts (*Linguistic Theory*, 1st, 196). Linguists argued that such phenomena were not so predictable after all, and further, that there were no syntactic reasons to posit performative verbs in deep structure (Newmeyer, *Linguistic Theory*, 1st, 214–19).[14] From the perspective of ordinary language philosophy, Searle noted that grammatical treatment of pragmatic knowledge was simply counterintuitive; it amounted to the claim that syntactic elements can refer only to other syntactic elements (the underlying "I" and performative verb) and not to actual persons and shared assumptions (*Expression* 166–69). Both points of view converged, as Newmeyer notes, to support the notion of a grammar with formal properties distinct from those of pragmatics (*Linguistic Theory*, 1st, 219).

Ironically, this perspective is actually one with which critics should agree. The argument for a strictly defined semantics and for distinct pragmatic and syntactic models with functionally different formalisms derives from the recognition that interpretive problems (in the literary sense) are not always illuminated by referring to sentence structure,

---

Fish, *Text* 106). Generative semantics did indeed collapse semantic and syntactic concerns; co-occurrence restrictions and causal relations, for example, were accounted for by an abstract syntax that now included semantic information (Newmeyer, *Linguistic Theory*, 1st, 112–14). Much of this research had a dubious relevance to literary issues, however, since a good deal of it focused on what are, from a critical perspective, narrow semantic concerns—on whether adjectives should be derived in the model from noun phrases, for instance, or whether pronouns replace noun phrases by means of transformations (Newmeyer, *Linguistic Theory*, 1st, 127, 134–35). (Many literary critics had meanwhile also developed some familiarity with pragmatics, since the literature on indirect speech acts was especially suggestive for literary problems [see Hancher, "Pragmatics"].)

[13] The expanded version of "Close the door," for example, would be "I hereby request that you close the door." In the deletion of the subject and auxiliary in questions—from "Have you seen John lately?" to "Seen John lately?"—the derived sentence requires interpretation as a request for information, whereas the original sentence is ambiguous, interpretable as a yes/no question, a request for information, or an exclamation (Newmeyer, *Linguistic Theory*, 1st, 213–14; see Susan Schmerling).

[14] Newmeyer summarizes other arguments against syntactic treatment of pragmatic phenomena which are too involved to detail here. One controversy centered on whether speech acts entailed their felicity conditions; since it was successfully argued they did not, felicity conditions seemed to require different treatment, an analysis outside the bounds of a syntactic-semantics. See *Linguistic Theory*, 1st, 215–16.

even though some pragmatic phenomena may be systematic.[15] The resulting modular account of language—consisting of separate but interacting components—in no way involves the assumption that *all* knowledge of interpretive significance is accessible, exhaustible by these or any models, or necessarily amenable to formal analysis. Now one could take another tack and say that it should have been clear at once that pragmatic concerns should not receive syntactic treatment. Yet this is obvious only if one is talking at the start about broader discourse issues; it takes considerable discussion of a different kind to demonstrate that the scope of quantifiers is pragmatically rather than syntactically determined, for one has to account for apparent syntactic relations.

Of course many discussions of the determinacy of meaning in linguistic theory refer not to the role of semantic concerns in generative grammar but more directly to Jacques Derrida's deconstruction of the Saussurean model, and the assumption is often that this critique applies to linguistics in general. As a theory of meaning, Saussure's account quite clearly fails, and it is a more legitimate object of attack than generative grammar on this score, for Saussure genuinely intends to engage general issues of representation. Most obviously problematic in the *Course in General Linguistics* is Saussure's vacillation between his differential scheme—meaning as a function of oppositional relationships—and moments in which signifiers stand in simple one-to-one correspondence to objects in the world. And Saussure ultimately posits a one-level model that does not articulate morphemes into larger utterances, imagine slippage between sentence and speech act, or embed speech acts within larger stretches of discourse. In other words, the *Course* represents a semiotic rather than a pragmatic or discourse theory.[16] Yet, again from the perspective of the model's significance for linguistic study, these problems do not affect the extremely productive applications of the model for phonology. "Linguistics" is not a simple, discrete term, and neither does any one linguistic model generate a single application or consequence.

---

[15] I am avoiding the term "semantic" here, since it is used quite differently in linguistics and criticism. In linguistics a semantic fact is one legitimately related to syntax (as opposed to a pragmatic phenomenon); in criticism "semantics" refers to any problem of meaning and is often more or less interchangeable with "pragmatics."

[16] There have been other attempts to turn the Saussurean model into a theory of meaning, but these are not generally known in American linguistics and have not been especially successful. The exception is Jakobson's development of "markedness" theory, but this now has a more restricted application to morphology. See Henkel, "Comment."

"LINGUISTICS": SOCIAL CONCERNS

Now the (more telling) second objection to linguistic study is that it does not address the social scene of language, that its theories of discourse and meaning rely on invariant abstractions irrespective of specific contexts. Again the initial aims are reasonable, but they are often cast in an isolating rhetoric. Linguistics in this view trades in a "linguistic alienation" that "trivialize[s] change and everyday linguistic creativity" (Stewart 44); it is "lacking a grip on the real world," "hamstrung by its idealisation and abstraction away from the specificities of time and physical and social space which characterise linguistic behaviour" (Fabb and Durant, "Introduction" 9).[17] This complaint in one sense contradicts some of the earlier objections, in that the antiempiricist cast of much deconstruction-influenced critical discussion would seem not to endorse the investigation of actual speech which a social study of language must entail.[18] In a more general sense, however, linguistic study should, by deconstructive example, interrogate its own categories, reassess its imagined speakers and speech communities (see Pratt, "Linguistic Utopias" 60). The (deconstructed) opposition between speech and writing should suggest, through Derrida's critique of Saussure, a linguistics of writing, an examination of the literariness and textuality of *all* language; such an investigation would quite naturally extend to its social significance.[19]

Now since it is obvious that at least some kinds of linguistic study focus on social issues, objections typically take either of two forms: sociolinguistic study, critics argue, is limited or suppressed. Again it will be useful to consider sociolinguistic matters in a discipline-internal context. The pressure to incorporate the study of social facts into linguistics developed in the 1960s, largely as a result of William Labov's early work, later collected in *Sociolinguistic Patterns* and *Language in the Inner City*. Labov's innovation was to apply sociological models and research methods to linguistic phenomena. In several

---

[17] See also Paul Hopper 20–22; Norris, "Theory" 96; Muecke 159–60. I am entirely in sympathy with Hopper's complaints about text grammars that attempt to "universally characterize narrative," and I agree that this impulse often results from attempts to apply the Chomskyan model to discourse theory (20). But I think his description of generative grammar as a theory of sentence meaning in isolation (21) is mistaken. Similarly, I have absolutely no objection to Muecke's call for attention to the political underpinnings of public discourse; again I simply question his account of the aims of grammatical models.

[18] There is also much anxiety within linguistic study itself about what it means to be a "science" and in what sense linguistics qualifies.

[19] See Culler, *On Deconstruction* 128; Hopper 22; Fabb and Durant, "Introduction" 9–10.

studies Labov impressively demonstrated the advantages of the sociolinguistic approach. Relying on more consistently collected data cate-
gorized by style, he documented the regular stratification of prestige
and stigmatized syntactic and phonological variables according to social class in large populations (the Lower East Side of New York City)
and according to finer status distinctions within smaller ones (by task
and floor within department stores, for instance) (*Sociolinguistic* 43–
69). The clear correlation of even phonetic variants (postvocalic [r],
simplification of word-final consonant clusters) with speakers' social
positions, and the sensitivity of such variables to subtle changes in
context, naturally suggested a variety of related issues. Research proliferated on sociolinguistic topics—on ethnic and urban dialects, on creoles, on social factors in linguistic change, on style variation, on bilin-
gualism and code switching, on social dialects and education issues, on
linguistic markers of group identity and covert prestige norms, on language variation and gender, on linguistic attitudes, on speech within
small social networks, on speech genres and language games, and—
under the further influence of ethnographic-anthropological models
and ordinary language philosophy—on conversational conventions and
the acquisition of pragmatic norms. This list is hardly exhaustive, but
it responds to the suggestion that linguistics did not move beyond Labov's paradigm or the discovery of a fixed correlation between language
behavior and social class.

Like any linguistic paradigm, Labov's variation model (as only one
approach to sociolinguistics) did indeed define problems and thus limit
answers. But investigation of language-class relationships also revealed
productive irregularities. For instance, Labov found that speakers did
not all shift upward in the production of prestige variables in the same,
predictable fashion from casual to formal speaking styles, and that this
behavior too could be explained in terms of contrasting class advantages and insecurities (*Sociolinguistic* 122–42). Whereas Labov re-
ported that New York City (especially middle-class) speakers tended to
underestimate their production of stigmatized forms, Peter Trudgill
found a more complicated pattern in Norwich (women underreporting
more than men, middle-class men overreporting) which signaled differences in American and British working-class identity and the association of working-class speech forms with masculinity. Early studies
documented a higher production of prestige variables for female speakers,
but in a South Carolina speech community Patricia Nichols found gen-
dered speech differences related to local sex- and age-associated em-
ployment opportunities as opposed to gender per se. While Jenny
Cheshire found that adolescents marked their loyalty to peer-groups

with stigmatized syntactic variables, she also discovered that speakers exploited vernacular norms unpredictably to achieve expressive effects. As one would expect, in short, the disciplinary conversation is ongoing.[20]

Critical discussion on sociolinguistic issues is again well intentioned. Often remarks are framed as arguments for regrounding linguistic study by restoring to a central focus that which has been marginalized (writing, discourse, social factors).[21] The problem is that since such discussions suppose these issues receive almost no attention in linguistic study, they never address the actual limitations of real attempts to deal with these topics. Thus one critic calls for the investi-

---

[20] Complicating literary pronouncements on linguistics is an overheard and genuine tension between sociolinguists and other linguists rather parallel to the once-palpable animosity between deconstructionists and New Critics. The argument with which literary critics are most familiar (indeed the one they echo) concerns linguistic competence; since all speech behavior is inherently social, involves complex contextual knowledge, the competence-performance distinction is suspect (see Labov, *Sociolinguistic* 186–87; *Language* 125). The narrow focus on an idealized speaker has inhibited linguists from examining actual speech communities (see Labov's 1970 remarks in *Sociolinguistic* 186–87); but because variation is an inevitable part of any language system, it constitutes essential linguistic knowledge and is a central and necessary object of study (Labov, *Sociolinguistic* 223, 226, 258–59). Early on much of this debate focused specifically on variable linguistic rules. Since speakers clearly know which social and linguistic constraints favor variability, sociolinguists argued, this knowledge is a part of competence and thus of rule formulation (Wolfram and Fasold 107; Labov, *Language* 93–101, 124–29). Later discussion rather diminished this specific argument, if not the overarching conflict. Sociolinguists themselves have questioned the status of variable rules. Such rules did not distinguish between stylistic variation and phonetic or syntactic optionality; statements about constraints did not illuminate the causes of variation; and probability calculations did not accurately depict differential speech behavior within communities (Fasold 244–57). This is not to say that documenting speech differences proved impossible or trivial, but incorporating such facts into a model of core linguistic knowledge—into the rule formulations of the syntactic model—finally obscured important facts about variation.

[21] Critics are correct, however, in saying that linguists rarely investigate writing. The nature of the relation between sociolinguists and theory-oriented linguists persists as an issue. One version (see Newmeyer, *The Politics of Linguistics* 143–50, for example), simply points to linguists with different academic interests. There are theoretical linguists and applied linguists in this view; generativists supply the apparatus—a developing model—for sociolinguistic projects, and applied linguists investigate and articulate the specific problems theory-oriented linguists must adapt their models to solve. It is true that many sociolinguists, especially—though not so many discourse theorists—are invested in mainstream theories and models. Labov is thoroughly a generativist, and creolists draw from studies of child language acquisition. It is also correct that theorists have responded to data developed from applied projects. Nevertheless, the overwhelming earlier focus on largely abstract matters naturally did detract from sociolinguistic investigations, and one can often observe considerable distance between these two groups, demonstrated at linguistic institutes, for instance, or by Talbot Taylor's review of Newmeyer's book. Yet the point here is that such discipline-internal disputes tend to translate into the sense in literary studies that social interests in linguistics are completely marginalized, a notion that the rich literature on sociolinguistic topics does not support.

gation of suprasegmentals and critiques distinctive features, without noting that suprasegmentals have been a major focus in phonology for many years and that the distinctive-feature system he discusses is outmoded. Another dismisses the Chomskyan revolution by attacking extended standard theory's "deep structure" and "surface structure," which he interprets as a distinction between meaning and effects, without acknowledging that the distinction has largely eroded, or how and why it has. A third writer calls for a linguistic phenomenology, but in arguments that focus on a grammatical model. And a critic who draws from sociolinguistic accounts themselves suggestions for future linguistic study, finds that work on creoles has largely been ignored.[22]

Even so, I do not object to a criticism—recast as a broader theory of signification—that attends to specific social contexts, local politics, and also defines discourse meaning according to those conditions. The problem lies not in such critical aims but in their rhetorical means. That is, such suggestions persuasively depend on the presumed target of the injunction to consider language in its social context. To comment on the social nature of language, that is, critics have frequently focused on generative grammar as the recalcitrant oppositional theory. They are quite right to note that generative grammar represents an inadequate theory of discourse, but it is surely important that generative grammar did not set out to be one. The question is really about what critics choose to call "linguistics"; much discussion on language and social concerns generates from linguistics departments, but such projects are seldom a topic of literary-critical discussion. Yet critics remark that attention to social concerns in linguistic study would fundamentally disturb the discipline's foundations, "open up a breach that penetrates to the very core of linguistics" (Culler, "Towards" 177), necessitating its dissolution or, more often, its reorganization according to principles suggested by literary studies.[23] Such a strategy allows critics to reiterate the legitimate demand for a cultural criticism but without specifically entering into interdisciplinary debate. My aim is not to attack critical goals and motives or to claim that critics and linguists can agree but merely to say that an enriching conversation between fields—about language and social class, language and ethnicity—has been missed.

We might pause to consider our disciplinary perspectives on each

---

[22] See Culler, "Towards"; Schleifer, "Responds" 332–33; Norris, "Theory" 96; Pratt, "Linguistic Utopias" 61. I question here only disciplinary characterizations, not critical aims.

[23] See Fabb and Durant, "Introduction" 2; Norris, "Theory" 91, 95; Schleifer, "Deconstruction" 394; MacCabe, "Language" 443–44.

other, here through the controversy over speech versus writing. Literary critics imagine linguists to be fully committed to the proposition that a logical calculus suffices to explain the complex everyday workings of speech. Linguists (often in introductory texts) invent English teachers who are politically naive enforcers of the standard language in particular and middle-class social norms in general, loyal adherents to unexamined notions of linguistic propriety and correctness. Critics sometimes hint that sociolinguists impose rigid categories on the populations they study.[24] And sociolinguists deplore the presumption that one may write on social issues without conducting fieldwork, without consulting the people one discusses. Critics have objected to linguistics for its simplistic conception of self, for privileging selfhood over textuality. Linguists take persons in English departments to be valorizing the texts of the standard language and high culture over speakers. I think it is safe to conclude that critics and linguists simply do not understand each other's projects.

PROSPECTS

I think everyone will agree that linguistics cannot, as Jakobson once suggested it could, absorb literary criticism and neatly focus and guide its development. Yet I also remain skeptical about a linguistics redesigned by critics. I certainly do not claim that the disciplines have nothing to say to each other. Indeed, interdisciplinary projects on both sides of the campus prove otherwise—Roger Fowler's literary theory, derived from a functional linguistics; Deborah Tannen's criticism-based poetics of everyday conversation; or Dan Sperber and Deirdre Wilson's extended application of H. P. Grice's work to literary and non-literary discourse alike. Many of the examples of this book speak to the productive effects of even mismatched aims across fields. However much critics may dispute the methods, no one has read Proust or thought through graduate programs the same way since Gérard Genette and Jonathan Culler wrote about them. But disciplinary boundaries, as Stanley Fish once remarked, are simply necessary to investigation of any kind, essential for the formulation of shared goals and problems ("Being" 21). Interdisciplinary rhetoric typically anticipates that barriers between academic fields will soon dissolve, but it is not clear that projects in linguistics and criticism are at all commensurate and that they may link in any transparent fashion. As much as we might hope for it, no single, mutually satisfying metatheory will be forthcoming.

[24] One imagines Vine Deloria's anthropologist (see 78–100).

I want to promote here neither an autonomously conceived literary theory nor an isolated and insulated linguistics. Indeed, as I mentioned at the outset, literary studies are necessarily in some sense interdisciplinary. Neither do I think we should, even if we could, return to some ideal of (perhaps Prague School) interdisciplinarity, become both critics and linguists, master multiple fields in order to practice criticism. I would wish, then, not for less model borrowing or always for less metaphorical treatment of what is borrowed but simply for more conscious extrapolation from the imported concepts—in short, for more genuine interactions with outside disciplines met on their own terms. The problem is not that linguistics-derived literary notions are construed too loosely or refashioned too dramatically in a literary context, for such terms begin as metaphors in the original field. Rather, the persisting challenge for critics is to distinguish between the linguistics-based and the literary versions. Disenchantment with linguistic models can be productive, I think, but only when an engagement with linguistic theory actually takes place.

Works Cited

Alfino, Mark. "Another Look at the Searle-Derrida Debate." *Philosophy and Rhetoric* 24.2 (1991): 143–52.

Anscombe, G. E. M. "On Brute Facts." *Analysis* 18 (1958): 69–72.

Attridge, Derek. "Closing Statement: Linguistics and Poetics in Retrospect." In *The Linguistics of Writing: Arguments between Language and Literature,* ed. Nigel Fabb, Derek Attridge, Alan Durant, and Colin MacCabe, 15–32. New York: Methuen, 1987.

———. "Language as History/History as Language: Saussure and the Romance of Etymology." In *Peculiar Language: Literature as Difference from the Renaissance to James Joyce,* 90–126. Ithaca: Cornell University Press, 1988.

———. "Literature as Imitation: Jakobson, Joyce, and the Art of Onomatopoeia." In *Peculiar Language: Literature as Difference from the Renaissance to James Joyce,* 127–57. Ithaca: Cornell University Press, 1988.

Austin, J. L. *How to Do Things with Words.* Ed. J. O. Urmson and Marina Sbisà. 2d ed. Cambridge: Harvard University Press, 1962.

———. "A Plea for Excuses." In *Philosophical Papers,* 3d ed., ed. J. O. Urmson and G. J. Warnock, 175–204. Oxford: Oxford University Press, 1979.

———. "Three Ways of Spilling Ink." In *Philosophical Papers,* 3d ed., ed. J. O. Urmson and G. J. Warnock, 272–87. Oxford: Oxford University Press, 1979.

Barry, Peter. "Linguistics and Literary Criticism: A Polytheism without Gods." *English* (1980): 133–43.

Bass, Alan. Translator's Introduction to *Writing and Difference,* by Jacques Derrida, ix–xx. Chicago: University of Chicago Press, 1978.

Bennington, Geoffrey, and Jacques Derrida. *Jacques Derrida.* Trans. Geoffrey Bennington. Chicago: University of Chicago Press, 1993. (Originally published as *Jacques Derrida.* Paris: Seuil, 1991.)

Benveniste, Emile. "Analytical Philosophy and Language." In *Problems in Gen-*

eral Linguistics, trans. Mary Elizabeth Meek, 231–38. Coral Gables: University of Miami Press, 1971. (Originally published as *Problèmes de linguistique génerale.* Paris: Gallimard, 1966.)

Bierwisch, Manfred. "Poetics and Linguistics." In *Linguistics and Literary Style,* ed. Donald C. Freeman, essay trans. Peter H. Salus, 96–115. New York: Holt, Rinehart, Winston, 1970. (Originally published as "Poetik und Linguistik." In *Mathematik und Dichtung,* ed. Helmut Kreuzer and Rul Gunzenhaüser. Munich: Nymphenburger, 1965, 1967, 49–65.)

Bizup, Joseph M., and Eugene Kintgen. "The Cognitive Paradigm in Literary Studies." *College English* 8 (1993): 841–57.

Black, Max. *Models and Metaphors: Studies in Language and Philosophy.* Ithaca: Cornell University Press, 1962.

Bloomfield, Leonard. *Language.* 1933. Chicago: University of Chicago Press, 1984.

Brooks, Cleanth. *The Well Wrought Urn: Studies in the Structure of Poetry.* 1947. Reprint, New York: Harcourt Brace Jovanovich, 1975.

Brooks, Peter. *Reading for the Plot: Design and Intention in Narrative.* Cambridge: Harvard University Press, 1984.

Brown, Penelope, and Stephen Levinson. "Universals in Language Use: Politeness Phenomena." In *Questions and Politeness,* ed. Esther Goody, 56–311. Cambridge: Cambridge University Press, 1978.

Butler, Judith. *Bodies That Matter: On the Discursive Limits of "Sex."* New York: Routledge, 1993.

Carter, Ronald, ed. *Language and Literature: An Introductory Reader in Stylistics.* London: George Allen and Unwin, 1982.

Cavell, Stanley. "Politics as Opposed to What?" In *The Politics of Interpretation,* ed. W. J. T. Mitchell, 181–202. Chicago: University of Chicago Press, 1983.

Chatman, Seymour. *Coming to Terms: The Rhetoric of Narrative in Fiction and Film.* Ithaca: Cornell University Press, 1990.

——. "New Ways of Analyzing Narrative Structure, with an Example from Joyce's *Dubliners.*" *Language and Style* 2.1 (1969): 3–36.

——. "Reply to Barbara Herrnstein Smith." In *On Narrative,* ed. W. J. T. Mitchell, 258–65. Chicago: University of Chicago Press, 1981.

——. *Story and Discourse: Narrative Structure in Fiction and Film.* Ithaca: Cornell University Press, 1978.

——. "What Can We Learn from Contextualist Narratology?" *Poetics Today* 11 (1990): 309–28.

——, ed. *Approaches to Poetics: Selected Papers From the English Institute.* New York: Columbia University Press, 1973.

Chatman, Seymour, and Samuel R. Levin, eds. *Essays on the Language of Literature.* Boston: Houghton Mifflin, 1967.

Cherry, Christopher. "Regulative Rules and Constitutive Rules." *Philosophical Quarterly* 23 (1973): 301–15.

Cheshire, Jenny. "Linguistic Variation and Social Function." In *Sociolinguistic Variation in Speech Communities,* ed. Suzanne Romaine, 153–69. London: Edward Arnold, 1982.

Chomsky, Noam. *Aspects of the Theory of Syntax*. Cambridge: MIT Press, 1965.

——. *Knowledge of Language: Its Nature, Origin, and Use*. New York: Praeger, 1986.

——. *Language and Responsibility*. Trans. John Viertel. New York: Pantheon, 1979. (Originally published as *Dialogues avec Mitsou Ronat*. Paris: Flammarion, 1977.)

——. *The Logical Structure of Linguistic Theory*. Chicago: University of Chicago Press, 1975.

——. "On the Nature of Language." In *Essays on Form and Interpretation*, ed. Noam Chomsky, 63–77. New York: North-Holland-Elsevier, 1977.

——. "Questions of Form and Interpretation." In *Essays on Form and Interpretation*, ed. Noam Chomsky, 25–59. New York: North-Holland-Elsevier, 1977.

——. *Syntactic Structures*. New York: Mouton, 1957.

——. *Towards a New Cold War: Essays on the Current Crisis and How We Got There*. New York: Pantheon, 1982.

Culler, Jonathan. "Convention and Meaning: Derrida and Austin." *New Literary History* 13 (1981): 15–30.

——. "Literature and Linguistics." In *Interrelations of Literature*, ed. Jean-Pierre Barricelli and Joseph Gibaldi, 1–24. New York: Modern Language Association, 1982.

——. *On Deconstruction: Theory and Criticism after Structuralism*. Ithaca: Cornell University Press, 1982.

——. "Political Criticism: Confronting Religion." In *Framing the Sign: Criticism and Its Institutions*, 69–82. Norman: University of Oklahoma Press, 1988.

——. *The Pursuit of Signs: Semiotics, Literature, Deconstruction*. Ithaca: Cornell University Press, 1981.

——. *Saussure*. Hassocks, England: Harvester Press, 1976.

——. "Structuralism and Grammatology." *boundary 2* 8.2 (1979): 75–93.

——. *Structuralist Poetics: Structuralism, Linguistics, and the Study of Literature*. Ithaca: Cornell University Press, 1975.

——. "Towards a Linguistics of Writing." In *The Linguistics of Writing: Arguments between Language and Literature*, ed. Nigel Fabb, Derek Attridge, Alan Durant, and Colin MacCabe, 173–84. New York: Methuen, 1987.

Darnton, Robert. *The Great Cat Massacre and Other Episodes in French Cultural History*. New York: Vintage Books-Random House, 1985.

Dasenbrock, Reed Way, ed. *Redrawing the Lines: Analytic Philosophy, Deconstruction, and Literary Theory*. Minneapolis: University of Minnesota Press, 1989.

——. "Redrawing the Lines: An Introduction." In *Redrawing the Lines: Analytic Philosophy, Deconstruction, and Literary Theory*, ed. Reed Way Dasenbrock, 3–26. Minneapolis: University of Minnesota Press, 1989.

Davis, Philip W. *Modern Theories of Language*. Englewood Cliffs, N.J.: Prentice-Hall, 1973.

Deloria, Vine, Jr. *Custer Died for Your Sins: An Indian Manifesto*. New York: Macmillan, 1969.

de Man, Paul. "Excuses (*Confessions*)." In *Allegories of Reading: Figural Language in Rousseau, Nietzsche, Rilke, Proust*, 278–301. New Haven: Yale University Press, 1979.

——. "The Resistance to Theory." *Yale French Studies* 63 (1982): 3–20.

——. "The Rhetoric of Blindness: Jacques Derrida's Reading of Rousseau." In *Blindness and Insight: Essays in the Rhetoric of Contemporary Criticism*, rev. 2d ed., 102–41. Minneapolis: University of Minnesota Press, 1983.

——. "Semiology and Rhetoric." In *Allegories of Reading: Figural Language in Rousseau, Nietzsche, Rilke, and Proust*, 3–19. New Haven: Yale University Press, 1979.

Derrida, Jacques. "Afterword: Toward an Ethic of Discussion." In *Limited Inc*, ed. Gerald Graff, essay trans. Sam Weber, 111–60. Evanston, Ill.: Northwestern University Press, 1988.

——. "Differance." In *Speech and Phenomena and Other Essays on Husserl's Theory of Signs*, trans. David B. Allison, 129–60. Evanston, Ill.: Northwestern University Press, 1973. (Originally published as "La Différance." *Bulletin de la Société française de philosophie* 62 [1968].)

——. "Force and Signification." In *Writing and Difference*, trans. Alan Bass, 3–30. Chicago: University of Chicago Press, 1978. (Originally published in *L'écriture et la différence*. Paris: Seuil, 1967.)

——. *Limited Inc*. Ed. Gerald Graff. Essays trans. Sam Weber, Sam Weber and Jeffrey Mehlman. Evanston, Ill.: Northwestern University Press, 1988. (Selections originally published 1972–88.)

——. "Limited Inc a b c . . ." In *Limited Inc*, ed. Gerald Graff, essay trans. Samuel Weber, 29–110. Evanston, Ill.: Northwestern University Press, 1988. (Originally published 1977.)

——. "The Linguistic Circle of Geneva." In *Margins of Philosophy*, trans. Alan Bass, 137–53. Chicago: University of Chicago Press, 1982. (Originally published in *Marges de la philosophie*. Paris: Minuit, 1972.)

——. "Mallarmé." In *Acts of Literature*, ed. Derek Attridge, essay trans. Christine Roulston, 110–26. New York: Routledge, 1992. (Originally published as "Mallarmé." In *Tableau de le littérature française: De Madame de Staël à Rimbaud*. Paris: Gallimard, 1974.)

——. *Of Grammatology*. Trans. Gayatri Chakravorty Spivak. Baltimore: Johns Hopkins University Press, 1976. (Originally published as *De la grammatologie*. Paris: Minuit, 1967.)

——. *Positions*. Trans. Alan Bass. Chicago: University of Chicago Press, 1981. (Originally published as *Positions*. Paris: Minuit, 1972.)

——. "Signature Event Context." In *Limited Inc*, ed. Gerald Graff, essay trans. Samuel Weber and Jeffrey Mehlman, 1–23. Evanston, Ill.: Northwestern University Press, 1988. (Originally published Paris: Minuit, 1972.)

——. "Some Questions and Responses." In *The Linguistics of Writing: Arguments between Language and Literature*, ed. Nigel Fabb, Derek Attridge, Alan Durant, and Colin MacCabe, 252–64. New York: Methuen, 1987.

———. *Speech and Phenomena and Other Essays on Husserl's Theory of Signs.* Trans. David B. Allison. Evanston, Ill.: Northwestern University Press, 1973. (Originally published as *La voix et le Phénomène.* Paris: Presses Universitaires de France, 1967.)

———. "Structure, Sign, and Play in the Discourse of the Human Sciences." In *Writing and Difference*, trans. Alan Bass, 178–93. Chicago: University of Chicago Press, 1978. (Originally published in *L'écriture et la différence.* Paris: Seuil, 1967.)

Dijk, Teun van, ed. *Pragmatics of Language and Literature.* New York: North-Holland and American Elsevier, 1976.

Dixon, R. M. W. "Ergativity." *Language* 55 (1979): 80–96.

Doležel, Lubomír. *Occidental Poetics: Tradition and Progress.* Lincoln: University of Nebraska Press, 1990.

Dowling, William C. "Intentionless Meaning." In *Against Theory: Literary Studies and the New Pragmatism*, ed. W. J. T. Mitchell, 89–94. Chicago: University of Chicago Press, 1985.

Eagleton, Terry. *Literary Theory: An Introduction.* Minneapolis: University of Minnesota Press, 1983.

Eco, Umberto. *The Role of the Reader: Explorations in the Semiotics of Texts.* Bloomington: Indiana University Press, 1979.

———. *Semiotics and the Philosophy of Language.* Bloomington: Indiana University Press, 1984.

Èjxenbaum, Boris M. "The Theory of the Formal Method." In *Readings in Russian Poetics: Formalist and Structuralist Views*, ed. Ladislav Matejka and Krystyna Pomorska, essay trans. Irwin R. Titunik, 3–37. Cambridge: MIT Press, 1978. (Originally published 1927.)

Erlich, Victor. *Russian Formalism: History-Doctrine.* The Hague: Mouton, 1955.

Fabb, Nigel. "Saussure and Literary Theory: From the Perspective of Linguistics." *Critical Quarterly* 30.2 (1988): 58–72.

Fabb, Nigel, Derek Attridge, Alan Durant, and Colin MacCabe, eds. *The Linguistics of Writing: Arguments between Language and Literature.* New York: Methuen, 1987.

Fabb, Nigel, and Alan Durant. "Introduction: The Linguistics of Writing: Retrospect and Prospect after Twenty-Five Years." In *The Linguistics of Writing: Arguments between Language and Literature*, ed. Nigel Fabb, Derek Attridge, Alan Durant, and Colin MacCabe, 1–14. New York: Methuen, 1987.

———. "Ten Years on in the Linguistics of Writing." *Prose Studies* 10.1 (1987): 51–71.

Fairclough, Norman. *Language and Power.* London: Longman, 1989.

Fasold, Ralph. *Sociolinguistics of Language.* Oxford: Basil Blackwell, 1990.

Felman, Shoshana. *The Literary Speech Act: Don Juan with J. L. Austin, or Seduction in Two Languages.* Trans. Catherine Porter. Ithaca: Cornell University Press, 1983. (Originally published as *Le scandale du corps parlant.* Paris: Seuil, 1980.)

Fish, Stanley. "Anti-foundationalism, Theory Hope, and the Teaching of Composition." In *The Current in Criticism: Essays on the Present and Future of Literary Theory*, ed. Clayton Koelb and Virgil Lokke, 65–79. West Lafayette, Ind.: Purdue University Press, 1987.

———. "Being Interdisciplinary Is So Very Hard to Do." *Profession 89*: 15–22.

———. "Consequences." In *Against Theory: Literary Studies and the New Pragmatism*, ed. W. J. T. Mitchell, 106–31. Chicago: University of Chicago Press, 1985.

———. *Doing What Comes Naturally: Change, Rhetoric, and the Practice of Theory in Literary and Legal Studies*. Durham, N.C.: Duke University Press, 1989.

———. "Fish v. Fizz." In *Doing What Comes Naturally: Change, Rhetoric, and the Practice of Theory in Literary and Legal Studies*, 120–40. Durham, N.C.: Duke University Press, 1989.

———. "Force." In *Doing What Comes Naturally: Change, Rhetoric, and the Practice of Theory in Literary and Legal Studies*, 503–24. Durham, N.C.: Duke University Press, 1989.

———. "How To Do Things with Austin and Searle: Speech-Act Theory and Literary Criticism." In *Is There a Text in This Class? The Authority of Interpretive Communities*, 197–245. Cambridge: Harvard University Press, 1980.

———. *Is There a Text in This Class? The Authority of Interpretive Communities*. Cambridge: Harvard University Press, 1980.

———. "Literature in the Reader: Affective Stylistics." In *Is There a Text in This Class? The Authority of Interpretive Communities*, 52–67. Cambridge: Harvard University Press, 1980.

———. "What Is Stylistics and Why Are They Saying Such Terrible Things about It?" In *Is There a Text in This Class? The Authority of Interpretive Communities*, 68–96. Cambridge: Harvard University Press, 1980.

———. "What Is Stylistics and Why Are They Saying Such Terrible Things about It? Part II." In *Is There a Text in This Class? The Authority of Interpretive Communities*, 246–67. Cambridge: Harvard University Press, 1980.

———. "With the Compliments of the Author: Reflections on Austin and Derrida." *Critical Inquiry* 8 (1982): 693–721.

Fowler, Roger. *Linguistic Criticism*. Oxford: Oxford University Press, 1986.

———. "Linguistics and, and Versus, Poetics." *Journal of Literary Semantics* 8.1 (1979): 3–21.

———. *Linguistics and the Novel*. London: Methuen, 1977.

———. "Linguistics, Stylistics; Criticism?" In *Contemporary Essays on Style: Rhetoric, Linguistics, and Criticism*, ed. Glen A. Love and Michael Payne, 165–74. Glenview, Ill.: Scott, Foresman, 1969.

———. "Linguistic Theory and the Study of Literature." In *Essays on Style and Language*, ed. Roger Fowler, 1–28. London: Kegan Paul, 1966.

———. *Literature as Social Discourse: The Practice of Linguistic Criticism*. Bloomington: Indiana University Press, 1981.

———, ed. *Essays on Style and Language*. London: Routledge-Kegan Paul, 1966.

Fraser, Bruce. "Hedged Performatives." In *Syntax and Semantics*, vol. 3: *Speech*

Acts, ed. Peter Cole and Jerry Morgan, 187–210. New York: Academic Press, 1975.

Freeman, Donald C. "Keats's 'To Autumn': Poetry as Process and Pattern." In *Essays in Modern Stylistics,* ed. Donald C. Freeman, 83–99. New York: Methuen, 1981.

——. "Linguistic Approaches to Literature." In *Linguistics and Literary Style,* ed. Donald C. Freeman, 3–17. New York: Holt, Rinehart, Winston, 1970.

——, ed. *Essays in Modern Stylistics.* New York: Methuen, 1981.

——, ed. *Linguistics and Literary Style.* New York: Holt, Rinehart, Winston, 1970.

Galan, F. W. *Historic Structures: The Prague School Project, 1928–1946.* Austin: University of Texas Press, 1985.

Garver, Newton. "Derrida on Rousseau on Writing." *Journal of Philosophy* 74 (1977): 663–73.

Garvin, Paul L., ed. and trans. *A Prague School Reader on Esthetics, Literary Structure, and Style.* Washington, D.C.: Georgetown University Press, 1964. (Selections originally published 1932–48.)

Genette, Gérard. "Fictional Narrative, Factual Narrative." *Poetics Today* 11 (1990): 755–74.

——. "Modern Mimology: The Dream of a Poetic Language." Trans. Thais E. Morgan. *PMLA* 104 (1989): 202–14.

——. *Narrative Discourse: An Essay in Method.* Trans. Jane E. Lewin. Ithaca: Cornell University Press, 1980. (Originally published with additional text as *Figures, Figures II, Figures III.* Paris: Seuil, 1966, 1969, 1972.)

Goodman, Nelson. "The Telling and the Told." In *On Narrative,* ed. W. J. T. Mitchell, 255–57. Chicago: University of Chicago Press, 1981.

Greimas, A. J. "Elements of a Narrative Grammar." *Diacritics* 7 (1977): 23–40.

——. "Narrative Grammar: Units and Levels." *MLN* 86 (1971): 793–806.

——. *Structural Semantics.* Trans. H. S. Gill. New Delhi: Bahri, 1989. (Originally published 1989.)

Grice, H. Paul. "Further Notes on Logic and Conversation." In *Syntax and Semantics,* vol. 9: *Pragmatics,* ed. Peter Cole, 183–98. New York: Academic Press, 1978.

——. "Logic and Conversation." In *Syntax and Semantics,* vol. 3: *Speech Acts,* ed. Peter Cole and Jerry Morgan, 41–58. New York: Academic Press, 1975.

——. "Utterer's Meaning, Sentence-Meaning, and Word-Meaning." In *The Philosophy of Language,* ed. John Searle, 54–70. London: Oxford University Press, 1971.

Gumperz, John J., ed. *Discourse Strategies.* Cambridge: Cambridge University Press, 1982.

Halliday, M. A. K. "Linguistic Function and Literary Style: An Inquiry into the Language of William Golding's *The Inheritors.*" In *Essays in Modern Stylistics,* ed. Donald C. Freeman, 325–60. New York: Methuen, 1981.

Hancher, Michael. "Beyond a Speech-Act Theory of Literary Discourse." *MLN* 92 (1977): 1081–98.

——. "The Law of Signatures." In *Law and Aesthetics*, ed. Roberta Kevelson, 227–43. New York: Peter Lang, 1992.

——. "Pragmatics in Wonderland." In *Rhetoric, Literature, and Interpretation*, ed. Harry R. Garvin and Steven Mailloux, 165–84. Lewisburg, Pa.: Bucknell University Press, 1983.

——. "Three Kinds of Intention." *MLN* 87 (1972): 827–51.

Harris, Roy. *Reading Saussure: A Critical Commentary on the "Cours de Linguistique Générale."* La Salle, Ill.: Open Court, 1987.

Hawkes, Terence. *Structuralism and Semiotics.* Berkeley: University of California Press, 1977.

Henkel, Jacqueline. "A Comment on 'Deconstruction and Linguistic Analysis.'" *College English* 50 (1988): 454–57.

——. "Promises According to Searle: Some Problems with Constitutive Rules." *1983 Mid-America Linguistics Conference Papers* (1984): 181–94.

Herman, Edward S., and Noam Chomsky. *Manufacturing Consent: The Political Economy of the Mass Media.* New York: Pantheon, 1988.

Hirsch, E. D., Jr. *The Aims of Interpretation.* Chicago: University of Chicago Press, 1976.

Hitchens, Christopher. "The Chorus and Cassandra: What Everyone Knows about Noam Chomsky." *Grand Street* 5.1 (1985): 106–31.

Hjelmslev, Louis. *Prolegomena to a Theory of Language.* Rev. ed. Trans. Francis J. Whitfield. Madison: University of Wisconsin Press, 1961. (Originally published 1943.)

Holdcroft, David. *Saussure: Signs, System, and Arbitrariness.* Cambridge: Cambridge University Press, 1991.

Holenstein, Elmar. *Roman Jakobson's Approach to Language: Phenomenological Structuralism.* Trans. Catherine Schelbert and Tarcisius Schelbert. Bloomington: Indiana University Press, 1974. (Originally published as *Jakobson, ou Le structuralism phénoménologique.* Paris: Seghers, 1974.)

Holland, Nancy Jean. "A Theory of Meaning after the End of Philosophy." Ph.D. dissertation, University of California, Berkeley, 1981.

Holland, Norman. *The Critical I.* New York: Columbia University Press, 1992.

Hollander, John. "Opening Statement." In *Style and Language*, ed. Thomas Sebeok, 396–407. Cambridge: MIT Press, 1960.

Hopper, Paul J. "Discourse Analysis: Grammar and Critical Theory in the 1980s." *Profession 88* (1988): 18–24.

Iser, Wolfgang. *The Act of Reading: A Theory of Aesthetic Response.* Baltimore: Johns Hopkins University Press, 1978.

Jakobson, Roman. "Anthony's Contribution to Linguistic Theory." In *Selected Writings: Word and Language* 2:285–88. The Hague: Mouton, 1971. (Originally published 1962.)

——. "Boas' View of Grammatical Meaning." In *Selected Writings: Word and Language* 2:489–96. The Hague: Mouton, 1971. (Originally published 1959.)

——. "Brain and Language." In *On Language*, ed. Linda R. Waugh and Monique Monville-Burston, 498–513. Cambridge: Harvard University Press, 1990. (Originally published 1980.)

——. *Child Language, Aphasia, and Phonological Universals.* The Hague: Mouton, 1968. Trans. Allan R. Keiler. (Originally published as *Kindersprache, Aphasie, und allgemeine Lautgesetze.* N.p., 1941.)

——. "Closing Statement: Linguistics and Poetics." In *Style and Language,* ed. Thomas Sebeok, 350–77. Cambridge: MIT Press, 1960.

——. "Dada." In *Language in Literature,* ed. Krystyna Pomorska and Stephen Rudy, essay trans. Stephen Rudy, 34–40. Cambridge: Belknap-Harvard University Press, 1987. (Originally published 1921.)

——. "The Dominant." In *Readings in Russian Poetics: Formalist and Structuralist Views,* ed. Ladislav Matejka and Krystyna Pomorska, essay trans. Herbert Eagle, 82–87. Cambridge: MIT Press, 1978. (Written 1935; published 1971.)

——. "Efforts towards a Means-Ends Model of Language in Interwar Continental Linguistics." In *Selected Writings: Word and Language* 2:522–26. The Hague: Mouton, 1971. (Originally published 1963.)

——. *The Framework of Language.* Ed. Irwin R. Titunik and Ladislav Matejka. Ann Arbor: Michigan Studies in the Humanities, 1980. (Selections originally published 1975–79.)

——. "Futurism." In *Language in Literature,* ed. Krystyna Pomorska and Stephen Rudy, essay trans. Stephen Rudy, 28–33. Cambridge: Belknap-Harvard University Press, 1987. (Originally published 1919.)

——. "A Glance at the Development of Semiotics." In *Language in Literature,* ed. Krystyna Pomorska and Stephen Rudy, essay trans. Patricia Baudoin, 436–54. Cambridge: Belknap-Harvard University Press, 1987. (Originally published as *Coup d'oeil sur le développement de la sémiotique.* Bloomington: Indiana University Press, 1975.)

——. *Language in Literature.* Ed. Krystyna Pomorska and Stephen Rudy. Cambridge: Belknap-Harvard University Press, 1987. (Selections originally published 1919–77.)

——. "Linguistic Glosses to Goldstein's 'Wortbegriff.'" In *Selected Writings: Word and Language* 2:267–71. The Hague: Mouton, 1971. (Originally published 1959.)

——. "Linguistics in Relation to Other Sciences." In *On Language,* ed. Linda R. Waugh and Monique Monville-Burston, 451–88. Cambridge: Harvard University Press, 1990. (Delivered 1967; revised and published 1974.)

——. *Main Trends in the Science of Language,* New York: Harper and Row, 1970.

——. "Marginal Notes on the Prose of the Poet Pasternak." In *Language in Literature,* ed. Krystyna Pomorska and Stephen Rudy, essay trans. Angela Livingstone, 301–17. Cambridge: Belknap-Harvard University Press, 1987. (Originally published as "Randbemerkungen zur Prosa des Dichters Pasternak." In *Slavische Rundschau* 6 [1935].)

——. *On Language.* Ed. Linda R. Waugh and Monique Monville-Burston. Cambridge: Harvard University Press, 1990. (Selections originally published 1936–80.)

——. "On the Linguistic Approach to the Problem of Consciousness and the

Unconscious." In *The Framework of Language,* ed. Irwin R. Titunik and Ladislav Matejka, 113–32. Ann Arbor: Michigan Studies in the Humanities, 1980. (Originally published 1978).

——. "On Linguistic Aspects of Translation." In *Selected Writings: Word and Language* 2:260–66. The Hague: Mouton, 1971. (Originally published 1959.)

——. "On Realism in Art." In *Readings in Russian Poetics: Formalist and Structuralist Views,* ed. Ladislav Matejka and Krystyna Pomorska, essay trans. Karol Magassy, 38–46. Cambridge: MIT Press, 1978. (Originally published 1921.)

——. "A Postscript to the Discussion on Grammar of Poetry." *Diacritics* 10.1 (1980): 22–35.

——. "Quest for the Essence of Language." In *On Language,* ed. Linda R. Waugh and Monique Monville-Burston, 407–21. Cambridge: Harvard University Press, 1990. (Originally published 1966.)

——. "Retrospect." In *Selected Writings: Phonological Studies* 1:631–58. The Hague: Mouton, 1962.

——. "Retrospect." In *Selected Writings: Poetry of Grammar and Grammar of Poetry* 3:765–89. The Hague: Mouton, 1981.

——. "Shifters and Verbal Categories." In *On Language,* ed. Linda R. Waugh and Monique Monville-Burston, 386–92. Cambridge: Harvard University Press, 1990. (Originally published 1950 and 1957.)

——. "Sign and System: A Reassessment of Saussure's Doctrine." In *Verbal Art, Verbal Sign, Verbal Time,* ed. Krystyna Pomorska and Stephen Rudy, essay trans. Benjamin Hrushovski, 28–33. Minneapolis: University of Minnesota Press, 1985. (Written 1959; originally published 1962.)

——. *Studies on Child Language and Aphasia.* The Hague: Mouton, 1971. (Selections originally published 1949–66.)

——. "Subliminal Verbal Patterning in Poetry." In *Language in Literature,* ed. Krystyna Pomorska and Stephen Rudy, 250–61. Cambridge: Belknap-Harvard University Press, 1987. (Originally published 1970.)

——. "Supraconscious Turgenev." In *Language in Literature,* ed. Krystyna Pomorska and Stephen Rudy, essay trans. Stephen Rudy, 262–66. Cambridge: Belknap-Harvard University Press, 1987. (Originally published 1979.)

——. "Two Aspects of Language and Two Types of Aphasic Disturbances." In *On Language,* ed. Linda R. Waugh and Monique Monville-Burston, 115–33. Cambridge: Harvard University Press, 1990. (Originally published 1956.)

——. *Verbal Art, Verbal Sign, Verbal Time.* Ed. Krystyna Pomorska and Stephen Rudy. Minneapolis: University of Minnesota Press, 1985. (Selections originally published 1928–81.)

——. "What Is Poetry?" In *Semiotics of Art: Prague School Contributions,* ed. Ladislav Matejka and Irwin R. Titunik, essay trans. Michael Heim, 164–75. Cambridge: MIT Press, 1976. (Originally published 1934.)

——, and Petr Bogatyrev. "On the Boundary between Studies of Folklore and Literature." In *Readings in Russian Poetics: Formalist and Structuralist Views,* ed. and trans. Ladislav Matejka and Krystyna Pomorska, essay trans.

Herbert Eagle, 91–93. Cambridge: MIT Press, 1978. (Originally published 1931.)

——, and Morris Halle, eds. *Fundamentals of Language.* The Hague: Mouton, 1956.

——, and Lawrence Jones. *Shakespeare's Verbal Art in "Th'Expence of Spirit."* The Hague: Mouton, 1970.

——, and Claude Lévi-Strauss. "Charles Baudelaire's 'Les Chats.'" In *Language in Literature*, ed. Krystyna Pomorska and Stephen Rudy, essay trans. Katie Furniss-Lane, revised Roman Jakobson, 180–97. Cambridge: Belknap-Harvard University Press, 1987. (Originally published in *L'Homme* 2 [1962].)

——, and Krystyna Pomorska. *Dialogues.* Cambridge: MIT Press, 1983. (Originally published 1980.)

——, and Jurij Tynjanov. "Problems in the Study of Language and Literature." In *Verbal Art, Verbal Sign, Verbal Time*, ed. Krystyna Pomorska and Stephen Rudy, essay trans. Herbert Eagle, 25–27. Minneapolis: University of Minnesota Press, 1985. (Originally published 1928.)

——, and Linda R. Waugh. "The Spell of Speech Sounds." In *Selected Writings: Major Works, 1976–1980*, vol. 8, ed. Stephen Rudy, 181–239. Amsterdam: Mouton de Gruyter, 1988. (Originally published 1979.)

Jameson, Fredric. *The Prison-House of Language: A Critical Account of Structuralism and Russian Formalism.* Princeton: Princeton University Press, 1972.

Jay, Gregory S. "Values and Deconstructions: Derrida, Saussure, Marx." *Cultural Critique* 8 (1987–88): 153–96.

Jefferson, Ann, and David Robey, eds. *Modern Literary Theory: A Comparative Introduction.* 2d ed. Totowa, N.J.: Barnes and Noble, 1986.

Kalish, Donald. "Semantics." In *The Encyclopedia of Philosophy* 7:148–58. New York: Macmillan, 1967.

Kamuf, Peggy. "Floating Authorship." *Diacritics* 16.4 (1986): 3–13.

Katz, Jerrold J. *Language and Other Abstract Objects.* Totowa, N.J.: Rowman and Littlefield, 1981.

Katz, Jerrold J., and Jerry A. Fodor. "The Structure of a Semantic Theory." In *The Structure of Language*, ed. Jerry A. Fodor and Jerrold Katz, 479–518. Englewood Cliffs, N.J.: Prentice-Hall, 1964.

Katz, Jerrold J., and Paul M. Postal. *An Integrated Theory of Linguistic Descriptions.* Cambridge: MIT Press, 1964.

Kinneavy, James L. *A Theory of Discourse: The Aims of Discourse.* New York: W. W. Norton, 1971.

Knapp, Steven, and Walter Benn Michaels. "Against Theory." In *Against Theory: Literary Studies and the New Pragmatism*, ed. W. J. T. Mitchell, 11–30. Chicago: University of Chicago Press, 1985.

——. "Against Theory 2: Hermeneutics and Deconstruction." *Critical Inquiry* 14 (1987): 49–68.

——. "A Reply to Our Critics." In *Against Theory: Literary Studies and the New Pragmatism*, ed. W. J. T. Mitchell, 95–105. Chicago: University of Chicago Press, 1985.

——. "A Reply to Richard Rorty: What Is Pragmatism?" In *Against Theory: Literary Studies and the New Pragmatism*, ed. W. J. T. Mitchell, 139–46. Chicago: University of Chicago Press, 1985.

Kristeva, Julia. "The Speaking Subject." In *On Signs*, ed. Marshall Blonsky, 210–20. Baltimore: Johns Hopkins University Press, 1985.

Kuhn, Thomas S. *The Structure of Scientific Revolutions.* Enlarged 2d ed. Chicago: University of Chicago Press, 1970.

Labov, William. *Language in the Inner City: Studies in the Black English Vernacular.* Philadelphia: University of Pennsylvania Press, 1972.

——. *Sociolinguistic Patterns.* Philadelphia: University of Pennsylvania Press, 1972.

Labov, William, and David Fanshel. *Therapeutic Discourse: Psychotherapy as Conversation.* New York: Academic Press, 1977.

Lanser, Susan Sniader. *The Narrative Act: Point of View in Prose Fiction.* Princeton: Princeton University Press, 1981.

Leech, Geoffrey. "Stylistics and Functionalism." In *The Linguistics of Writing: Arguments between Language and Literature*, ed. Nigel Fabb, Derek Attridge, Alan Durant, and Colin MacCabe, 76–88. New York: Methuen, 1987.

Leitch, Vincent B. *Deconstructive Criticism: An Advanced Introduction.* New York: Columbia University Press, 1983.

Levin, Samuel R. "Concerning What Kind of Speech Act a Poem Is." In *Pragmatics of Language and Literature*, ed. Teun A. van Dijk, 141–60. New York: North-Holland-American Elsevier, 1976.

——. "Coupling in a Shakespearean Sonnet." In *Linguistic Structures in Poetry*, 51–58. The Hague: Mouton, 1962.

——. *Linguistic Structures in Poetry.* The Hague: Mouton, 1962.

Lévi-Strauss, Claude. *The Savage Mind.* Chicago: University of Chicago Press, 1966. (Originally published as *Pensée sauvage.* Paris: Plon, 1962.)

——. "The Structural Study of Myth." In *Structural Anthropology*, vol. 1, trans. Claire Jacobson and Brooke Grundfest Schoepf, 206–31. New York: Basic Books, 1963. (Originally published 1958.)

Lodge, David. "Analysis and Interpretation of the Realist Text: A Pluralistic Approach to Ernest Hemingway's 'Cat in the Rain.'" *Poetics Today* 1.4 (1990): 5–22.

Love, Glen A., and Michael Payne, eds. *Contemporary Essays on Style: Rhetoric, Linguistics, and Criticism.* Glenview, Ill.: Scott, Foresman, 1969.

Lyons, John. *Noam Chomsky.* New York: Viking Press, 1970.

MacCabe, Colin. "Language, Linguistics, and the Study of Literature." In *Modern Criticism and Theory: A Reader*, ed. David Lodge, 432–44. New York: Longman, 1988.

——. "Opening Statement: Theory and Practice." In *The Linguistics of Writing: Arguments between Language and Literature*, ed. Nigel Fabb, Derek Attridge, Alan Durant, and Colin MacCabe, 286–306. New York: Methuen, 1987.

Mackey, Louis H. "An Exchange on Deconstruction." *New York Review of Books*, October 27, 1983, 74–79.

Macksey, Richard, and Eugenio Donato, eds. *The Structuralist Controversy: The Languages of Criticism and the Sciences of Man*. Baltimore: Johns Hopkins University Press, 1970.

Maclean, Ian. "Un Dialogue de Sourds? Some Implications of the Austin-Searle-Derrida Debate." *Paragraph*, March 5, 1985, 1–26.

Mailloux, Steven. "Convention and Context." *New Literary History* 14 (1983): 399–407.

——. *Interpretive Conventions: The Reader in the Study of American Fiction*. Ithaca: Cornell University Press, 1982.

Manley, Lawrence. "Concepts of Convention and Models of Critical Discourse." *New Literary History* 13 (1981): 31–52.

Martin, Wallace. *Recent Theories of Narrative*. Ithaca: Cornell University Press, 1986.

Matejka, Ladislav, and Krystyna Pomorska, eds. *Readings in Russian Poetics: Formalist and Structuralist Views*. Cambridge: MIT Press, 1978. (Selections originally published 1921–35.)

Matejka, Ladislav, and Irwin R. Titunik, eds. *Semiotics of Art: Prague School Contributions*. Cambridge: MIT Press, 1976. (Selections orginally published 1934–73.)

Mathesius, Vilém. "Functional Linguistics." In *Praguiana: Some Basic and Lesser Known Aspects of the Prague Linguistic School*, vol. 12 of *Linguistic and Literary Studies in Eastern Europe*, ed. and trans. Josef Vachek and Libuše Dušková, essay trans. Libuše Dušková, 121–42. Philadelphia: John Benjamins, 1983. (Originally published 1929.)

McCawley, James D. Review of *Knowledge of Language: Its Nature, Origin, and Use*, by Noam Chomsky. *Language* 64 (1988): 355–65.

Michaels, Walter Benn. "The Interpreter's Self: Peirce on the Cartesian 'Subject.'" *Georgia Review* 31 (1977): 383–402.

Mitchell, W. J. T., "Introduction: Pragmatic Theory." In *Against Theory: Literary Studies and the New Pragmatism*, ed. W. J. T. Mitchell, 1–10. Chicago: University of Chicago Press, 1985.

——, ed. *Against Theory: Literary Studies and the New Pragmatism*. Chicago: University of Chicago Press, 1985.

——, ed. *On Narrative*. Chicago: University of Chicago Press, 1981.

Morson, Gary Saul. "Who Speaks for Bakhtin?" In *Bakhtin: Essays and Dialogues on His Work*, ed. Gary Saul Morson, 1–19. Chicago: University of Chicago Press, 1986.

Muecke, Stephen. "Language as a Series of Statements." *Southern Review* (Australia) 17.2 (1984): 150–65.

Mukařovský, Jan. *Aesthetic Function, Norm, and Value as Social Facts*. Trans. Mark E. Suino. Ann Arbor: University of Michigan Press, 1970. (Originally published 1935 and 1936.)

——. "Art as Semiotic Fact." In *Semiotics of Art: Prague School Contributions*, ed. Ladislav Matejka and Irwin R. Titunik, essay trans. Irwin R. Titunik, 3–9. Cambridge: MIT Press, 1976. (Originally published 1936.)

——. "On Poetic Language." In *The Word and Verbal Art: Selected Essays by*

Jan Mukařovský, ed. and trans. John Burbank and Peter Steiner, 1–64. New Haven: Yale University Press, 1977. (Originally published 1940.)

——. "Standard Language and Poetic Language." In *A Prague School Reader on Esthetics, Literary Structure, and Style*, ed. and trans. Paul L. Garvin, 17–30. Washington, D.C.: Georgetown University Press, 1964. (Originally published 1932.)

——. *Structure, Sign, and Function*. Ed. and trans. John Burbank and Peter Steiner. New Haven: Yale University Press, 1978. (Selections originally published 1931–66.)

——. "Two Studies of Poetic Designation." In *Word and Verbal Art: Selected Essays by Jan Mukařovský*, ed. and trans. John Burbank and Peter Steiner, 65–80. New Haven: Yale University Press, 1977. (Originally published 1938 and 1941.)

——. *The Word and Verbal Art: Selected Essays by Jan Mukařovský*. Ed. and trans. John Burbank and Peter Steiner. New Haven: Yale University Press, 1977. (Selections originally published 1933–45.)

Newmeyer, Frederick. *Grammatical Theory: Its Limits and Its Possibilities*. Chicago: University of Chicago Press, 1983.

——. "Has There Been a Chomskyan Revolution in Linguistics?" *Language* 62 (1986): 1–18.

——. *Linguistic Theory in America: The First Quarter-Century of Transformational Generative Grammar*. New York: Academic Press, 1980.

——. *Linguistic Theory in America*. 2d ed. San Diego: Academic Press, 1986.

——. *The Politics of Linguistics*. Chicago: University of Chicago Press, 1986.

Nichols, Patricia C. "Linguistic Options and Choices for Black Women in the Rural South." In *Language, Gender and Society*, ed. Barrie Thorne, Cheris Kramarae, and Nancy Henley, 54–68. Rowley, Mass.: Newbury House, 1983.

Norris, Christopher. "Deconstruction and 'Ordinary Language': Speech versus Writing in the Text of Philosophy." In *The Deconstructive Turn: Essays in the Rhetoric of Philosophy*, 1–33. New York: Methuen, 1983.

——. *Deconstruction: Theory and Practice*. London: Methuen, 1982.

——. *Derrida*. Cambridge: Harvard University Press, 1987.

——. "Home Thoughts from Abroad: Derrida, Austin, and the Oxford Connection." *Philosophy and Literature* 10.1 (1986): 1–25.

——. "Philosophy as *Not* Just a 'Kind of Writing': Derrida and the Claim of Reason." In *Redrawing the Lines: Analytic Philosophy, Deconstruction, and Literary Theory*, ed. Reed Way Dasenbrock, 189–203. Minneapolis: University of Minnesota Press, 1989.

——. "That the Truest Philosophy Is the Most Feigning: Austin on the Margins of Literature." In *The Deconstructive Turn: Essays in the Rhetoric of Philosophy*, 59–84. New York: Methuen, 1983.

——. "Theory of Language and the Language of Literature." *Journal of Literary Semantics* 7.2 (1978): 90–98.

Ohmann, Richard. "Generative Grammars and the Concept of Literary Style." In *Contemporary Essays on Style: Rhetoric, Linguistics, and Criticism*, ed. Glen A. Love and Michael Payne, 133–48. Glenview, Ill.: Scott, Foresman, 1969.

——. "Literature as Act." In *Approaches to Poetics: Selected Papers from the English Institute*, ed. Seymour Chatman, 81–107. New York: Columbia Univerty Press, 1973.

——. "Literature as Sentences." In *Contemporary Essays on Style: Rhetoric, Linguistics, and Criticism*, ed. Glen A. Love and Michael Payne, 149–57. Glenview, Ill.: Scott, Foresman, 1969.

——. "Speech Acts and the Definition of Literature." *Philosophy and Rhetoric* 4 (1971): 1–19.

——. "Speech, Literature, and the Space Between." *New Literary History* 5 (1974): 37–63.

On Convention: I. Special issue of *New Literary History* 13 (1981): 1–177.

On Convention: II. Special issue of *New Literary History* 14 (1983): 397–594.

Pavel, Thomas G. *The Feud of Language: A History of Structuralist Thought*. Trans. Linda Jordan and Thomas G. Pavel. Oxford: Basil Blackwell, 1989. (Originally published as *Le mirage linguistique*. Paris: Minuit, no date given.)

——. "Narrative Tectonics." *Poetics Today* 11 (1990): 349–64.

Pepper, Stephen C. *World Hypotheses*. Berkeley: University of California Press, 1942.

Petrey, Sandy. *Speech Acts and Literary Theory*. New York: Routledge, 1990.

Pettit, Philip. *The Concept of Structuralism: A Critical Analysis*. Berkeley: University of California Press, 1975.

Pinker, Steven. *The Language Instinct: How the Mind Creates Language*. New York: William Morrow, 1994.

Porter, James I. "Saussure and Derrida on the Figure of the Voice." *MLN* 101 (1986): 871–94.

Pratt, Mary Louise. "Ideology and Speech-Act Theory." *Poetics Today* 7.1 (1986): 59–72.

——. "Interpretive Strategies/Strategic Interpretations: On Anglo-American Reader Response Criticism." *boundary 2* 11 (1982): 201–31.

——. "Linguistic Utopias." In *The Linguistics of Writing: Arguments between Language and Literature*, ed. Nigel Fabb, Derek Attridge, Alan Durant, and Colin MacCabe, 48–66. New York: Methuen, 1987.

——. *Toward a Speech Act Theory of Literary Discourse*. Bloomington: Indiana University Press, 1977.

Prince, Gerald. "Aspects of a Grammar of Narrative." *Poetics Today* 1 (1980): 49–63.

——. *A Grammar of Stories*. The Hague: Mouton, 1973.

——. *Narrative as Theme: Studies in French Fiction*. Lincoln: University of Nebraska Press, 1992.

——. *Narratology: The Form and Functioning of Narrative*. Amsterdam: Mouton, 1982.

——. "On Narrative Studies and Narrative Genres." *Poetics Today* 11 (1990): 271–82.

Propp, Vladimir. "Fairy Tale Transformations." In *Readings in Russian Poetics: Formalist and Structuralist Views*, ed. Ladislav Matejka and Krystyna Pomorska, essay trans. C. H. Severens, 94–114. Cambridge: MIT Press, 1978.

——. *Morphology of the Folktale.* 2d ed. Ed. Louis A. Wagner. Trans. Laurence Scott. Austin, Tex.: University of Texas Press, 1968.

Putnam, Hilary. "Convention: A Theme in Philosophy." *New Literary History* 13 (1981): 1–14.

Rawls, John. "Two Concepts of Rule." *Philosophical Review* 69 (1955): 3–32.

Reichert, John. "Do Poets Ever Mean What They Say?" *New Literary History* 13 (1981): 53–68.

Richards, I. A. "Factors and Functions in Poetry." In *Poetries: Their Media and Ends*, ed. Trevor Eaton, 1–16. The Hague: Mouton, 1974.

——. "Linguistics into Poetics." In *Poetries: Their Media and Ends*, ed. Trevor Eaton, 39–49. The Hague: Mouton, 1974.

——. *Principles of Literary Criticism.* New York: Harvest-Harcourt Brace Jovanovich, 1925.

——. *Speculative Instruments.* London: Kegan Paul, 1955.

Riemsdijk, Henk van, and Edwin Williams. *Introduction to the Theory of Grammar.* Cambridge: MIT Press, 1986.

Riffaterre, Michael. "Describing Poetic Structures: Two Approaches to Baudelaire's 'Les Chats.'" *Yale French Studies* 36–37 (1966): 200–242.

Rimmon-Kenan, Shlomith. *Narrative Fiction: Contemporary Poetics.* London: Methuen, 1983.

Robey, David. "Modern Linguistics and the Language of Literature." In *Modern Literary Theory: A Comparative Introduction*, 2d ed., ed. Ann Jefferson and David Robey, 38–64. Totowa, N.J.: Barnes and Noble, 1986.

——, ed. *Structuralism: An Introduction.* Oxford: Clarendon-Oxford University Press, 1973.

Rorty, Richard. "Derrida on Language, Being, and Abnormal Philosophy." *Journal of Philosophy* 74.2 (1977): 673–81.

——. "Philosophy as a Kind of Writing: An Essay on Derrida." *New Literary History* 10 (1978): 141–60.

——. "Philosophy without Principles." In *Against Theory: Literary Studies and the New Pragmatism*, ed. W. J. T. Mitchell, 132–38. Chicago: University of Chicago Press, 1985.

——. "Two Meanings of 'Logocentrism': A Reply to Norris." In *Redrawing the Lines: Analytic Philosophy, Deconstruction, and Literary Theory*, ed. Reed Way Dasenbrock, 204–16. Minneapolis: University of Minnesota Press, 1989.

Saporta, Sol. "The Application of Linguistics to the Study of Poetic Language." In *Style and Language*, ed. Thomas Sebeok, 82–93. Cambridge: MIT Press, 1960.

Saussure, Ferdinand de. *Course in General Linguistics.* Trans. Wade Baskin 1959. Ed. Charles Bally and Albert Sechehaye. Rev. ed. London: Peter Owen, 1974.

Schauber, Ellen, and Ellen Spolsky. *The Bounds of Interpretation: Linguistic Theory and Literary Text.* Stanford: Stanford University Press, 1986.

——. "Stalking a Generative Poetics." *New Literary History* 12 (1981): 397–413.

Schleifer, Ronald. "Deconstruction and Linguistic Analysis." *College English* 49 (1987): 381–95.

——. "Ronald Schleifer Responds." *College English* 51 (1989): 331–33.

Schmerling, Susan. "Subjectless Sentences and the Notion of Surface Structure." In *Papers from the Ninth Regional Meeting of the Chicago Linguistic Society* (1973): 577–86.

Scholes, Robert. "Deconstruction and Communication." *Critical Inquiry* 14 (1988): 278–295.

——. *Structuralism in Literature: An Introduction.* New Haven: Yale University Press, 1974.

Seamon, Roger. "Poetics against Itself: On the Self-Destruction of Modern Scientific Criticism." *PMLA* 104 (1989): 294–305.

Searle, John R. "The Background of Meaning." In *Speech Act Theory and Pragmatics*, ed. John Searle, Ferenc Kiefer, and Manfred Bierwisch, 221–32. Boston: D. Reidel, 1980.

——. "Chomsky's Revolution in Linguistics." In *On Noam Chomsky: Critical Essays*, ed. Gilbert Harman, 2–33. Garden City, N.Y.: Anchor-Doubleday, 1974.

——. "An Exchange on Deconstruction." *New York Review of Books*, February 2, 1984, 48–49.

——. *Expression and Meaning: Studies in the Theory of Speech Acts.* London: Cambridge University Press, 1979.

——. "Indirect Speech Acts." In *Expression and Meaning: Studies in the Theory of Speech Acts*, 30–57. London: Cambridge University Press, 1979.

——. "The Logical Status of Fictional Discourse." In *Expression and Meaning: Studies in the Theory of Speech Acts*, 58–75. Cambridge University Press, 1979.

——. "Reiterating the Differences: A Reply to Derrida." In *Glyph 1*, ed. Sam Weber and Henry Sussman, 198–208. Johns Hopkins Textual Studies. Baltimore: Johns Hopkins University Press, 1977.

——. *Speech Acts: An Essay in the Philosophy of Language.* London: Cambridge University Press, 1969.

——. "The Word Turned Upside Down." Review of *On Deconstruction: Theory and Criticism after Structuralism*, by Jonathan Culler. *New York Review of Books*, October 27, 1983, 74–79.

——, ed. *The Philosophy of Language.* London: Oxford University Press, 1971.

Sebeok, Thomas A., ed. *Style and Language.* Cambridge: MIT Press, 1960.

Sedgwick, Eve Kosofsky. "Queer Performativity: Henry James's *The Art of the Novel.*" *GLQ* 1.1 (1993): 1–16.

Sinclair, J. McH. "Taking a Poem to Pieces." In *Essays on Style and Language*, ed. Roger Fowler, 68–81. Routledge and Kegan Paul, 1966.

Smith, Barbara Herrnstein. "Narrative Versions, Narrative Theories." In *On Narrative*, ed. W. J. T. Mitchell, 209–32. Chicago: University of Chicago Press, 1981.

Sperber, Dan, and Deirdre Wilson. *Relevance: Communication and Cognition.* Cambridge: Harvard University Press, 1986.

Spivak, Gayatri Chakravorty. "Revolutions That as Yet Have No Model: Derrida's 'Limited Inc.'" Review of "Limited Inc a b c . . . ," by Jacques Derrida. *Diacritics* (December 1980): 29–49.

Spolsky, Ellen. *Gaps in Nature: Literary Interpretation and the Modular Mind.* Albany: State University of New York Press, 1993.

Stankiewicz, Edward. "Linguistics and the Study of Poetic Language." In *Style and Language,* ed. Thomas Sebeok, 69–81. Cambridge: MIT Press, 1960.

Steiner, Peter. "In Defense of Semiotics: The Dual Asymmetry of Cultural Signs." *New Literary History* 12 (1981): 415–35.

——. *The Prague School: Selected Writings, 1929–1946.* Trans. John Burbank, Olga Hasty, Manfred Jacobson, Bruce Kochis, and Wendy Steiner. Austin: University of Texas Press, 1982.

——. *Russian Formalism: A Metapoetics.* Ithaca: Cornell University Press, 1984.

Stewart, Susan. "Shouts on the Street: Bakhtin's Anti-Linguistics." In *Bakhtin: Essays and Dialogues on His Work,* ed. Gary Saul Morson, 41–57. Chicago: University of Chicago Press, 1986.

Strauss, Barrie Ruth. "Influencing Theory: Speech Acts." In *Tracing Literary Theory,* ed. Joseph Natoli, 213–47. Urbana: University of Illinois Press, 1987.

Strawson, P. F. "Intention and Convention in Speech Acts." In *The Philosophy of Language,* ed. John Searle, 23–38. London: Oxford University Press, 1971.

Striedter, Jurij. *Literary Structure, Evolution, and Value: Russian Formalism and Czech Structuralism Reconsidered.* Cambridge: Harvard University Press, 1989.

Suleiman, Susan R. "Introduction: Varieties of Audience-Oriented Criticism." In *The Reader in the Text: Essays on Audience and Interpretation,* ed. Susan Suleiman and Inge Crosman, 3–45. Princeton: Princeton University Press, 1980.

Tannen, Deborah. "Ethnic Style in Male-Female Conversation." In *Language and Social Identity,* ed. John Gumperz, 317–30. Cambridge: Cambridge University Press, 1983.

——. *Talking Voices: Repetition, Dialogue, and Imagery in Conversational Discourse.* Cambridge: Cambridge University Press, 1989.

Taylor, Talbot J. Review of *The Politics of Linguistics,* by Frederick J. Newmeyer. *Language* 66 (1990): 159–62.

Thorne, James Peter. "Stylistics and Generative Grammars." In *Linguistics and Literary Style,* ed. Donald C. Freeman, 182–96. New York: Holt, Rinehart, Winston, 1970.

Todorov, Tzvetan. *Grammaire du "Decameron."* The Hague: Mouton, 1969.

——. *Introduction to Poetics.* Trans. Richard Howard. Minneapolis: University of Minnesota Press, 1981. (Originally published in *Qu'est-ce que le structuralisme: Poétique* and revised in *Poétique.* Paris: Seuil, 1968 and 1973.)

——. "Jakobson's Poetics." In *Theories of the Symbol,* trans. Catherine Porter, 271–84. Ithaca: Cornell University Press, 1982. (Originally published in *Théories du symbole.* Paris: Seuil, 1977.)

——. "Poetic Language: The Russian Formalists." In *Literature and Its Theorists: A Personal View of Twentieth-Century Criticism,* trans. Catherine Porter, 10–28. Ithaca: Cornell University Press, 1987. (Originally published in *Critique de la critique.* Paris: Seuil, 1984.)

———. "Saussure's Semiotics." In *Theories of the Symbol*, trans. Catherine Porter, 255–70. Ithaca: Cornell University Press, 1982. (Originally published in *Théories du symbole*. Paris: Seuil, 1977.)

———. "The Two Principles of Narrative." In *Genres in Discourse*, trans. Catherine Porter, 27–38. New York: Cambridge University Press, 1990. (Originally published as *Genres du Discourse*. Paris: Seuil, 1978.)

Tompkins, Jane P., ed. *Reader-Response Criticism: From Formalism to Post-Structuralism*. Baltimore: Johns Hopkins University Press, 1980.

Toolan, Michael J. *Narrative: A Critical Linguistic Introduction*. London: Routledge, 1988.

Trudgill, Peter. "Sex, Covert Prestige and Linguistic Change in the Urban British English of Norwich." *Language in Society* 1.2 (1972): 179–95.

Tyler, Stephen A. *The Said and the Unsaid: Mind, Meaning, and Culture*. New York: Academic Press, 1978.

Vachek, Josef. *The Linguistic School of Prague: An Introduction to Its Theory and Practice*. Bloomington: Indiana University Press, 1966.

Vodička, Felix. "Response to Verbal Art." In *Semiotics of Art: Prague School Contributions*, ed. Ladislav Matejka and Irwin R. Titunik, 197–208. Cambridge: MIT Press, 1976.

Wardhaugh, Ronald. *An Introduction to Sociolinguistics*. 2d ed. Oxford: Basil Blackwell, 1992.

Waugh, Linda R. *Roman Jakobson's Science of Language*. Dordrecht, Netherlands: Peter de Ridder Press, 1976.

Waugh, Linda R., and Monique Monville-Burston. "Introduction: The Life, Work, and Influence of Roman Jakobson." In *On Language*, ed. Linda R. Waugh and Monique Monville-Burston, 1–45. Cambridge: Harvard University Press, 1990.

Weber, Samuel. "Saussure and the Apparition of Language: The Critical Perspective." *MLN* 91 (1976): 913–38.

———. "A Stroke of Luck." *Enclitic* 6.2 (1982): 29–31.

Wellek, René. "Closing Statement." In *Style and Language*, ed. Thomas A. Sebeok, 408–19. Cambridge: MIT Press, 1960.

———. Foreword to *The Word and Verbal Art: Selected Essays by Jan Mukařovský*, by Jan Mukařovský, ed. and trans. John Burbank and Peter Steiner, vii–xiii. New Haven: Yale University Press, 1977.

———. "The Literary Theory and Aesthetics of the Prague School." In *Discriminations*, 275–303. New Haven: Yale University Press, 1970.

———. "The Main Trends of Twentieth-Century Criticism." In *Concepts of Criticism*, ed. Stephen G. Nichols Jr., 344–64. New Haven: Yale University Press, 1963.

Wimsatt, W. K., and Monroe C. Beardsley. "The Affective Fallacy." In *The Verbal Icon: Studies in the Meaning of Poetry*, by W. K. Wimsatt, 20–39. Lexington: University of Kentucky Press, 1954. New York: Noonday-Farrar, Straus, 1964.

———. "The Intentional Fallacy." In *The Verbal Icon: Studies in the Meaning of Poetry*, by W. K. Wimsatt, 2–18. Lexington: University of Kentucky Press, 1954. New York: Noonday-Farrar, Straus, 1964.

Winner, Thomas G. "The Aesthetics and Poetics of the Prague Linguistic Circle." *Poetics* 8 (1973): 77–96.

Winspur, Steven. "Text Acts: Recasting Performatives with Wittgenstein and Derrida." In *Redrawing the Lines: Analytic Philosophy, Deconstruction, and Literary Theory*, ed. Reed Way Dasenbrock, 169–88. Minneapolis: University of Minnesota Press, 1989.

Wolfram, Walt, and Ralph W. Fasold. *The Study of Social Dialects in American English*. Englewood Cliffs, N.J.: Prentice-Hall, 1974.

Wortman, Marc. "Shattering the Urn." *Yale Alumni Magazine* (December 1990): 32–39.

Index